Open Source and Management

Fabien **Pinckaers**
Geoff **Gardiner**

Open ERP for Retail and Industrial Management

Open Object Press

Open Source and Management

Open ERP

Open ERP for Retail and Industrial Management:

Steps towards Sales, Logistics and Manufacturing integration.

by Fabien Pinckaers and Geoff Gardiner

First Edition

Many of the designations used by manufacturers and suppliers to distinguish their products are claimed as trademarks. Where those designations appear in this book, and Open Object Press was aware of a trademark claim, the designations have been printed in initial capitals.

While every precaution has been taken in the preparation of this book, the publisher and the authors assume no responsibility for errors or omissions, or for damages resulting from the use of the information contained herein.

Open Object Press

Open Object Press is a division of **Tiny S.P.R.L.** (www.openerp.com)

Copyright © 2009 Fabien Pinckaers and Geoff Gardiner

First edition April 2009   **ISBN** : 978-2-9600876-0-4

Open Object Press

40, Chaussée de Namur
1367 Grand-Rosière
http://openerp.com/

Contents

Foreword

Information Systems have played an increasingly visible role over the past several years in improving the competitiveness of business. More than just tools for handling repetitive tasks, they're used to guide and advance all of a company's daily activities. Integrated management software is today very often a key source of significant competitive advantage.

Such software is commonly called an ERP (Enterprise Resource Planning) system. This book is about the use of Open ERP, a leading ERP system, for manufacturing and stock management. It's one of a series of books from Open Object Press on the use of Open ERP in a range of enterprise settings.

Open Source software at the service of management

Risks and integration costs are important barriers to all the advantages you gain from such systems. That's why, today, few small- and medium-sized companies use ERP. In addition, the larger ERP vendors such as SAP, Microsoft and Oracle haven't been able to reconcile the power and comprehensive cover of an ERP system with the simplicity and flexibility wanted by the users. But this is exactly what small and medium enterprises are looking for.

The development processes of open source software, and the new business models adopted by their developers, provide a new way of resolving such problems of cost and quality for this kind of enterprise software.

To make an ERP system fully available to small and medium enterprises, cost reduction is the first priority. Open source software makes it possible to greatly reduce development costs by aggressive reuse of open source software libraries; to eliminate intermediaries (the distributors), with all of their expensive sales overhead; to cut out selling costs by free publication of the software; and to considerably reduce the marketing overhead.

Since there is open interaction among thousands of contributors and partners working on the same project, the quality of the resulting software benefits greatly from the scrutiny. And you can't be everything at once: accountant, software developer, salesperson, ISO 9001 quality professional, specialist in agricultural products, expert in the customs and habits of pharmaceutical vendors, just as a start.

Faced with these wide-ranging requirements, what could be better than a world network of partners and contributors? Everyone adds their own contribution according to their professional competence. Throughout this book you'll see that the results exceed any reasonable expectations when such work is well organized.

But the real challenge of development is to make this solution simple and flexible, as well as complete. And to reach this level of quality you need a leader and co-ordinator who can organize all of these activities. So the development team of Tiny ERP, today called Open ERP, is responsible for most of the organization, synchronization and coherence of the software.

And Open ERP offers great performance in all these areas!

The Open ERP Solution

Because of its modularity, collaborative developments in Open ERP have been cleanly integrated, enabling any company to choose from a large list of available functions. As with most open source software, accessibility, flexibility, and simplicity are important keywords for development. Experience has shown that there's no need to train users for several months on the system, because they can just download it and use it directly.

So you'll find the modules for all types of needs, allowing your company to build its customized system by simply grouping and configuring the most suitable modules. Hundreds of modules are available.

They range from specific modules like the EDI interface for agricultural products, which has been used to interface with Match and Leclerc stores, up to the generic demonstration automation module for ordering sandwiches, which can take care of the eating preference of your staff.

The results are impressive. Open ERP (once called Tiny ERP when it started out) is management software that is downloaded more than any other in the world, with over 600 downloads per day. It's available today in 18 languages and has a world network of partners and contributors. More than 800 developers participate in the projects on the collaborative development system of Tiny Forge.

To our knowledge, Open ERP is the only management system which is routinely used not only by big companies but also by very small companies and independent companies. This diversity is an illustration of the software's flexibility: a rather elegant coordination between people's functional expectations of the software and great simplicity in its use.

And diversity is also found in the various sectors and trades which use the software, including agricultural products, textiles, public auctions, IT, and trade associations.

Lastly, such software has arisen from the blend of high code quality, well-judged architecture and use of free technologies. In fact, you may be surprised (if you're an IT person) to find that the size of Open ERP is less than 4 MB when you've installed the software. We've moved a long way from the days when the only people who could be expected to benefit from ERP were the owners of a widget factory on some remote industrial estate.

Why this book ?

Many books set out to tell readers about the management of enterprise, and equally many aim to instruct the reader in the use of a piece of specialized software. We're not aiming to add to those lists because our approach is intended to be different.

Having restructured and reorganized many businesses, we wanted our management experience to generate a work that is both instructive and practical. It was important for us not to write a manual about Open ERP, but instead a work that deals with advanced management techniques realized through these IT tools. You'll see what management practices might be useful, what's possible, and then how you could achieve that in Open ERP.

It's this that we'll consider Open ERP for: not as an end in itself but just the tool you use to put an advanced management system into place.

Who's it for ?

Written by two CEOs who have been successful with new technologies, this book is aimed at directors and managers who have an ambition to improve the performance of their whole company's management team. They're likely already to have significant responsibilities and possess the influence to get things done in their company.

It's likely that most readers will come from small- and medium-sized enterprises (up to a few hundred staff), and independent companies, because of the breadth of functions that need to be analyzed and involved in change. The same principles also apply to larger companies, however.

Structure of this book

Part I, *First steps with Open ERP*, starts with the installation of Open ERP. If you have already installed Open ERP you can directly take your first steps on a guided tour in the *Guided Tour* chapter. If you're already familiar with Open ERP or Tiny ERP you can use the *Developing a real case* chapter to find out how to create a new workflow from scratch in an empty database with nothing to distract you. Or you can skip directly to the *Management of Sales* chapter in the *Sales and Purchasing* part, to start with details of Open ERP's functional modules.

Part II, *Sales and Purchasing*, deals with Selling and Purchasing goods and services.

Part III, *Stock and Manufacturing*, describes the physical movement of Stocks and their Manufacture (the transformation or products and services into other products).

Part IV, *Process Management*, is focused on the Process description that Open ERP manages.

Finally Part V, *System Administration and Implementation*, structured in two chapters, explains first how to administer and configure Open ERP then provides a methodology for implementing Open ERP in the enterprise.

About the authors

Fabien Pinckaers

Fabien Pinckaers was only eighteen years old when he started his first company. Today, over ten years later, he has founded and managed several new technology companies, all based on Free / Open Source software.

He originated Tiny ERP, now Open ERP, and is the director of two companies including Tiny sprl, the editor of Open ERP. In three years he has grown the Tiny group from one to eighty-five employees without loans or external fund-raising, and while making a profit.

He has also developed several large scale projects, such as Auction-in-Europe.com, which become the leader in the art market in Belgium. Even today people sell more art works there than on ebay.be.

He is also the founder of the LUG (Linux User Group) of Louvain-la-Neuve, and of several free projects like OpenReport, OpenStuff and Tiny Report. Educated as a civil engineer (polytechnic), he has won several IT prizes in Europe such as Wired and l'Inscene.

A fierce defender of free software in the enterprise, he is in constant demand as a conference speaker and he is the author of numerous articles dealing with free software in the management of the enterprise.

Geoff Gardiner

Geoff has held posts as director of services and of IT systems for international companies and in manufacturing. He was senior Industrial Research Fellow at Cambridge University's Institute for Manufacturing where he focused on innovation processes.

He founded Seath Solutions Ltd (http://www.seathsolutions.com/) to provide services in the use of Open Source software, particularly Open ERP, for business management.

Author of articles and books focusing on the processes and technology of innovation, Geoff is also an active contributor to the Open ERP project. He holds an MBA from Cranfield School of Management and an MA in Engineering and Electrical Sciences from Trinity Hall, Cambridge. He is a member of the Institution of Engineering and Technology and of the Society of Authors.

Having observed, suffered from, and led process implementation projects in various organizations, he has many thoughts about the successful adoption of an effective management automation tool.

Acknowledgements

From Geoff Gardiner

My gratitude goes to my co-author, Fabien Pinckaers, for his vision and tenacity in developing Tiny ERP and Open ERP, and the team at Tiny for its excellent work on this.

Open ERP relies on a philosophy of Open Source and on the technologies that have been developed and tuned over the years by numerous talented people. Their efforts are greatly appreciated.

Special thanks to my family for their encouragement, their tolerance and their constant presence.

From Fabien Pinckaers

My thanks to all of the team at Tiny for their hard work in preparing, translating and re-reading the book in its various forms. My particular thanks to Laurence Henrion and my family for supporting me throughout all this effort.

Part I

First steps with Open ERP

Open ERP is an impressive software system, being simple to use and yet providing great benefits in helping you manage your company. It's easy to install under both Windows and Linux compared with other enterprise-scale systems, and offers unmatched functionality.

The objective of this first part of the book is to help you to start discovering it in practice.

The first chapter, *Installation and Initial Setup*, gives detailed guidance for installing it. Next, in *Guided Tour*, you're taken on a step-by-step guided tour using the information in its demonstration database. Then in *Developing a real case* you can try out a real case, from scratch in a new database, by developing a complete business workflow that runs from purchase to sale of goods.

Installation and Initial Setup
1

Installing Open ERP under Windows or Linux for familiarization use should take you only half an hour or so and needs only a couple of operations.

The first operation is installation of the application and database server on a server PC (that's a Windows or Linux or Macintosh computer).

You've a choice of approaches for the second operation: either install a web server (most probably on the original server PC) to use with standard web clients that can be found on anybody's PC, or install application clients on each intended user's PC.

When you first install Open ERP you'll set up a database containing a little functionality and some demonstration data to test the installation.

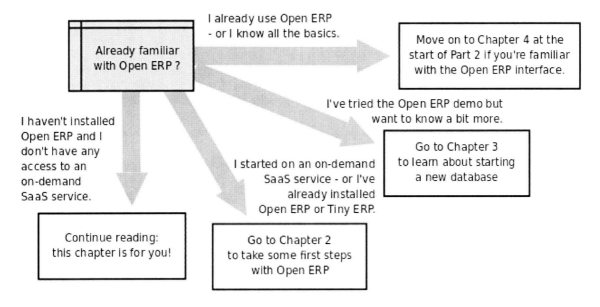

Figure 1.1: *Options for reading this part of the book*

This chapter, *Installation and Initial Setup*, focuses on the installation of Open ERP so that you can begin to familiarize yourselves with its use. If you're not a systems administrator, or if you've already installed Open ERP, or if you're planning to use an online SaaS provider, then you can skip this chapter and move straight to the next chapter, *Guided Tour*. If you've already used Open ERP (or Tiny ERP) a bit then you can move past that to the third chapter in this part of the book, *Developing a real case*.

Renaming from Tiny ERP to Open ERP

Tiny ERP was renamed to Open ERP early in 2008 so somebody who's already used Tiny ERP should be equally at home with Open ERP. The two names refer to the same software, so there's no functional difference between versions 4.2.X of Open ERP and 4.2.X of Tiny ERP. This book applies to versions of Open ERP from 5.0.0 onwards, with references to earlier versions from time to time.

The SaaS, or "on-demand", offer

SaaS (Software as a Service) is delivered by a hosting supplier and paid in the form of a monthly subscription that includes hardware (servers), system maintenance, provision of hosting services, and support.

You can get a month's free trial on Tiny's http://ondemand.openerp.com, which enables you to get started quickly without incurring costs for integration or for buying computer systems. Many of Tiny's partner companies will access this, and some may offer their own similar service.

This service should be particularly useful to small companies that just want to get going quickly and at low cost. It gives them immediate access to an integrated management system that's been built on the type of enterprise architecture used in banks and other large organizations. Open ERP is that system, and is described in detail throughout this book.

Whether you want to test Open ERP or to put it into full production, you have at least two starting points:

- evaluate it on line at http://www.openerp.com and ask Tiny for an SaaS trial hosted at http://ondemand.openerp.com, or the equivalent service at any of Tiny's partner companies,

- install it on your own computers to test it in your company's systems environment.

There are some differences between installing Open ERP on Windows and on Linux systems, but once installed, it gives the same functions from both so you won't generally be able to tell which type of server you're using.

Linux, Windows, Mac

Although this book deals only with installation on Windows and Linux systems, the same versions are also available for the Macintosh on the official website of Open ERP.

Web sites for Open ERP

- Main Site: http://www.openerp.com,

- SaaS or "on-demand" Site: http://ondemand.openerp.com,

- Documentation Site: http://doc.openerp.com/,

- Community discussion forum where you can often receive informed assistance: http://www.openobject.com/forum.

Current documentation

The procedure for installing Open ERP and its web server are sure to change and improve with each new version, so you should always check each release's documentation – both packaged with the release and on the website – for exact installation procedures.

Once you've completed this installation, create and set up a database to confirm that your Open ERP installation is working. You can follow these early chapters in this part of the book to achieve this.

1.1 The architecture of Open ERP

To access Open ERP you can:

- use a web browser pointed at the Open ERP client-web server, or

- use an application client (the GTK client) installed on each computer.

The two methods of access give very similar facilities, and you can use both on the same server at the same time. It's best to use the web browser if the Open ERP server is some distance away (such as on another continent) because it's more tolerant of time delays between the two than the GTK client is. The web client is also easier to maintain, because it's generally already installed on users' computers.

Conversely you'd be better off with the application client (called the GTK client because of the technology it's built with) if you're using a local server (such as in the same building). In this case the GTK client will be more responsive, so more satisfying to use.

Web client and GTK client

The main functional difference between the two Open ERP clients is the presence of the calendar view in the web client, which doesn't exist in the GTK client at present (versions 4.x and 5.0). Apart from that you will find that there are small differences in their general usability.

When you're changing the structure of your Open ERP installation (adding and removing modules, perhaps changing labels) you'll find the web client to be irritating because of its use of **caching**.

Caching speeds it all up by keeping a copy of data somewhere between the server and your client, which is usually good. But you may have made changes to your installation that you cannot immediately see in your browser. Many apparent faults are caused by this! The workaround is to use the GTK client during development and implementation where possible.

The Tiny company will continue to support two clients for the foreseeable future, so you can use whichever client you prefer.

An Open ERP system is formed from three main components:

- the PostgreSQL database server, which contains all of the databases, each of which contains all data and most elements of the Open ERP system configuration,

- the Open ERP application server, which contains all of the enterprise logic and ensures that Open ERP runs optimally,

- the web server, a separate application called the Open Object client-web, which enables you to connect to Open ERP from standard web browsers and is not needed when you connect using a GTK client.

Terminology: client-web – server or client?

The client-web component can be thought of as a server or a client depending on your viewpoint.

It acts as a web server to an end user connecting from a web browser, but it also acts as a client to the Open ERP application server just as a GTK application client does.

So in this book its context will determine whether the client-web component is referred to as a server or a client.

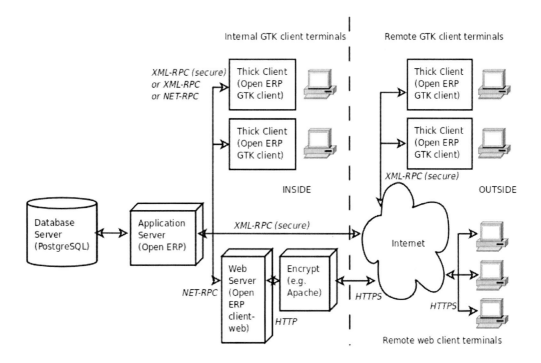

Figure 1.2: *The architecture of Open ERP*

eTiny

The web application used to be known as "eTiny". Its name changed to "client-web" as Tiny ERP was renamed to Open ERP, but its characteristics have generally stayed the same.

PostgreSQL, the relational and object database management system.

It's a free and open-source high-performance system that compares well with other database management systems such as MySQL and FirebirdSQL (both free), Sybase, DB2 and Microsoft SQL Server (all proprietary). It runs on all types of Operating System, from Unix/Linux to the various releases of Windows, via Mac OS X, Solaris, SunOS and BSD.

These three components can be installed on the same server or can be distributed onto separate computer servers if performance considerations require it.

If you choose to run only with GTK clients you won't need the third component – the client-web server – at all. In this case Open ERP's GTK client must be installed on the workstation of each Open ERP user in the company.

1.2 The installation of Open ERP

Whether you're from a small company investigating how Open ERP works, or on the IT staff of a larger organization and have been asked to assess Open ERP's capabilities, your first requirement is to install it or to find a working installation.

The table below summarizes the various installation methods that will be described in the following sections.

Table 1.1: Comparison of the different methods of installation on Windows or Linux

Method	Average Time	Level of Complexity	Notes
All-in-one Windows Installer	A few minutes	Simple	Very useful for quick evaluations because it installs all of the components pre-configured on one computer (using the GTK client).
Independent installation on Windows	Half an hour	Medium	Enables you to install the components on different computers. Can be put into production use.
Ubuntu Linux packages	A few minutes	Simple	Simple and quick but the Ubuntu packages aren't always up to date.
From source, for all Linux systems	More than half an hour	Medium to slightly difficult	This is the method recommended for production environments because it's easy to keep it up to date.

Each time a new release of Open ERP is made, Tiny supplies a complete Windows auto-installer for it. This contains all of the components you need – the PostgreSQL database server, the Open ERP application server and the GTK application client.

This auto-installer enables you to install the whole system in just a few mouse-clicks. The initial configuration is set up during installation, making it possible to start using it very quickly as long as you don't want to change the underlying code. It's aimed at the installation of everything on a single PC, but you can later connect GTK clients from other PCs, Macs and Linux boxes to it as well.

The first step is to download the Open ERP installer. At this stage you must choose which version to install – the stable version or the development version. If you're planning to put it straight into production you're strongly advised to choose the stable version.

Stable versions and development versions

Open ERP development proceeds on two parallel tracks: stable versions and development versions.

New functionality is integrated into the development branch. This branch is more advanced than the stable branch, but it can contain undiscovered and unfixed faults. A new development release is made every month or so, and Tiny have made the code repository available so you can download the very latest revisions if you want.

The stable branch is designed for production environments. Releases of new functionality there are made only about once a year after a long period of testing and validation. Only fault fixes are released through the year on the stable branch.

To download the version of Open ERP for Windows, follow these steps:

1. Navigate to the site http://openerp.com.

2. Click *Downloads* on the menu at the left then, under **Windows Installers**, *All in One*.

3. This brings up the demonstration version Windows installer, currently **openerp-allinone-setup-5.0.0-3**.

4. Save the file on your PC - it's quite a substantial size because it downloads everything including the PostgreSQL database system, so will take some time.

To install Open ERP and its database you must be signed in as an Administrator on your PC. Double- click the installer file to install it and accept the default parameters on each dialog box as you go.

If you had previously tried to install the all-in-one version of Open ERP, you have to uninstall that first because various elements of a previous installation could interfere with your new installation. Make sure that all Tiny ERP, Open ERP and PostgreSQL applications are removed: you're likely to have to restart your PC to finish removing all traces of them.

The Open ERP client can be opened, ready to use the Open ERP system, once you have completed the all–in-one installation. The next step consists of setting up the database, and is covered in the final section of this chapter *Creating the database*.

1.2.1 Independent installation on Windows

System administrators can have very good reasons for wanting to install the various components of a Windows installation separately. For example, your company may not support the version of PostgreSQL or Python that's installed automatically, or you may already have PostgreSQL installed on the server you're using, or you may want to install the database server, application server and web server on separate hardware units.

For this situation you can get separate installers for the Open ERP server and client from the same location as the all-in-one auto-installer. You'll also have to download and install a suitable version of PostgreSQL independently.

You must install PostgreSQL before the Open ERP server, and you must also set it up with a user and password so that the Open ERP server can connect to it. Tiny's web-based documentation gives full and current details.

Connecting users on other PCs to the Open ERP server

To connect other computers to the Open ERP server you must set the server up so that it's visible to the other PCs, and install a GTK client on each of the those PCs:

1. Make your Open ERP server visible to other PCs by opening the Windows Firewall in the Control Panel, then asking the firewall to make an exception of the Open ERP server. In the **Exceptions** tab of Windows Firewall click on **Add a program...** and choose **Open ERP Server** in the list provided. This step enables other computers to see the Open ERP application on this server.

2. Install the Open ERP client (**openerp-client-5.X.exe**), which you can download in the same way as you downloaded the other Open ERP software, onto the other PCs.

Version matching

You must make sure that the version of the client matches that of the server. The version number is given as part of the name of the downloaded file. Although it's possible that some different revisions of client and server will function together, there's no certainty about that.

To run the client installer on every other PC you'll need to have administrator rights there. The installation is automated, so you just need to guide it through its different installation steps.

To test your installation, start by connecting through the Open ERP client on the server machine while you're still logged in as administrator.

Why sign in as a PC Administrator?

You'd not usually be signed on as a PC administrator when you're just running the Open ERP client, but if there have been problems in the installation it's easier to remain as an administrator after the installation so that you can make any necessary fixes than to switch user as you alternate between roles as a tester and a software installer.

Start the GTK client on the server through the Windows Start menu there. The main client window appears, identifying the server you're connected to (which is `localhost` – your own server PC – by default). If the message **No database found, you must create one** appears then you've **successfully connected** to an Open ERP server containing, as yet, no databases.

Connection modes

In its default configuration at the time of writing, the Open ERP client connects to port 8069 on the server using the XML-RPC protocol (from Linux) or port 8070 using the NET-RPC protocol instead (from Windows). You can use either protocol from either operating system. NET-RPC is quite a bit quicker, although you may not notice that on the GTK client in normal use. Open ERP can run XML-RPC, but not NET-RPC, as a secure connection.

OPEN SOURCE MANAGEMENT SOLUTION

http://openerp.com

Server: http://192.168.0.131:8069   [Change]

Database: **No database found, you must create one !**

User: admin

Password:

❌ Cancel   OK

Figure 1.3: *Dialog box on connecting a GTK client to a new Open ERP server*

The all-in-one installer also provides a web server, but this was not yet working at the time of writing.

Resolving errors with a Windows installation

If you can't get Open ERP to work after installing your Windows system you'll find some ideas for resolving this below:

1. Is the Open ERP application working? Signed in to the server as an administrator, stop and restart the service using **Stop Service** and **Start Service** from the menu *Start → Programs → OpenERP Server* .

2. Is the Open ERP application server set up correctly? Signed in to the server as Administrator, open the file `openerp-server.conf` in `C:\Program Files\OpenERP AllInOne` and check its content. This file is generated during installation with information derived from the database. If you see something strange it's best to entirely reinstall the server from the demonstration installer rather than try to work out what's happening.

3. Is your PostgreSQL server running? Signed in as administrator, select **Stop Service** from the menu *Start → Programs → PostgreSQL*. If, after a couple of seconds, you can read **The PostgreSQL4OpenERP service has stopped** then you can be reasonably sure that the database server was working. Restart PostgreSQL.

4. Does PostgreSQL work at all? Still in the PostgreSQL menu, start the pgAdmin III application which you can use to explore the database. Double-click on the `PostgreSQL4OpenERP` connection. You can find the password in the Open ERP server configuration file. If the database server is working you'll be able to see some information about the empty database. If it's not then an error message will appear.

5. Are your client programs correctly installed? If your Open ERP GTK clients haven't started then the swiftest approach is to reinstall them.

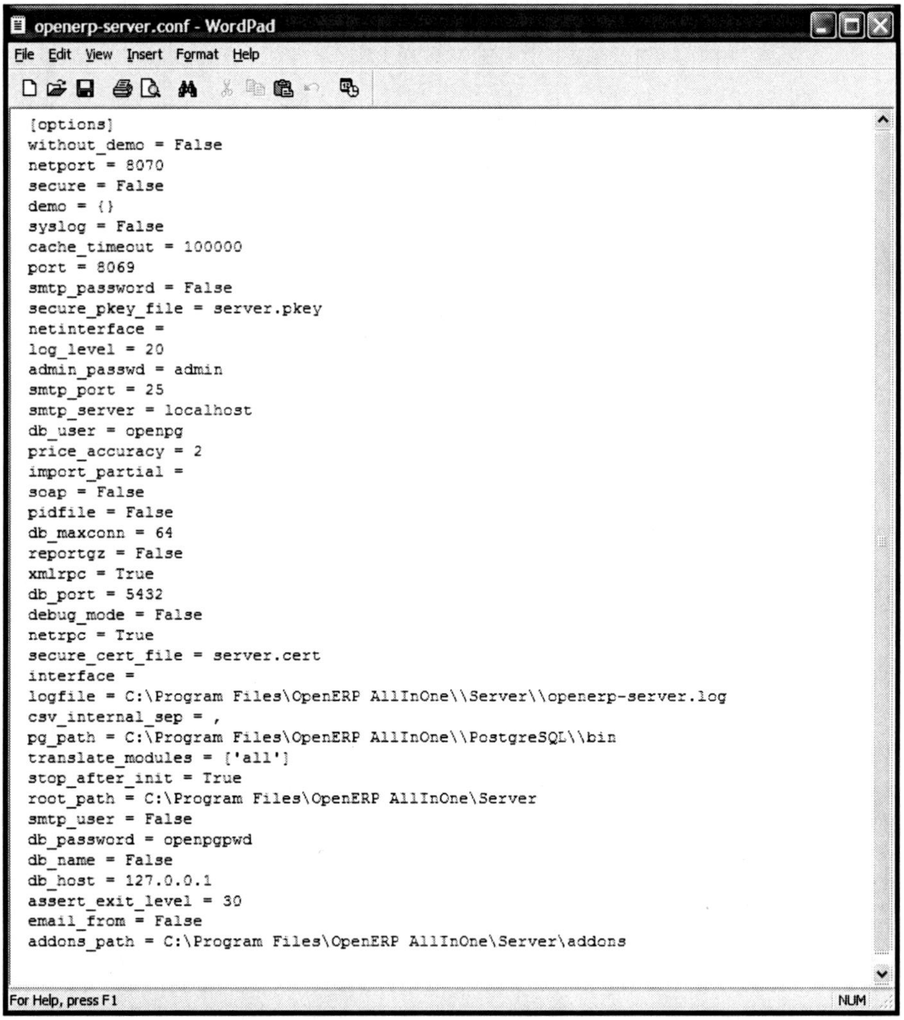

```
[options]
without_demo = False
netport = 8070
secure = False
demo = {}
syslog = False
cache_timeout = 100000
port = 8069
smtp_password = False
secure_pkey_file = server.pkey
netinterface =
log_level = 20
admin_passwd = admin
smtp_port = 25
smtp_server = localhost
db_user = openpg
price_accuracy = 2
import_partial =
soap = False
pidfile = False
db_maxconn = 64
reportgz = False
xmlrpc = True
db_port = 5432
debug_mode = False
netrpc = True
secure_cert_file = server.cert
interface =
logfile = C:\Program Files\OpenERP AllInOne\\Server\\openerp-server.log
csv_internal_sep = ,
pg_path = C:\Program Files\OpenERP AllInOne\\PostgreSQL\\bin
translate_modules = ['all']
stop_after_init = True
root_path = C:\Program Files\OpenERP AllInOne\Server
smtp_user = False
db_password = openpgpwd
db_name = False
db_host = 127.0.0.1
assert_exit_level = 30
email_from = False
addons_path = C:\Program Files\OpenERP AllInOne\Server\addons
```

Figure 1.4: *Typical Open ERP configuration file*

6. Can remote client computers see the server computer at all? Check this by opening a command prompt window (enter `cmd` in the window *Start → Run...*) and enter `ping <address of server>` there (where `<address of server>` represents the IP address of the server). The server should respond with a reply.

7. Have you changed any of the server's parameters? At this point in the installation the port number of the server must be 8069 using the protocol XML-RPC.

8. Is there anything else in the server's history that can help you identify the problem? Open the file `openerp-server.log` in `C:\Program Files\OpenERP AllInOne`(which you can only do when the server is stopped) and scan through the history for ideas. If something looks strange there, contributors to the Open ERP forums can often help identify the reason.

1.2.2 Installation on Linux (Ubuntu)

This section guides you through installing the Open ERP server and client on Ubuntu, one of the most popular Linux distributions. It assumes that you're using a recent release of Desktop Ubuntu with its graphical user interface on a desktop or laptop PC.

Other Linux distributions

Installation on other distributions of Linux is fairly similar to installation on Ubuntu. Read this section of the book so that you understand the principles, then use the online documentation and the forums for your specific needs on another distribution.

For information about installation on other distributions, visit the documentation section by following *Product → Documentation* on http://www.openerp.com. Detailed instructions are given there for different distributions and releases, and you should also check if there are more up to date instructions for the Ubuntu distribution as well.

Installation of Open ERP from packages

At the time of writing this book, Ubuntu hadn't yet published packages for Open ERP, so this section describes the installation of version 4.2 of Tiny ERP. This is very similar to Open ERP and so can be used to test the software.

Here's a summary of the procedure:

1. Start Synaptic Package Manager, and enter your root password as required.

2. Check that the repositories `main universe` and `restricted` are enabled.

3. Search for a recent version of PostgreSQL, for example `postgresql-8.3`then select it for installation along with its dependencies.

4. Search for `tinyerp` then select `tinyerp-client` and `tinyerp-server` for installation along with their dependencies. Click **Update Now** to install it all.

5. Close Synaptic Package Manager.

Installing PostgreSQL results in a database server that runs and restarts automatically when the PC is turned on. If all goes as it should with the tinyerp-server package then tinyerp-server will also install, and restart automatically when the PC is switched on.

Start the Tiny/Open ERP GTK client by clicking its icon in the *Applications* menu, or by opening a terminal window and typing `tinyerp-client`. The Open ERP login dialog box should open and show the message **No database found you must create one!**.

Although this installation method is simple and therefore an attractive option, it's better to install Open ERP using a version downloaded from http://openerp.com. The downloaded revision is likely to be far more up to date than that available from a Linux distribution.

 Package versions

Maintaining packages is a process of development, testing and publication that takes time. The releases in Open ERP (or Tiny ERP) packages are therefore not always the latest available. Check the version number from the information on the website before installing a package. If only the third digit group differs (for example 5.0.1 instead of 5.0.2) then you may decide to install it because the differences may be minor – fault fixes rather than functionality changes between the package and the latest version.

Manual installation of the Open ERP server

In this section you'll see how to install Open ERP by downloading it from the site http://openerp.com, and how to install the libraries and packages that Open ERP depends on, onto a desktop version of Ubuntu. Here's a summary of the procedure:

1. Navigate to the page http://openerp.com with your web browser,

2. Click *Downloads* on the left menu,

3. Download the client and server files from the *Sources (Linux)* section into your home directory (or some other location if you've defined a different download area).

To download the PostgreSQL database and all of the other dependencies for Open ERP from packages:

1. Start Synaptic Package Manager, and enter the root password as required.

2. Check that the repositories `main universe` and `restricted` are enabled.

3. Search for a recent version of PostgreSQL (such as `postgresql-8.3` then select it for installation along with its dependencies.

4. Select all of Open ERP's dependences, an up-to-date list of which should be found in the installation documents on Tiny's website, then click **Update Now** to install them.

Python programming language

Python is the programming language that's been used to develop Open ERP. It's a dynamic, non-typed language that is object-oriented, procedural and functional. It comes with numerous libraries that provide interfaces to other languages and has the great advantage that it can be learnt in only a few days. It's the language of choice for large parts of NASA's, Google's and many other enterprises' code.

For more information on Python, explore http://www.python.org.

Once all these dependencies and the database are installed, install the server itself using the instructions on the website.

Open a terminal window to start the server with the command `sudo -i -u postgres openerp-server` , which should result in a series of log messages as the server starts up. If the server is correctly installed, the message **[...] waiting for connections...** should show within 30 seconds or so, which indicates that the server is waiting for a client to connect to it.

```
File  Edit  View  Terminal  Tabs  Help
gsg@u804srv1:~$ sudo -i -u postgres openerp-server
[sudo] password for gsg:
[2009-03-07 17:25:10,110] INFO:server:version - 5.0.0
[2009-03-07 17:25:10,111] INFO:server:addons path - /usr/lib/python2.5/site-packages/openerp-server/addons
[2009-03-07 17:25:10,111] INFO:server:database hostname - localhost
[2009-03-07 17:25:10,112] INFO:server:database port - 5432
[2009-03-07 17:25:10,112] INFO:server:database user - postgres
[2009-03-07 17:25:10,113] INFO:objects:initialising distributed objects services
[2009-03-07 17:25:10,422] INFO:web-services:starting XML-RPC services, port 8069
[2009-03-07 17:25:10,423] INFO:web-services:starting NET-RPC service, port 8070
[2009-03-07 17:25:10,424] INFO:web-services:the server is running, waiting for connections...
```

Figure 1.5: *Open ERP startup log in the console*

Manual installation of Open ERP GTK clients

To install an Open ERP GTK client, follow the steps outline on the website installation document for your particular operating system.

Survey: Don't Cancel!

When you start the GTK client for the first time, a dialog box appears asking for various details that are intended to help the Tiny company assess the prospective user base for its software.

If you click the **Cancel** button, the window goes away – but Open ERP will ask the same questions again next time you start the client. It's best to click **OK**, even if you choose to enter no data, to prevent that window reappearing next time.

Open a terminal window to start the client using the command openerp-client. When you start the client on the same Linux PC as the server you'll find that the default connection parameters will just work without needing

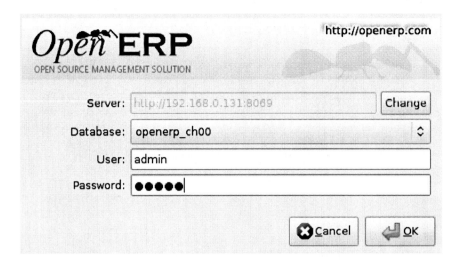

Figure 1.6: *Open ERP client at startup*

any change. The message **No database found, you must create one!** shows you that the connection to the server has been successful and you need to create a database on the server.

Creating the database

You can connect other GTK clients over the network to your Linux server. Before you leave your server, make sure you know its network address – either by its name (such as mycomputer.mycompany.net) or its IP address (such as 192.168.0.123).

> **Different networks**
>
> Communications between an Open ERP client and server are based on standard protocols. You can connect Windows clients to a Linux server, or vice versa, without problems. It's the same for Mac versions of Open ERP – you can connect Windows and Linux clients and servers to them.

To install an Open ERP client on a computer under Linux, repeat the procedure shown earlier in this section. You can connect different clients to the Open ERP server by modifying the connection parameters on each client. To do that, click the **Change** button on the connection dialog and set the following field as needed:

- **Server** : name or IP address of the server over the network,

- **Port** : the port, whose default is 8069 or 8070,

- **Connection protocol** : XML-RPC or NET-RPC .

It's possible to connect the server to the client using a secure protocol to prevent other network users from listening in, but the installation described here is for direct unencrypted connection.

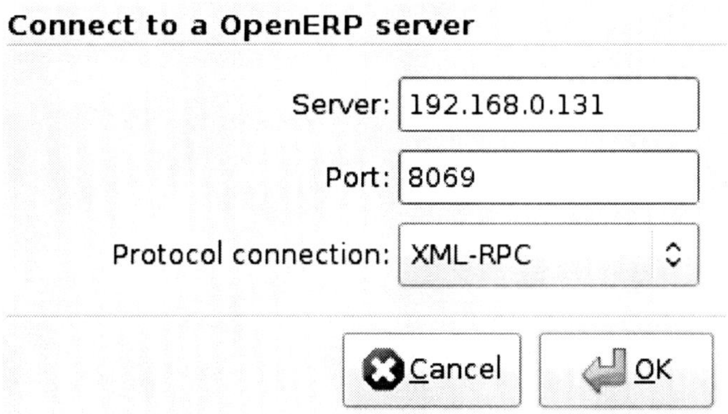

Connect to a OpenERP server

Server: 192.168.0.131

Port: 8069

Protocol connection: XML-RPC ⟳

❌ Cancel   ↩ OK

Figure 1.7: *Dialog box for defining connection parameters to the server*

If your Linux server is protected by a firewall you'll have to provide access to port 8069or 8070for users on other computers with Open ERP GTK clients.

Installation of an Open ERP web server

Just as you installed a GTK client on a Linux server, you can also install the Open ERP client-web server. You can install it from sources after installing its dependencies from packages as you did with the Open ERP server, but Tiny have provided a simpler way to do this for eTiny – using a system known as ez_setup.

Before proceeding, confirm that your Open ERP installation is functioning correctly with a GTK client. If it's not you'll need to go back now and fix it, because you need to be able to use it fully for the next stages.

To install client-web follow the up-to-date instructions in the installation document on the website.

Ez tool

Ez is the packaging system used by Python. It enables the installation of programs as required just like the packages used by a Linux distribution. The software is downloaded across the network and installed on your computer by ez_install.

ez_setup is a small program that installs ez_install automatically.

The Open ERP Web server connects to the Open ERP server in the same way as an Open ERP client using the NET-RPC protocol. Its default setup corresponds to that of the Open ERP server you've just installed, so should connect directly at startup.

1. At the same console as you've just been using, go to the Openerp web directory by typing **cd openerp-web-5.X**.

2. At a terminal window type **start-openerp-web** to start the Open ERP Web server.

You can verify the installation by opening a web browser on the server and navigating to http://localhost:8080 to connect to eTiny as shown in the figure *Open ERP web client at startup*. You can also test this from another

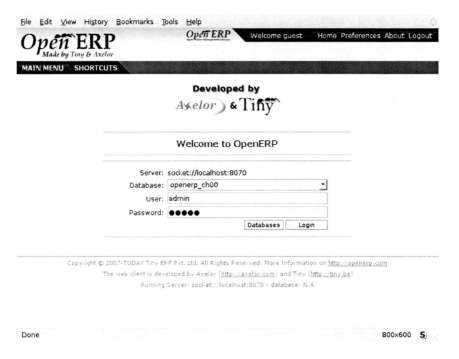

Figure 1.8: *Open ERP web client at startup*

computer connected to the same network if you know the name or IP address of the server over the network – your browser should be set to http://<server_address>:8080 for this.

Verifying your Linux installation

You've used default parameters so far during the installation of the various components. If you've had problems, or you just want to set this up differently, the following points provide some indicators about how you can set your installation up.

psql and pgAdmin tools

psql is a simple client, executed from the command line, that's delivered with PostgreSQL. It enables you to execute SQL commands on your Open ERP database.

If you prefer a graphical utility to manipulate your database directly you can install pgAdmin III (it is commonly installed automatically with PostgreSQL on a windowing system, but can also be found at http://www.pgadmin.org/).

1. The PostgreSQL database starts automatically and listens locally on port 5432 as standard: check this by entering sudo netstat -anpt at a terminal to see if port 5432 is visible there.

2. The database system has a default role of postgres accessible by running under the Linux postgres user: check this by entering sudo su postgres -c psql at a terminal to see the psql startup

message – then type `\q` to quit the program.

3. Start the Open ERP server from the postgres user (which enables it to access the PostgreSQL database) by typing `sudo su postgres -c tinyerp-server`.

4. If you try to start the Open ERP server from a terminal but get the message `socket.error: (98, 'Address already in use')` then you might be trying to start Open ERP while an instance of Open ERP is already running and using the sockets that you've defined (by default 8069 and 8070). If that's a surprise to you then you may be coming up against a previous installation of Open ERP or Tiny ERP, or something else using one or both of those ports.

   Type `sudo netstat -anpt` to discover what is running there, and record the PID. You can check that the PID orresponds to a program you can dispense with by typing `ps aux | grep <PID>` and you can then stop the program from running by typing `sudo kill <PID>`. You need additional measures to stop it from restarting when you restart the server.

5. The Open ERP server has a large number of configuration options. You can see what they are by starting the server with the argument `-help` By efault the server configuration is stored in the file `.terp_serverrc` in the user's home directory (and for the postgres user that directory is `/var/lib/postgresql`.

6. You can delete the configuration file to be quite sure that the Open ERP server is starting with just the default options. It is quite common for an upgraded system to behave badly because a new version server cannot work with options from a previous version. When the server starts without a configuration file it will write a new one once there is something non-default to write to it – it will operate using defaults until then.

7. To verify that the system works, without becoming entangled in firewall problems, you can start the Open ERP client from a second terminal window on the server computer (which doesn't pass through the firewall). Connect using the XML-RPC protocol on port 8069 or NET-RPC on port 8070. The server can use both ports simultaneously. The window displays the log file when the client is started this way.

8. The client setup is stored in the file `.terprc` in the user's home directory. Since a GTK client can be started by any user, each user would have their setup defined in a configuration file in their own home directory.

9. You can delete the configuration file to be quite sure that the Open ERP client is starting with just the default options. When the client starts without a configuration file it will write a new one for itself.

10. The web server uses the NET-RPC protocol. If a GTK client works but the web server doesn't then the problem is either with the NET-RPC port or with the web server itself, and not with the Open ERP server.

One server for several companies

You can start several Open ERP application servers on one physical computer server by using different ports. If you have defined multiple database roles in PostgreSQL, each connected through an Open ERP instance to a different port, you can simultaneously serve many companies from one physical server at one time.

1.3 Database creation

Use the technique outlined in this section to create a new database, `openerp_ch01`. This database will contain the demonstration data provided with Open ERP and a large proportion of the core Open ERP functionality. You'll need to know your super administrator password for this – or you'll have to find somebody who does have it to create this seed database.

The super-administrator password

Anyone who knows the super-administrator password has complete access to the data on the server – able to read, change and delete any of the data in any of the databases there.

After first installation, the password is `admin`. You can change it through the GTK client from the menu *File → Databases → Administrator Password*, or through the web client by logging out (click the **Logout** link), clicking **Databases** on the login screen, and then clicking the **Password** button on the Management screen. This password is stored in a configuration file outside the database, so a server systems administrator can change it if you forget it.

Figure 1.9: *Changing the super-administrator password through the web client*

1.3.1 Creating the database

If you're using the GTK client, choose *Files → Databases → New database* in the menu at the top left. Enter the super-administrator password, then the name of the new database you're creating.

If you're using the web client, click **Databases** on the login screen, then **Create** on the database management page. Enter the super-administrator password, and the name of the new database you're creating.

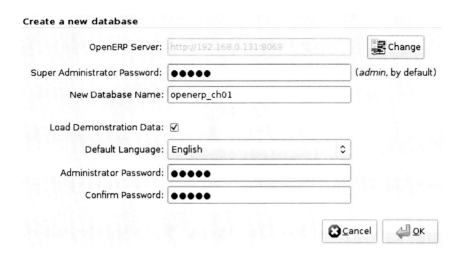

Figure 1.10: *Creating a new database through the GTK client*

In both cases you'll see a checkbox that determines whether you load demonstration data or not. The consequences of checking this box or not affect the **whole use** of this database.

In both cases you'll also see that you can choose the Administrator password. This makes your database quite secure because you can ensure that it is unique from the outset. (In fact many people find it hard to resist `admin` as their password!)

1.3.2 Database openerp_ch01

Wait for the message showing that the database has been successfully created, along with the user accounts and passwords (`admin/XXXX` and `demo/demo`). Now you've created this seed database you can extend it without having to know the super-administrator password.

User Access

The combination of username/password is specific to a single database. If you have administrative rights to a database you can modify all users. Alternatively you can install the `users_ldap` module, which manages the authentication of users in LDAP (the Lightweight Directory Access Protocol, a standard system), and connect it to several Open ERP databases. Using this, many databases can share the same user account details.

Failure to create a database

How do you know if you've successfully created your new database? You're told if the database creation has been unsuccessful. If you have entered a database name using prohibited characters (or no name, or too short a name) you will be alerted by the dialog box **Bad database name!** explaining how to correct the error. If you've entered the wrong super-administrator password or a name already in use (some names can be reserved without your knowledge), you'll be alerted by the dialog box **Error during database creation!**.

Connect to the database `openerp_ch01` that you just created, using the default administrator account.

If this is the first time you've connected to this database you'll be asked a series of questions to define the database parameters:

1. **Select a profile** : select `Minimal Profile` and click **Next**.

2. **Company Details** : replace the proposed default of `Tiny sprl` by your own company name, complete as much of your address as you like, and add some lines about your company, such as a slogan and any statutory requirements, to the header and footer fields. Click **Next**.

3. **Summary** : check the information and go back to make any modifications you need before installation. Then click **Install**.

4. **Installation Completed** : click **Ok**.

Once configuration is complete you're connected to your Open ERP system. Its functionality is very limited because you've selected a minimal installation, but this is sufficient to demonstrate that your installation is working.

1.3.3 Managing databases

As a super-administrator you've not only got rights to create new databases, but also to:

• delete databases,

• backup databases,

• restore databases.

All of these operations can be carried out from the menu *File → Databases... → Backup databases* in the GTK client, or from the **Database** button in the web client's **Login** screen.

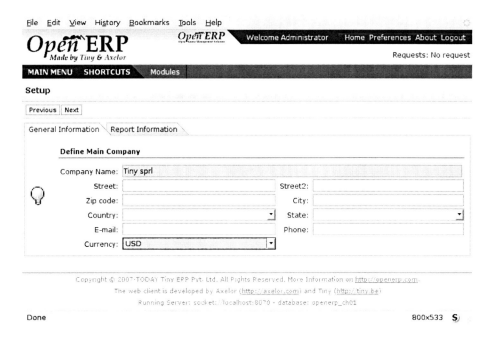

Figure 1.11: *Defining your company during initial database configuration*

Duplicating a database

To duplicate a database you can:

1. make a backup file on your PC from this database.

2. restore this database from the backup file on your PC, giving it a new name as you do so.

This can be a useful way of making a test database from a production database. You can try out the operation of a new configuration, new modules, or just the import of new data.

A system administrator can configure Open ERP to restrict access to some of these database functions so that your security is enhanced in normal production use.

You are now ready to use databases from your installation to familiarize yourself with the administration and use of Open ERP.

1.4 New Open ERP functionality

The database you've created and managed so far is based on the core Open ERP functionality that you installed. The core system is installed in the file system of your Open ERP application server, but only installed into an Open ERP database as you require it, as is described in the next chapter, *Guided Tour*.

What if want to update what's there, or extend what's there with additional modules?

- To update what you have, you'd install a new instance of Open ERP using the same techniques as described earlier in this section, *Database creation*.

- To extend what you have, you'd install new modules in the `addons` directory of your current Open ERP installation. There are several ways of doing that.

In both cases you'll need briefly to be a `root` user or `Administrator` of your Open ERP application server.

1.4.1 Extending Open ERP

To extend Open ERP you'll need to copy modules into the `addons` directory. That's in your server's `openerp-server` directory (which differs between Windows, Mac and some of the various Linux distributions and not available at all in the Windows all-in-one installer). If you look there you'll see existing modules such as `product` and `purchase`. A module can be provided in the form of files within a directory or a a zip-format file containing that same directory structure.

You can add modules in two main ways – through the server, or through the client. To add new modules through the server is a conventional systems administration task. As `root` user or other suitable user, you'd put the module in the `addons` directory and change its permissions to match those of the other modules.

To add new modules through the client you must first change the permissions of the `addons` directory of the server, so that it is writable by the server. That will enable you to install Open ERP modules using the Open ERP client (a task ultimately carried out on the application server by the server software).

> **Changing permissions**
>
> A very simple way of changing permissions on the Linux system you're using to develop an Open ERP application is to execute the command sudo chmod 777 <path_to_addons> (where <path_to_addons> is the full path to the addons directory, a location like /usr/lib/python2.5/site-packages/openerp- server/addons).

Any user of Open ERP who has access to the relevant administration menus can then upload any new functionality, so you'd certainly disable this capability for production use. You'll see examples of this uploading as you make your way through this book.

Guided Tour 2

Starting to discover Open ERP, using demonstration data supplied with the system, is a good way to familiarize yourself with the user interface. This guided tour provides you with an introduction to many of the available system features.

You'd be forgiven a flicker of apprehension when you first sit at your computer to connect to Open ERP, since ERP systems are renowned for their complexity and for the time it takes to learn how to use them. These are, after all, Enterprise Resource Planning systems, capable of managing most elements of global enterprises, so they should be complicated, shouldn't they? But even if this is often the case for proprietary software, Open ERP is a bit of an exception in the class of management software.

Despite its comprehensiveness, Open ERP's interface and workflow management facilities are quite simple and intuitive to use. For this reason Open ERP is one of the few software packages with reference customers in both very small businesses (typically requiring simplicity) and large accounts (typically requiring wide functional coverage).

A two-phase approach provides a good guide for your first steps with Open ERP:

1. Using a database containing demonstration data to get an overview of Open ERP's functionality (described in this chapter, *Guided Tour*)

2. Setting up a clean database to configure and populate a limited system for yourself (described in the next chapter, *Developing a real case*).

To read this chapter effectively, make sure that you have access to an Open ERP server. The description in this chapter assumes that you're using the Open ERP web client unless it states otherwise. The general functionality differs little from one client to the other.

2.1 Database creation

Use the technique outlined in *Installation and Initial Setup* to create a new database, `openerp_ch02` . This database will contain the demonstration data provided with Open ERP and a large proportion of the core Open ERP functionality. You'll need to know your super administrator password for this – or you'll have to find somebody who does have it to create this seed database.

Start the database creation process from the **Welcome** page by clicking **Databases** and then completing the following fields on the **Create new database** form:

- **Super admin password** : by default it's `admin` , if you or your system administrator haven't changed it,

- **New database name** : `openerp_ch02` ,

- **Load Demonstration data** checkbox: `checked` ,

- **Default Language** : `English` ,

- **Administrator password** : `admin` (because it's easiest to remember at this stage, but obviously completely insecure),

- **Confirm password** : `admin` .

2.2 To connect to Open ERP

Since this is the first time you've connected to it you'll have to go through the Setup wizard in steps:

1. **Select a profile** : select `Minimal Profile` and click **Next**.

2. At the **Define Main Company** step you should select your own **Company Name** and **Currency**, and address details on the first tab **General Information**; and add more details on the second tab **Report Information** including a logo, if you have one, that appears on reports. Click **Next**.

3. At the **Summary** page you can go back to change details if you need. Click the **Install** button.

4. Finally, at the **Installation done** page, click **Start Configuration**.

Configuration consists of a set of wizards that help you through options for the installed modules. Hardly anything is installed so this is a very simple process at the moment.

1. At the first screen click **Continue** to go into the first wizard. Choose **View Mode** : **Simplified Interface** and then click **Set** to save it.

2. Click **Skip Step** to step over the next wizard, which would enable you to add other users.

3. You've now reached the end of the configuration so click **Continue** to start using the system as the Administrator.

Once you're displaying the main menu you're able to see the following screen items, as shown in screenshot *The Main Menu of the openerp_ch02 database*:

- the **Preferences** toolbar to the top right, showing the user name, links to the **Home** page, **Preferences**, **About** and **Logout**,

- just below you'll find information about the **Request** system,

- links to the **MAIN MENU** and the **SHORTCUTS**,

- information about copyright and the database you're logged into at the bottom of the page,

- the main contents of the window with by the menu toolbar to the left: links generally line up on the right but there are none to show at the moment.

Two menus are available on the left:

- *Partners*,

- *Administration*.

Figure 2.1: *The Main Menu of the openerp_ch02 database*

2.2.1 Preferences toolbar

When you're connected to Open ERP the Preferences toolbar indicates which user you're connected as. So it should currently be showing **Welcome Administrator** (unless you logged in as another user and it's reflecting the name of that user instead).

You'll find a link to the **Home** page to its right. This takes you to either the dashboard or the available menus, depending on the user configuration. In the case of the openerp_ch02database so far the Home page is the Main Menu. But in general each user of the system is presented with a dashboard that's designed to show performance indicators and urgent documents that are most useful to someone of the user's position in the company. You'll see how to assign dashboards to different users in a later chapter, *Configuration & Administration*.

Multi-nationals and time zones

If you have users in different countries, they can configure their own timezone. Timestamp displays are then adjusted by reference to the user's own localization setting.

So if you have a team in India and a team in England, the times will automatically be converted. If an Indian employee sets her working hours from 9 to 6 that will be converted and saved in the server's timezone. When the English users want to set up a meeting with an Indian user, the Indian user's available time will be converted to English time.

The next element in the Toolbar is a link to **Preferences**. By clicking that link you reach a page where the current user can set their password, a timezone, a working language, and a signature:

- The **Password** field gives the user the opportunity to change their own password. You should take steps (perhaps written policies) to prevent users making these too trivial.

- The **Language** field enables the user's working language to be changed. But first the system must be loaded with other languages for the user to be able to choose an alternative, which is described in the next subsection of this chapter. This is a mandatory field, although might initially be set as blank.

- The **Timezone** setting indicates the user's location to Open ERP. This can be different from that of the server. All of the dates in the system are converted to the user's timezone automatically.

- The **Signature** field gives the user a place for the signature attached to messages sent from within Open ERP.

The **About** link gives information about the development of the Open ERP software and various links to other information.

The **Logout** link enables you to logout and return to the original login page. You can then login to another database, or to the same database as another user. This page also gives you access to the super-administrator functions for managing databases on this server.

The **Requests** link sits just below this toolbar. It is only visible if you're logged into a database. If your database is new it will say **No request**. You can click on that link to look at requests that have been sent to you at any time.

Installing a new language

Each user of the system can work in his or her own language. More than twenty languages are currently available besides English. Users select their working language using the Preferences link. You can also assign a language to a partner (customer or supplier), in which case all the documents sent to that partner will be automatically translated into that language.

More information about languages

The base version of Open ERP is translated into the following languages: English, German, Chinese, Spanish, Italian, Hungarian, Dutch, Portuguese, Romanian, Swedish and Czech.

But other languages are also available: Arabic, Afghan, Austrian, Bulgarian, Indonesian, Finnish, Thai, Turkish and Vietnamese..

As administrator you can install a new main working language into the system.

1. Select *Administration* in the Menu Toolbar and click *Translations → Load an Official Translation* in the main menu window,

2. Select the language to install, French for example, and click on **Start Installation**,

3. When the message **Installation done** appears in the **Language file loaded** window, click **OK** to return to the menu. (Your system will actually need the French locale loaded to be able to do this, so you may not be successful here.)

To see the effects of this installation change the preferences of your user to change the working language (you may first need to ensure that you have explicitly selected English as your language, rather than keep the default, before you're given the French option). The main menu is immediately translated in the selected language. If you're using the GTK client you'll first have to close the menu then open a new main menu to start seeing things in the new language.

Navigating the menu

From this point in the book navigation from the main menu is written as a series of menu entries connected by the → character. Instead of seeing " Select Administration in the Menu toolbar then click Translations > Load an Official Translation " you'll just get " use menu *Administration → Translations → Load an Official Translation* ".

Requests as a mechanism for internal communication

Requests are a powerful communication mechanism between users of the system. They're also used by Open ERP itself to send system messages to users.

They have distinct advantages over traditional emails:

- requests are linked to other Open ERP documents,

- an event's history is attached to the request,

- you can monitor events effectively from the messages they've sent.

Open ERP uses this mechanism to inform users about certain system events. For example if there's a problem concerning the procurement of a product a request is sent by Open ERP to the production manager.

Send a request to get an understanding of its functionality:

1. Click on the **Requests** link that should currently be showing **No Requests**. This opens a window that lists all of your waiting requests.

2. Click **New** to create and send a new request.

3. Complete the subject of the request, such as `How are things?` then give a description of the enquiry in the field.

4. Click the **Search** button to the right of the **To** field and select **Administrator** in the window that opens (that's the user that you're already connected as).

5. You can then link this request to other system documents using the **References** field, which could, for example, be a partner or a quotation or a disputed invoice.

6. Click **Send** to send the request to the intended recipient – that's yourself in this case. Then click **MAIN MENU** to return to the original screen.

To check your requests:

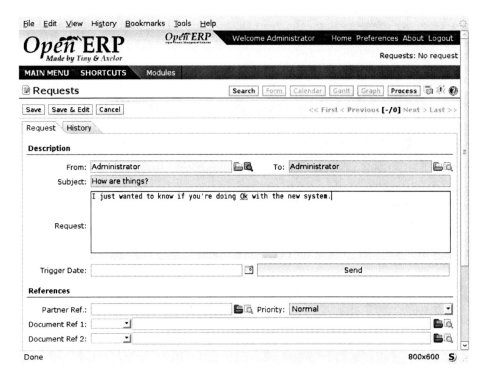

Figure 2.2: *Creating a new request*

1. Click on the link to the right of the **Requests** label to open a list of your requests. (It's possible that you'll still see the statement **No Requests** because this information is updated periodically ather than instantly.) The list of requests then opens and you can see the requests you've been sent there.

2. Click the **Edit** icon, represented by a pencil, at the right hand end of the request line. That opens the request in edit mode.

3. You can then click the **Reply** button and make your response in the **Request** field that appears in place of the original message.

4. Click **Send** to save your response and send it to the original sender.

Requests vs. email

The advantage of an Open ERP request compared with a set of emails about one thread of discussion is that a request contains all of the conversation in one place. You can easily monitor a whole discussion with the appropriate documents attached, and quickly review a list of incomplete discussions with the history within each request.

Look at the request and its history, then close it.

1. Click on the **History** tab in the **Request** form to see the original request and all of the responses. By clicking on each line you could get more information on each element.

2. Return to the first tab, **Request** and click **End of Request** to set it to `closed`. This then appears greyed out.

The request is no longer active. It's not visible to searches and won't appear in your list of waiting requests.

Trigger dates

You can send a request with a future date. This request won't appear in the recipient's waiting list until the indicated date. This mechanism is very useful for setting up alerts before an important event.

2.2.2 Configuring Users

The database you created contains minimal functionality but can be extended to include all of the potential functionality available to Open ERP. About the only functions actually available in this minimal database are Partners and Currencies – and these only because the definition of your main company required this. And because you chose to include demonstration data, both Partners and Currencies were installed with some samples. Because you logged in as Administrator, you have all the access you need to configure users. Click *Administration → Users → Users* to display the list of users defined in the system. A second user, `Demo User` , is also present in the system as part of the demonstration data. Click the `Demo User` name to open a non-editable form on that user.

Click the **Security** tab to see that the demo user is a member of only the `Employee` group, has no roles and is subject to no specialized rules. The `admin` user is different, as you can see if you follow the same sequence to review the its definition. It's a member of the `admin` group, which gives it more advanced rights to configure new users.

Roles, Groups and Users

Users and groups provide the structure for specifying access rights to different documents. Their setup answers the question "Who has access to what?"

Roles are used in business processes for permitting or blocking certain steps in the workflow of a given document. For example you can assign the role of approving an invoice. Roles answer the question "Who should do what?"

Click *Administration → Users → Groups* below the main menu to open the list of groups defined in the system. If you open the form view of the `admin` group by clicking its name in the list, the first tab give you the list of all the users who belong to this group.

Click the Security tab and it gives you details of the access rights for that group. These are detailed later in *Configuration & Administration*, but you can already see there further up in the window, the list of menus reserved for the admin group. By convention, the `admin` in Open ERP has rights of access to the *Configuration* menu in each section. So `Partners / Configuration` is found in the list of access rights but `Partners` isn't found there because it's accessible to all users.

You can create some new users to integrate them into the system. Assign them to predefined groups to grant them certain access rights. Then try their access rights when you login as these users. Management defines these access rights as described in *Configuration & Administration*.

Changes to default access rights

New versions of Open ERP differ from earlier versions of Open ERP and Tiny ERP in this area: many groups have been predefined and access to many of the menus and objects are keyed to these groups by default. This is quite a contrast to the rather liberal approach in 4.2.2 and before, where access rights could be defined but were not activated by default.

2.2.3 Managing partners

In Open ERP, a partner represents an entity that you do business with. That can be a prospect, a customer, a supplier, or even an employee of your company.

List of partners

Click *Partners* → *Partners* in the main menu to open the list of partners. Then click the name of the first partner to get hold of the details – a form appears with several tabs on it:

- the **General** tab contains the main information about the company, such as its corporate name, its primary language, your different contacts at that partner and the categories it belongs to.

- the **Sales & Purchases** tab contains information that's slightly less immediate.

- the *History* tab contains the history of all the events that the partner has been involved in. These events are created automatically by different system documents: invoices, orders, support requests and so on, from a list that can be configured in the system. These give you a rapid view of the partner's history on a single screen.

- the *Notes* tab is an area for free text notes.

To the right of the form is a list of Reports, Actions and Links related to a partner. Click some of them to get a feel for their use.

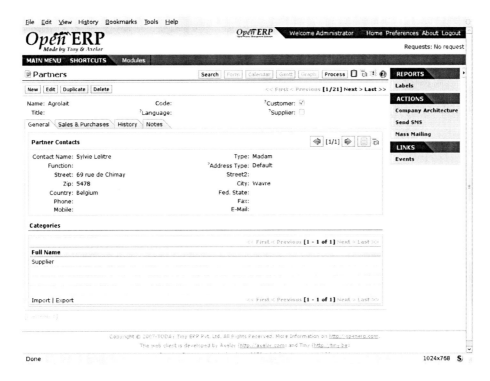

Figure 2.3: *Partner form*

Partner Categories

Partner Categories enable you to segment different partners according to their relation with you (client, prospect, supplier, and so on). A partner can belong to several categories – for example it may be both a customer and supplier at the same time.

But there are also Customer, Supplier and Rental checkboxes on the partner form, which are different. These checkboxes are designed to enable Open ERP to quickly select what should appear on some of the system drop-down selection boxes. They, too, need to be set correctly.

Partner Categories

You can list your partners by category using the menu *Partners → Partners by category* . This opens a hierarchical structure of categories where each category can be divided into sub-categories. Click a category to obtain a list of partners in that category. For example, click all of the partners in the category *Supplier* or *Supplier → Components Supplier*. You'll see that if a company is in a subcategory (such as **Components Supplier**) then it will also show up when you click the parent category (such as **Supplier**).

The administrator can define new categories. So you'll create a new category and link it to a partner:

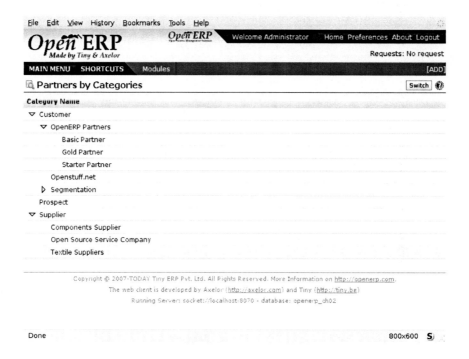

Figure 2.4: *Categories of partner in a hierarchical structure, for example Customer, Prospect, Supplier*

1. Use *Partners → Configuration → Partner Categories* to reach a list of the same categories as above but in a list view rather than a hierarchical tree structure.

2. Click **New** to open an empty form for creating a new category

3. Enter `My Prospects` in the field **Name of Category**. Then click on the **Search** icon to the right of the **Parent Category** field and select `Prospect` in the list that appears.

4. Then save your new category using the **Save** button.

> **Required Fields**
>
> Fields colored blue are required. If you try to save the form while any of these fields are empty the field turns red to indicate that there's a problem. It's impossible to save the form until you've completed every required field.

You can review your new category structure using *Partners → Partners by category*. You should see the new structure of `Prospects / My Prospects` there.

To create a new partner and link it to this new category open a new partner form to modify it.

1. In the **General** tab, type `New Partner` into the **Name** field.

2. Then click on the search icon to the right of the **Categories** field and select your new category from the list that appears: `Prospect / My Prospects`

Figure 2.5: *Creating a new partner category*

3. Then save your partner by clicking **Save** The partner now belongs in the category `Prospect / My prospects`.

4. Monitor your modification in the menu *Partners → Partners by category*. Select the category **My Prospect**. The list of partners opens and you'll find your new partner there in that list.

Searching for documents

If you need to search through a long list of partners it's best to use the available search criteria rather than scroll through the whole partner list. It's a habit that'll save you a lot of time in the long run as you search for all kinds of documents.

Example Categories of partners

A partner can be assigned to several categories. These enable you to create alternative classifications as necessary, usually in a hierarchical form.

Here are some structures that are often used:

- geographical locations,

- interest in certain product lines,

- subscriptions to newsletters,

- type of industry.

2.3 Installing new functionality

All of Open ERP's functionality is contained in its many and various modules. Many of these, the core modules, are automatically loaded during the initial installation of the system and can be updated online later. Although they're mostly not installed in your database at the outset, they're available on your computer for immediate installation. Additional modules can also be loaded online from the official Open ERP site http://openerp.com. These modules are inactive when they're loaded into the system, and can then be installed in a separate step.

You'll start by checking if there are any updates available online that apply to your initial installation. Then you'll install a CRM module to complete your existing database.

2.3.1 Updating the Modules list

Click *Administration → Modules Management → Update Modules List* to start the updating tool. The **Scan for new modules** window opens showing the addresses that Open ERP will look in for downloading new modules (known as the repositories), and updating existing ones.

Remote module repositories

If the repository list doesn't reflect your needs then you can edit it from *Administration → Modules Management → Repository List*. There you can link to new repositories by adding their URLs and disable listed ones by unchecking their **Active** checkbox. If you're not connected to the Internet then you probably want to disable anything there.

Your Open ERP installation must be configured with its `addons` directory as writable for you to be able to download anything at all. If it hasn't been, then you may need the assistance of a systems administrator to change your server's settings so that you can install new modules.

Click **Check New Modules** to start the download from the specified locations. When it's complete you'll see a **New Modules** window indicating how many new modules were downloaded and how many existing modules were updated. Click **OK** to return to the updated list.

It won't matter in this chapter if you can't download anything, but some of the later chapters refer to modules that aren't part of the core installation and have to be obtained from a remote repository.

Modules

All the modules available on your computer can be found in the addons directory of your Open ERP server. Each module there is represented by a directory carrying the name of the module or by a file with the module name and .zip appended to it. The file is in ZIP archive format and replicates the directory structure of unzipped modules.

Searching through the whole list

The list of modules shows only the first available modules. In the web client you can search or follow the First / Previous / Next / Last links to get to any point in the whole list, and you can change the number of entries listed by clicking the row number indicators between **Previous** and **Next** and selecting a different number from the default of 20.

If you use the GTK client you can search, as you would with the web client, or use the + icon to the top left of the window to change the number of entries returned by the search from its default limit of 80, or its default offset of 0 (starting at the first entry) in the whole list.

2.3.2 Installing a module

You'll now install a module named `product`, which will enable you to manage the company's products. This is part of the core installation, so you don't need to load anything to make this work, but isn't installed in the Minimal Profile.

Open the list of uninstalled modules from *Administration → Modules Management → Modules → Uninstalled modules*. Search for the module by entering the name `product` in the search screen then clicking it in the list that appears below it to open it. The form that describes the module gives you useful information such as its version number, its status and a review of its functionality. Click **Schedule for Installation** and the status of the module changes to **To be installed**.

Technical Guide

If you select a module in any of the module lists by clicking on a module line and then on **Technical Guide** at the top right of the window, Open ERP produces a technical report on that module. It's helpful only if the module is installed, so the menu *Administration → Modules Management → Modules → Installed Modules* produces the most fruitful list.

This report comprises a list of all the objects and all the fields along with their descriptions. The report adapts to your system and reflects any modifications you've made and all the other modules you've installed.

Click **Apply Scheduled Upgrades** then **Start Upgrade** on the **System Upgrade** form that appears. Close the window when the operation has completed. Return to the main menu you'll see the new menu *Products* has become available.

Refreshing the menu in the GTK client

After an update in the GTK client you'll have to open a new menu to refresh the content – otherwise you won't see the new menu item. To do that use the window menu *Form → Refresh/Cancel*.

Figure 2.6: *Installation of the product module*

2.3.3 Installing a module with its dependencies

Now install the CRM module (Customer Relationship Management) using the same process as before. Start from *Administration → Modules Management → Modules → Uninstalled modules.*

1. Get the list of modules to install, and search for the crm module in that list.

2. Schedule the module for installation by clicking **Schedule for Installation**.

3. Do the same for account.

4. Click **Apply Scheduled Upgrades** on the action toolbar to the right.

5. Click **Start Upgrade** to install both modules.

6. After a wait, when the installation is complete, click **Start Configuration**.

7. Accept the defaults for accounts setup and select None for the chart of accounts.

8. You'll see details of all the features installed by the modules on a new **Features** tab on the module form.

When you return to the main menu you'll find the new customer relationship management menu *CRM & SRM*. You'll also see all the accounting functions that are now available in the *Financial Management* menu.

There is no particular relationship between the modules installed and the menus added. Most of the core modules add complete menus but some also add submenus to menus already in the system. Other modules add menus and submenus as they need. Modules can also add additional fields to existing forms, or simply additional demonstration data or some settings specific to a given requirement.

Dependencies between modules

The module form shows two tabs before it's installed. The first tab gives basic information about the module and the second gives a list of modules that this module depends on. So when you install a module, Open ERP automatically selects all the necessary dependencies to install this module.

That's also how you develop the profile modules: they simply define a list of modules that you want in your profile as a set of dependencies.

Although you can install a module and all its dependencies at once, you can't remove them in one fell swoop – you'd have to uninstall module by module. Uninstalling is more complex than installing because you have to handle existing system data.

Uninstalling modules

Although it works quite well, uninstalling modules isn't perfect in Open ERP. It's not guaranteed to return the system exactly to the state it was in before installation.

So it's recommended that you make a backup of the database before installing your new modules so that you can test the new modules and decide whether they're suitable or not. If they're not then you can return to your backup. If they are, then you'll probably still reinstall the modules on your backup so that you don't have to delete all your test data.

If you wanted to uninstall you would use the menu *Administration → Modules Management → Modules → Installed Modules* and then uninstall them in the inverse order of their dependencies: `crm`, `account`, `product`.

2.3.4 Installing additional functionality

To discover the full range of Open ERP's possibilities you can install many additional modules. Installing them with their demonstration data provides a convenient way of exploring the whole core system. When you build on the `openerp_ch02` database you'll automatically include demonstration data because you checked the **Load Demonstration Data** checkbox when you originally created the database. Click *Administration → Modules Management → Modules → Uninstalled modules* to give you an overview of all of the modules available for installation.

To test several modules you won't have to install them all one by one. You can use the dependencies between modules to load several at once. For example, try loading the following modules:

- `profile_accounting`,
- `profile_crm`,
- `profile_manufacturing`,
- `profile_service`.

To find these quickly, enter the word `profile` in the **Name** field of the search form and click **Filter** to search for the relevant modules. Then install them one by one or all at once.

As you update you'll see thirty or so modules to be installed. Move on from the **System upgrade done** form by clicking **Start configuration** and then accepting the default crm configuration and picking configuration in turn,

Finally install the additional modules **Analytic Accounting** and **Document Management** when you're offered that configuration option. Don't install any more - you now have quite a fully-loaded system to look at.

Click **Home** and you'll be returned to a dashboard, not the main menu you had before. To get to the main menu, use the **MAIN MENU** link.

2.4 Guided Tour of Open ERP

You'll now explore the database `openerp_ch02` with these profile modules installed to give you an insight into the coverage of the core Open ERP software.

Translating new modules

When you've installed a new module and are using additional languages to English you have to reload the translation file. New terms introduced in these modules aren't translated by default. To do this use *Administration → Translations → Load an Official Translation.*

Depending on the user you're connected as the page appears differently from the Main Menu that showed before. Using the installation sequence above, certain dashboards may be assigned as various users' home pages. They show a summary of the information required to start the day effectively. A project dashboard might contains:

- a list of the next tasks to carry out,
- a list of the next deadlines,
- public notes about projects,
- a planning chart of hours required,
- the timesheet.

Each of the lists can be reordered by clicking on the heading of a column – first in ascending then in descending order as you click repeatedly. To get more information about any particular entry click on the name in the first column, or if you want to show a particular panel click **Zoom** above it.

Users' home pages are automatically reassigned during the creation or upgrading of a database. It's usual to assign a dashboard to someone's home page but any Open ERP screen can be assigned to the home page of any user.

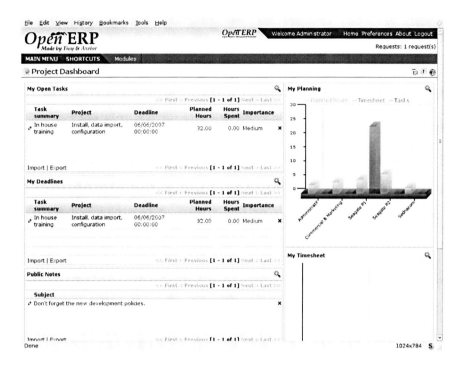

Figure 2.7: *Project Dashboard*

Creating shortcuts

Each user has access to many menu items throughout all of the available menu hierarchy. But in general an employee uses only a small part of the system's functions.

So you can define shortcuts for the most-used menus. These shortcuts are personal for each user. To create a new shortcut open the select menu and click on the **Add** link to the far right of **SHORTCUTS**.

To change or replace a link click **SHORTCUTS**. Open ERP then opens a list of editable shortcuts.

The following sections present an overview of the main functions of Open ERP. Some areas are covered in more detail in the following chapters of this book and you'll find many other functions available in the optional modules. Functions are presented in the order that they appear on the main menu.

2.4.1 Partners

To familiarize yourself with Open ERP's interface, you'll start work with information about partners. Clicking *Partners → Partners* brings up a list of partners that were automatically loaded when you created the database with **Load Demonstration Data** checked.

Search for a partner

Above the partner list you'll see a search form that enables you to quickly filter the partners. Two tabs are available for searching – **Basic Search** and **Advanced Search**. The latter simply shows more fields to narrow your selection.

If you've applied no filter, the list shows every partner in the system. For space reasons this list shows only the first few partners. If you want to display other records you can search for them or navigate through the whole list using the **First**, **Previous**, **Next**, **Last** arrows.

Figure 2.8: *Standard partner search*

 List limits

By default the list in the GTK client shows only the first 80 records, to avoid overloading the network and the server.

But you can change that limit by clicking the + icon to the left of the search criteria, and you can change the offset so that it starts further down the whole list than the first entry.

Similarly the list in the web client shows only the first 20, 40, 60, 80 or 100 records.

The actual number can be switched by clicking on the number and selecting one of the other limits, but you can't select any other limit (so, unlike the GTK client you can't select hundreds or thousands).

If you click on the name of a partner the form view corresponding to that partner opens in Read-Only mode. In the list you could alternatively click the pencil icon to open the same form in Edit mode. Once you have a form you can toggle between the two modes by clicking **Save** or **Cancel** when in Edit mode and **Edit** when in Read-Only mode.

When you're in Read-Only mode you can navigate through the whole list you selected, as though you were in the List view. In Read-Only mode you can also click **Search** to see the form in List view again.

Partner form

The partner form contains several tabs, all referring to the current record:

- **General**,
- **Suppliers & Customers**,
- **History**,
- **Notes**.

The fields in a tab aren't all of the same type – some (such as **Name**) contain free text, some (such as the **Language**) enable you to select a value from a list of options, others give you a view of another object (such as **Partner Contacts** – because a partner can have several contacts) or a list of link to another object (such as **Categories**). There are checkboxes (such as the **Active** field in the **Suppliers & Customers** tab), numeric fields (such as **Credit Limit**) and date fields (such as **Date**).

The **History** tab gives a quick overview of things that have happened to the partner – an overview of useful information such as orders, open invoices and support requests. Events are generated automatically by Open ERP from changes in other documents that refer to this partner.

It's possible to add events manually, such as a note recording a phone call. To add a new event click **Create new record.** to the right of the **Partner Events** field. That opens a new **Partner Events** dialog box enabling an event to be created and added to the current partner.

Actions possible on a partner

To the right of the partner form is a toolbar containing a list of possible **Reports** , **Actions**, and quick **Links** about the partner displayed in the form.

You can generate PDF documents about the selected object (or, in list view, about one or more selected objects) using certain buttons in the **Reports** section of the toolbar:

- **Labels** : print address labels for the selected partners,

Certain actions can be started by the following buttons in the **Actions** section of the toolbar:

- **Company Architecture** : opens a window showing the partners and their children in a hierarchical structure.

- **Send SMS** : enables you to send an SMS to selected partners. This system uses the bulk SMS facilities of the Clickatell® company http://clickatell.com.

- **Mass Mailing** : enables you to send an email to a selection of partners.

> **Reports, Actions and Links in the GTK client**
>
> When you're viewing a form in the GTK client, the buttons to the right of the form are shortcuts to the same Reports, Actions and Links as described in the text. When you're viewing a list (such as the partner list) those buttons aren't available to you. Instead, you can reach Reports and Actions through two of the buttons in the toolbar at the top of the list – Print and Action.

Partners are used throughout the Open ERP system in other documents. For example, the menu *Sales Management → Sales Orders → All Sales Orders* brings up all the Sales Orders in list view. Click the name of a partner rather than the order number on one of those lines and you'll get the Partner form rather than the Sales Order form.

> **Right clicks and shortcuts**
>
> In the GTK client you don't get hyperlinks to other document types. Instead, you can right-click in a list view to show the linked fields (that is fields having a link to other forms) on that line.
>
> In the web client you'll see hyperlink shortcuts on several of the fields on a form that's in Read- Only mode, so that you can move onto the form for those entries. When the web form is in Edit mode, you can instead hold down the control button on the keyboard and right-click with the mouse button in the field, to get all of the linked fields in a pop-up menu just as you would with the GTK client.
>
> You can quickly try this out by going to any one of the sales orders in *Sales Management → Sales Order → All Sales Orders* and seeing what you can reach from the **Customer** field on that sales order form using either the web client with the form in both read-only and in edit mode, or with the GTK client.

Before moving on to the next module, take a quick look into the *Partners → Configuration* menu, particularly *Partner Categories* and *Localisation* menus. They contain some of the demonstration data that you installed when you created the database.

2.4.2 Financial Management

The chapters in *General Accounting (which can be found in a companion volume to this book and in the online book)* in this book are dedicated to general and analytic accounting. A brief overview of the functions provided by these modules is given here as an introduction.

Accounting is totally integrated into all of the company's functions, whether it's general, analytic, budgetary or auxiliary accounting. Open ERP's accounting function is double-entry and supports multiple company divisions and multiple companies, as well as multiple currencies and languages.

Figure 2.9: *Links for a partner appear in an order form*

Accounting that's integrated throughout all of the company's processes greatly simplifies the work of entering accounting data, because most of the entries are generated automatically while other documents are being processed. You can avoid entering data twice in Open ERP, which is commonly a source of errors and delays.

So Open ERP's accounting isn't just for financial reporting – it's also the anchorpoint for many of a company's management processes. For example if one of your accountants puts a customer on credit hold then that will immediately block any other action related to that company's credit (such as a sale or a delivery).

Open ERP also provides integrated analytical accounting, which enables management by business activity or project and provides very detailed levels of analysis. You can control your operations based on business management needs, rather than on the charts of accounts that generally meet only statutory requirements.

2.4.3 Dashboards

Dashboards give you an overview of all the information that's important to you on a single page. The *Dashboards* menu gives you access to predefined boards for *Financial Management*, *Manufacturing* and *Project Management*.

Dashboards

Unlike most other ERP systems and classic statistically-based systems, Open ERP can provide dashboards to all of the system's users, and not just to a select few such as directors and accountants.

Users can each have their own dashboard, adapted to their needs, to enable them to manage their own work effectively. For example a developer using the **Project Dashboard** can see such information as a list of the next tasks, task completion history and an analysis of the state of progress of the relevant projects.

Dashboards are dynamic, which lets you navigate easily around the whole information base. Using the icons above a graph, for example, you can filter the data or zoom into the graph. You can click on any element of the list to get detailed statistics on the selected element.

Dashboards are adaptable to the needs of each user and each company.

Construction of dashboards

Open ERP contains a dashboard editor. It lets you construct your own dashboard to fit your specific needs using only a few clicks.

2.4.4 Products

In Open ERP, product means a raw material, a stockable product, a consumable or a service. You can work with whole products or with templates that separate the definition of products and variants.

For example if you sell t-shirts in different sizes and colors:

- the product template is the "T-shirt" which contains information common to all sizes and all colors,

- the variants are "Size:S" and "Color:Red", which define the parameters for that size and color,

- the final product is thus the combination of the two – t-shirt in size S and color Red.

The value of this approach for some sectors is that you can just define a template in detail and all of its available variants briefly rather than every item as an entire product.

Example Product templates and variants

A product can be defined as a whole or as a product template and several variants. The variants can be in one or several dimensions, depending on the installed modules.

For example, if you work in textiles, the variants on the product template for "T-shirt" are:

- Size (S, M, L, XL, XXL),
- Colour (white, grey, black, red),
- Quality of Cloth (125g/m2, 150g/m2, 160g/m2, 180g/m2),
- Collar (V, Round).

This separation of variant types requires the optional module `product_variant_multi`. Using it means that you can avoid an explosion in the number of products to manage in the database. If you take the example above it's easier to manage a template with 15 variants in four different types than 160 completely different products. This module is available in the `addons-extra` list (it had not been updated, at the time of writing, to work in release 5.0 of Open ERP).

The _Products_ menu gives you access to the definition of products and their constituent templates and variants, and to price lists.

Consumables

In Open ERP a consumable is a physical product which is treated like a stockable product except that stock management isn't taken into account by the system. You could buy it, deliver it or produce it but Open ERP will always assume that there's enough of it in stock. It never triggers a procurement exception.

Open a product form to see the information that describes it. Several different types of product can be found in the demonstration data, giving quite a good overview of the possible options.

Price lists (_Products_ → _Pricelists_) determine the purchase and selling prices and adjustments derived from the use of different currencies. The _Default Purchase Pricelist_ uses the product's **Cost** field to base a Purchase price on. The _Default Sale Pricelist_ uses the product's **List Price** field to base a Sales price on when issuing a quote.

Price lists are extremely flexible and enable you to put a whole price management policy in place. They're composed of simple rules that enable you to build up a rule set for most complex situations: multiple discounts, selling prices based on purchase prices, price reductions, promotions on whole product ranges and so on.

You can find many optional modules to extend product functionality through the Open ERP website, such as:

- `membership` : for managing the subscriptions of members of a company,

- `product_electronic` : for managing electronic products,

- `product_extended` : for managing production costs,

- `product_expiry` : for agro-food products where items must be retired after a certain period,

- `product_lot_foundry` : for managing forged metal products.

2.4.5 Human Resources

Open ERP's Human Resources Management modules provide such functionality as:

- management of staff and the holiday calendar,

- management of employment contracts,

- benefits management,

- management of holiday and sickness breaks,

- managing claims processes,

- management of staff performance,

- management of skills and competencies.

Most of these functions are provided from optional modules whose name starts with `hr_`rather than the core `hr` module, but they're all loaded into the main *Human Resources* menu.

The different issues are handled in detail in the fourth part of this book *Effective Management of Operations (which can be found in a companion volume to this book and in the online book)*, dedicated to internal organization and to the management of a services business.

2.4.6 Stock Management

The various sub-menus under *Stock Management* together provide operations you need to manage stock. You can:

- define your warehouses and structure them around locations and layouts of your choosing,

- manage inventory rotation and stock levels,

- execute packing orders generated by the system,

- execute deliveries with delivery notes and calculate delivery charges,

- manage lots and serial numbers for traceability,

- calculate theoretical stock levels and automate stock valuation,

- create rules for automatic stock replenishment.

Packing orders and deliveries are usually defined automatically by calculating requirements based on sales. Stores staff use picking lists generated by Open ERP, produced automatically in order of priority.

Stock management is, like accounting, double-entry. So stocks don't appear and vanish magically within a warehouse, they just get moved from place to place. And, just like accounting, such a double-entry system gives you big advantages when you come to audit stock because each missing item has a counterpart somewhere.

Most stock management software is limited to generating lists of products in warehouses. Because of its double-entry system Open ERP automatically manages customer and suppliers stocks as well, which has many advantages: complete traceability from supplier to customer, management of consigned stock, and analysis of counterpart stock moves.

Furthermore, just like accounts, stock locations are hierarchical, so you can carry out analyses at various levels of detail.

2.4.7 Customer and Supplier Relationship Management

Open ERP provides many tools for managing relationships with partners. These are available through the *CRM & SRM* menu.

CRM & SRM

CRM stands for Customer Relationship Management, a standard term for systems that manage client and customer relations. SRM stands for Supplier Relationship Management, and is commonly used for functions that manage your communications with your suppliers.

The concept of a "case" is used to handle arbitrary different types of relationship, each derived from a generic method. You can use it for all types of communication such as order enquiries, quality problems, management of a call center, record tracking, support requests and job offers.

Open ERP ensures that each case is handled effectively by the system's users, customers and suppliers. It can automatically reassign a case, track it for the new owner, send reminders by email and raise other Open ERP documentation and processes.

All operations are archived, and an email gateway lets you update a case automatically from emails sent and received. A system of rules enables you to set up actions that can automatically improve your process quality by ensuring that open cases never escape attention.

As well as those functions, you've got tools to improve the productivity of all staff in their daily work:

- a document editor that interfaces with OpenOffice.org,

- interfaces to synchronize your contacts and Outlook Calendar with Open ERP,

- an Outlook plugin enabling you to automatically store your emails and their attachments in a Document Management System integrated with Open ERP,

- a portal for your suppliers and customers that enables them to access certain data on your system.

You can implement a continuous improvement policy for all of your services, by using some of the statistical tools in Open ERP to analyze the different communications with your partners. With these, you can execute a real improvement policy to manage your service quality.

The management of customer relationships is detailed in the second section of this book (see *Managing Customer Relationships (which can be found in a companion volume to this book and in the online book)*).

2.4.8 Purchase Management

Purchase management enables you to track your suppliers' price quotations and convert them into Purchase Orders as you require. Open ERP has several methods of monitoring invoices and tracking the receipt of ordered goods.

You can handle partial deliveries in Open ERP, so you can keep track of items that are still to be delivered on your orders, and you can issue reminders automatically.

Open ERP's replenishment management rules enable the system to generate draft purchase orders automatically, or you can configure it to run a lean process driven entirely by current production needs.

2.4.9 Project Management

Open ERP's project management tools enable you to handle the definition of tasks and the specification of requirements for those tasks, efficient allocation of resources to the requirements, project planning, scheduling and automatic communication with partners.

All projects are hierarchically structured. You can review all of the projects from the menu *Project Management → All Projects*. To view a project's plans, select a project line and then click **Print**. Then select **Gantt diagram** to obtain a graphical representation of the plan.

You can run projects related to Services or Support, Production or Development – it's a universal module for all enterprise needs.

Project Management is described in *Internal Organization and Project Management (which can be found in a companion volume to this book and in the online book)*.

2.4.10 Manufacturing

Open ERP's production management capabilities enable companies to plan, automate, and track manufacturing and product assembly. Open ERP supports multi-level bills of materials and lets you substitute subassemblies dynamically, at the time of sales ordering. You can create virtual sub- assemblies for reuse on several products with phantom bills of materials.

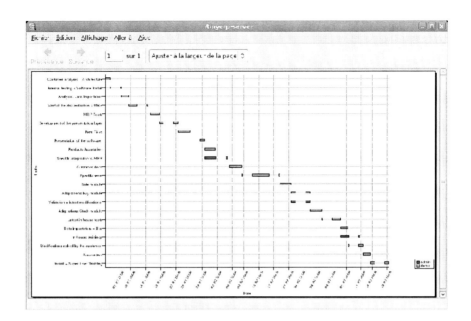

Figure 2.10: *Project Planning*

 BoMs, routing, workcenters

These documents describe the materials that make up a larger assembly. They're commonly called Bills of Materials or BoMs.

They're linked to routings which list the operations needed to carry out the manufacture or assembly of the product.

Each operation is carried out at a workcenter, which can be a machine, a tool, or a person.

Production orders based on your company's requirements are scheduled automatically by the system, but you can also run the schedulers manually whenever you want. Orders are worked out by calculating the requirements from sales, through bills of materials, taking current inventory into account. The production schedule is also generated from the various lead times defined throughout, using the same route

The demonstration data contains a list of products and raw materials with various classifications and ranges. You can test the system using this data.

2.4.11 Sales Management

The *Sales Management* menu gives you roughly the same functionality as the *Purchase Management* menu – the ability to create new orders and to review the existing orders in their various states – but there are important differences in the workflows.

Confirmation of an order triggers delivery of the goods, and invoicing timing is defined by a setting in each individual order.

Delivery charges can be managed using a grid of tariffs for different carriers.

2.4.12 Document Management

Open ERP integrates a complete document management system that not only carried out the functions of a standard DMS, but also integrates with all of its system-generated documents such as Invoices and Quotations. What's more it keeps all of this synchronized.

2.4.13 Process Management

Many documents have a workflow of their own, and also take part in cross-functional processes. Take a document that could be expected to have a workflow, such as a Sales Order, and then click the **Process** button above its form to see the full process.

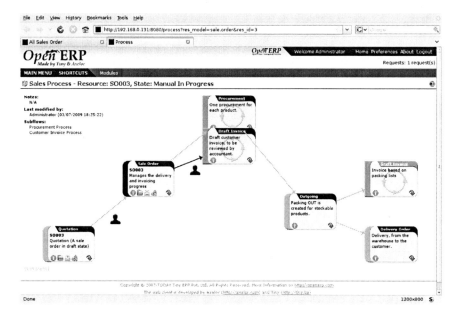

Figure 2.11: *Process for a Sales Order*

You can see the position of that particular document in its process, if you have selected a single document, by the solid bar on one of the process nodes. You also link to documents and menus for each of the stages.

There is a clear distinction between a cross-functional process (that is currently only shown in the web client) and the detailed document workflow (that is shown in both the web client from a process node, and the GTK client from the *Plugins > Execute a Plugin...* menu and clicking either the **Print Workflow** or the the **Print Workflow (Complex)** option.

Alongside the document management system, the process visualization features make Open ERP far better for documentation than similar systems.

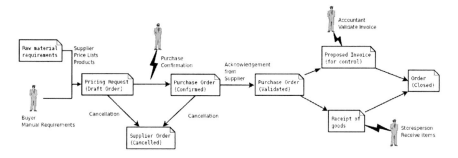

Figure 2.12: *Workflow for a Purchase Order*

2.4.14 Other functions

You've been through a brisk, brief overview of many of the main functional areas of Open ERP. Some of these – a large proportion of the core modules – are treated in more detail in the following chapters.

You can use the menu *Administration → Modules Management → Modules → Uninstalled modules* to find the remaining modules that have been loaded into your installation but not yet installed in your database. Some modules have only minor side-effects to Open ERP (such as `base_iban`), some have quite extensive effects (such as the various charts of accounts), and some make fundamental additions (such as `multi_company`).

But there are now more than three hundred modules available. If you've connected to the Internet, and if your `addons` directory is writable as described at the beginning of this chapter, you can download new modules using the menu *Administration → Modules Management → Update Modules List*.

A brief description is available for each module, but the most thorough way of understanding their functionality is to install one and try it. So, pausing only to prepare another test database to try it out on, just download and install the modules that appear interesting.

Developing a real case 3

Now that you've discovered some of the many possibilities of Open ERP from a tour of the demonstration database, you'll develop a real case. An empty database provides the starting point for testing a classic workflow from product purchase to sale, completing your guided tour and your familiarization with Open ERP.

A database loaded with demonstration data is very useful for understanding Open ERP's general capabilities. But to explore Open ERP through a lens of your own company's needs you should start with an empty database. You'll work in this chapter on a minimal database containing no demonstration data so that there is no confusion about what you created. And you'll keep the database you've created so that you can build on it throughout the rest of this book if you want to.

You'll develop a real case through the following phases:

1. Specify a real case.

2. Describe the functional needs.

3. Configure the system with the essential modules.

4. Carry out the necessary data loading.

5. Test the system with your database.

The case is deliberately extremely simple to provide you with a foundation for the more complex situations you'll handle in reality. Throughout this chapter it's assumed that you're accessing Open ERP through its web interface.

3.1 Use case

Configure a system that enables you to:

- buy products from a supplier,

- stock the products in a warehouse,

- sell these products to a customer.

The system should support all aspects of invoicing, payments to suppliers and receipts from customers.

3.2 Functional requirements

For working out the business case you'll have to model:

- the suppliers,

- the customers,

- some products,

- inventory for despatch,

- a purchase order,

- a sale order,

- invoices,

- payments.

To test the system you'll need at least one supplier, one customer, one product, a warehouse, a minimal chart of accounts and a bank account.

3.3 Database creation

Use the technique outlined in *Database creation* to create a new database, openerp_ch03 . This database will be free of data and contain the least possible amount of functionality as a starting point. You'll need to know your super administrator password for this – or you'll have to find somebody who does have it to create this seed database. You won't be able to use the openerp_ch1 or openerp_ch2 databases that you might have created so far in this book because they both contain demonstration data.

Start the database creation process from the **Welcome** page by clicking **Databases** and then completing the following fields on the **Create new database** form, as shown in *Creating a blank database*:

- **Super admin password** : by default it's admin , if you or your system administrator haven't changed it,

- **New database name** : openerp_ch03 ,

- **Load Demonstration data** checkbox: not checked (**this step is very important, but catches out many people**),

- **Default Language** : English ,

- **Administrator password** : admin (because it's easiest to remember at this stage, but obviously completely insecure),

- **Confirm password** : admin .

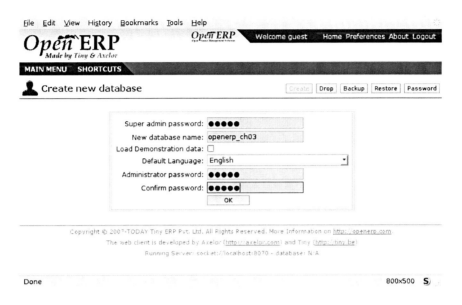

Figure 3.1: *Creating a blank database*

File Edit View History Bookmarks Tools Help

Setup

Cancel | Next

Select a Profile

Profile: | Minimal Profile   ▾ |

A profile sets a pre-selection of modules for specific needs. These profiles have been setup to help you discover the different aspects of OpenERP. This is just an overview, we have 300+ available modules.

You'll be able to install more modules later through the Administration menu.

Copyright © 2007-TODAY Tiny ERP Pvt. Ltd. All Rights Reserved. More information on http://openerp.com
The web client is developed by Axelor (http://axelor.com) and Tiny (http://tiny.be)
Running Server: socket://localhost:8070 - database: openerp_ch03

Done   800x453 S

Figure 3.2: *Setting up a blank database - first screen*

Then click **OK** to create the database and move to the setup screen *Setting up a blank database - first screen.*

After a short delay you are connected to the new `openerp_ch03` database as user `admin` with the password you gave it. You'll have to go through the Setup wizard in steps:

1. **Select a profile** : select `Minimal Profile` and click **Next**.

2. At the **Define Main Company** step you could select your own **Company Name** and **Currency**, and address details on the first tab **General Information**; and you can add more details on the second tab **Report Information** including a logo that would appear on reports. In this test you should leave everything untouched for the moment and just click **Next**: you'll change them later.

3. At the **Summary** page you can go back to change details if you need. Click the **Install** button.

4. Finally, at the **Installation done** page, click **Start Configuration**.

Configuration consists of a set of wizards that help you through options for the installed modules. Since you chose the minimal database hardly anything is installed so this is a very simple process at the moment, starting with the menu layout *Configuring a minimal database - first screen* .

Figure 3.3: *Configuring a minimal database - first screen*

1. At the first screen click **Continue** to go into the first wizard. Choose **View Mode** : **Extended Interface** so that you can see everything and then click **Set** to save it.

2. Click **Skip Step** to step over the next wizard, which would enable you to add other users.

3. You've now reached the end of the configuration so click **Continue** to start using the system as the Administrator as shown in the screenshot *Starting the minimal database.*

3.4 Installing and configuring modules

All of the functional needs are provided by core modules from Open ERP:

- product management (the `product` module),

Figure 3.4: *Starting the minimal database*

- inventory control (the `stock` module),

- accounting and finance (the `account` module),

- purchase management (the `purchase` module),

- sales management (the `sale` module).

Use the menu *Administration* → *Modules Management* → *Modules* → *Uninstalled modules* to show the list of all modules that are registered within Open ERP but as yet uninstalled. Then:

1. Enter `product` into the **Name** field and click **Filter** to list the `product` module.

2. Click the name `product` in the list to display the product module in form view, rather than the list view that a search displays.

3. Click the **Schedule for Installation** button on the product module form.

4. Click the **Search** button at the top of the form to toggle back to the list view with search selection fields on it.

5. Search for the `sale` module then select it, too, as you did with product, to show it in form view.

6. Click the **Dependencies** tab to see that you'll automatically be loading the `product`, `stock`, `mrp`, and `process` modules along with the `sale` module. `product` and `process` are both already marked for installation as a result of the first steps.

7. Return to the **Module** tab and then click its **Schedule for Installation** button.

8. Click **Apply Scheduled Upgrades** in the **Action** toolbar to the right.

9. When the **System Upgrade** form appears, review the list of Modules to update – it may be longer than you had expected, and now includes all the modules you need, because the dependencies themselves had their own dependencies.

10. Click **Start Upgrade**, wait for **System upgrade done** to be displayed, then click **Start Configuration** on that form.

Configuration is required for both the accounts setup and the sales defaults.

1. Accept the defaults for the **Fiscal Year** and choose the **Charts of Account** to be **None** then click **Continue**.

2. The sales defaults are shown in the screenshot *The module form once a module is installed*. The selections you make determine how Open ERP's processes work by setting its default behaviour (although you can override any of them for any sales order, so you are not strictly bound by these defaults). Accept the initial set by clicking **Set default behaviour**.

3. You've reached the end of this configuration stage so click **Continue** to continue using the system as the Administrator. You first reach a new tab **Features** that lists the new menus and views as shown in the figure *The module form once a module is installed*. Each of the modules that were installed has its own new tab - it's not only the one you see displayed in front of you. Click **Next** and **Previous** to move between them.

4. The main menu now displays all of the menu items that were loaded by the modules you installed. Click **MAIN MENU** to see this, shown in the screenshot *Continuing with the database after installing new modules*.

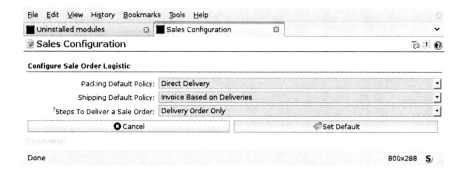

Figure 3.5: *The module form once a module is installed*

3.5 Database setup

You'll create all the elements in the database that you need to carry out the use case. These are specified in the functional requirements.

3.5.1 Configuring Accounts

You need to start off with a minimal set of accounts, and to do that you will need a couple of account types. You can structure your accounts into a chart at any time (and, in fact, you can structure them into several

Figure 3.6: *Continuing with the database after installing new modules*

additional charts at the same time as you'll see in the chapter *Configuring Accounts from A to Z (which can be found in a companion volume to this book and in the online book))*, so you don't need to be concerned unduly about structure.

Account Types

Create account types using *Financial Management → Configuration → Financial Accounting → Financial Accounts → Account Types* and then clicking the **New** button. You'll need the following four types, the first of which is shown in figure *New Account Type*.

Table 3.1: Defining Account Types

Acc. Type Name	Code	Sequence	Sign on Reports	Deferral Method	Partner Account
View	view	5	Positive	None	unchecked
Income	income	5	Positive	Unreconciled	unchecked
Expense	expense	5	Positive	Unreconciled	unchecked
Cash	cash	5	Positive	Balance	unchecked

Figure 3.7: *New Account Type*

Accounts

Create accounts using *Financial Management* → *Configuration* → *Financial Accounting* → *Financial Accounts* → *List of Accounts* and then clicking the **New** button.

You need accounts to handle the purchase and sales orders that haven't yet been paid, two more for the receipt and shipping of goods, and one for the payment and receipt of funds. And one 'organizing' account that's just a view of the other five. So you'll need the following six accounts, one of which is shown in *New Account*.

Table 3.2: Defining Accounts

Name	Code	Internal Type	Parent	Account Type	Reconcile
Minimal Chart	0	View		View	unchecked
Payable	AP	Payable	0 Minimal Chart	Expense	checked
Receivable	AR	Receivable	0 Minimal Chart	Income	checked
Cash	C	Others	0 Minimal Chart	Cash	unchecked
Purchases	P	Others	0 Minimal Chart	Expense	unchecked
Sales	S	Others	0 Minimal Chart	Income	unchecked

The **Account Type** entry is taken from the list of types that you just created. Although it looks a bit like a text box, it doesn't behave in quite the same way. A single `Del` or `Backspace` keystroke is all you need to delete the whole text, and when you type the name (or part of the name) you still need to associate that text with the entry by clicking the **Search** icon to the right of the field.

Properties

You now define some default properties so that you don't have to think about which account is used for which transaction every time you do something. The main new properties are the four that associate accounts payable and receivable to partners, and expenses and income to product categories.

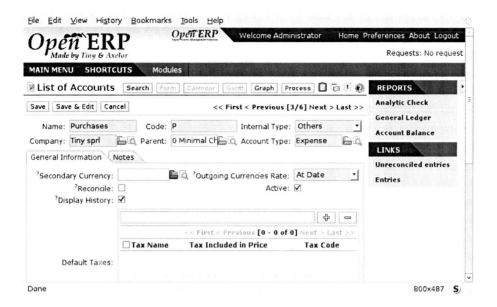

Figure 3.8: *New Account*

Create properties using *Administration → Configuration → Properties → Default Properties* and then clicking the **New** button.

Table 3.3: Defining Properties

Name	Company	Fields	Value	Parent Resource
property_account_payable	Tiny sprl	Account Payable	(account.account) AP Payable	(None)
property_account_receivable	Tiny sprl	Account Receivable	(account.account) AR Receivable	(None)
property_account_expense_categ	Tiny sprl	Expense Account	(account.account) P Purchases	(None)
property_account_income_categ	Tiny sprl	Income Account	(account.account) S Sales	(None)

Mistakes in configuring accounts and properties

It's easy to make mistakes in configuring the accounts and their properties, but the consequences are not immediately obvious. You'll mostly discover mistakes when trying to make a Purchase or Sale Order (see later, for example, *Purchase Order*), where the accounts are required fields or, if you're diligent, when you set up Partners.

If you configure them correctly at this stage then fields will be completed automatically and you'll never know a thing. If you don't configure all this correctly then you won't be able to save the order form until you have corrected the problem or until you manually set the accounts.

Since this configuration is quite tedious you'd be best finding a certified Chart of Accounts that that has already been set up to meet your needs, if you can find one.

3.5.2 Configuring Journals

You'll also need to configure some journals, which are used to record the transactions from one account to another when invoices are raised and then paid. Create journals from the menu *Financial Management → Configuration → Financial Accounting → Financial Journals* and then clicking the **New** button.

Table 3.4: Defining Journals

Journal Name	Code	Type	View	Entry Sequence	Default Debit Account	Default Credit Account
Purchase Journal	PUJ	Purchase	Journal View	Purchase Journal	P Purchases	P Purchases
Sale Journal	SAJ	Sale	Journal View	Sale Journal	S Sales	S Sales
Bank Journal	BNK	Cash	Cash Journal View	Account Journal	C Cash	C Cash

Mistakes in configuring journals

It's easy to make mistakes in configuring the journals, too, and the consequences are also not immediately obvious. You'll mostly discover mistakes when creating an invoice (which happens at different points in the process depending on your configuration). In this example, validating a Purchase Order creates a draft invoice (see later, again for example, *Purchase Order*), where a journal is required.

As with accounts and properties, if you configure them correctly at this stage then the fields will be completed automatically and you'll never know a thing. If you don't configure all this correctly then there will be errors with the order form or corresponding draft invoice until you have corrected the problem or until you manually set the journal.

3.5.3 Configuring the Main Company

Start to configure your database by renaming the **Main Company** from its default of `Tiny sprl` to the name of your own company or (in this case) another example company. When you print standard documents such as quotations, orders and invoices you'll find this configuration information used in the document headers and footers.

To do this, click *Partners → Partners* and click the name of the only company there, which is `Tiny sprl`. This gives you a read-only view form view of the company, so make it editable by clicking the **Edit** button to the upper left of the form.

> **Editable form in the web client**
>
> When toggling from the list view to the form view of an item, you can generally click its name in the list view to show a non-editable view or the pencil icon by the left-hand edge of the line to open it in an editable view. You can toggle between editable and non-editable once you're in form view.

Change the following:

- **Name** : `Ambitious Plumbing Enterprises,`
- **Contact Name** : `George Turnbull.`

Before you save this, look at the partner's accounting setup by clicking the fifth tab **Accounting**. The fields **Account Receivable** and **Account Payable** have account values in them that were taken from the account properties you just created. You don't have to accept those values: you can enter any suitable account you like at this stage, although Open ERP constrains the selection to ones that make accounting sense.

Back at the first tab, **General'change any other fields you like, such as the address and phone numbers, then :guilabel:'Save**. This changes one Contact for the Partner, which is sufficient for the example.

From the **MAIN MENU**, click *Administration → Users → Company Structure → Companies* and edit the only entry there:

- **Company Name** : `AmbiPlum,`
- **Partner** : should already show `Ambitious Plumbing Enterprises,`
- **Report Header** : `Ambitious Plumbing,`
- **Report Footer 1** : `Best Plumbing Services, Great Prices,`
- **Report Footer 2** : `Ambitious - our Registered Company Details.`

Figure *Changing company details* shows the effect of this. You can also change various other company-wide parameters for reports and scheduling in the other tabs, and you can upload a company logo of a specific size for the reports. Click **Save** to store this.

You can leave the currency at its default setting of `EUR`for this example. Or you can change it in this Company and the two default Pricelists (*Products → Pricelists → Pricelists*) if you feel compelled to do that.

Figure 3.9: *Changing company details*

Currency

The examples in this book are in USD and EUR. You, the reader, could use your home currency (perhaps CAD, CNY, GBP, or IDR) in their place.

3.5.4 Creating partner categories, partners and their contacts

You'll now create a suppliers category and a customers category. Partner categories are useful for organizing groups of partners but have no special behavior that affects partners, so you can assign them as you like. Then you'll define one supplier and one customer, with a contact for each.

To do this use the menu *Partners → Configuration → Partner Categories'and click :guilabel:'New* to open a new form for defining **Partner Categories**. Define the two categories that follow by just entering their **Category Name** and saving them:

- Suppliers,
- Customers.

Then create two partners from the menu *Partners → Partners*. Click on the **New** button to open a blank form and then add the following data for the first partner first:

- **Name** : Plumbing Component Suppliers,
- **Customer** checkbox : unchecked,
- **Supplier** checkbox : checked,
- **Contact Name** : Jean Poolley,
- **Address Type** : Default,

- add `Suppliers` to the **Categories** field by selecting it from the Search List,

- then save the partner by clicking the **Save** button.

Figure *New Partner Form* shows the result.

Figure 3.10: *New Partner Form*

 Contact Types

If you've recorded several contacts for the same partner you can specify which contact is used for various documents by specifying the Address Type.

For example the delivery address can differ from the invoice address for a partner. If the Address Types are correctly assigned, then Open ERP can automatically select the appropriate address during the creation of the document – an invoice is addressed to the contact that's been assigned the Address Type of Invoice, otherwise to the Default address.

For the second partner, proceed just as you did for the first, with the following data:

- **Name** : `Smith and Offspring`,

- **Customer** checkbox : `checked`,

- **Supplier** checkbox : `unchecked`,
- **Contact Name** : `Stephen Smith`,
- **Address Type** : `Default`.

Then add `Customers` in the **Categories** field. **Save** the form. To check your work you can go to the menu *Partners → Partner Categories* and click on each category in turn to see the companies in the category.

> **Multiple Partner Categories**
>
> If this partner was also a supplier then you'd add Suppliers to the categories as well, but there's no need to do so in this example. You can assign a partner to multiple categories at all levels of the hierarchy.

3.5.5 Creating products and their categories

Unlike partner categories and their assigned partners, product categories do have an effect on the products assigned to them – and a product may belong to only one category. Select the menu *Products → Configuration → Product Categories* and click **New** to get an empty form for defining a product category.

Enter `Radiators` in the **Name** field. You'll see that other fields, specifically those in the **Accounting Properties** section, have been automatically filled in with values of accounts and journals. These are the values that will affect products – equivalent fields in a product will take on these values if they, too, are blank when their form is saved. Click **Save**.

> **Properties fields**
>
> Properties have a rather unusual behavior. They're defined by parameters in the menus in *Administration → Configuration → Properties*, and they update fields only when a form is saved, and only when the fields are empty at the time the form is saved. You can manually override any of these properties as you need.
>
> Properties fields are used all over the Open ERP system and particularly extensively in a multi- company environment. There, property fields in a partner form can be populated with different values depending on the user's company.
>
> For example the payment conditions for a partner could differ depending on the company from which it's addressed.

> **UOM**
>
> UOM is an abbreviation for Unit of Measure. Open ERP manages multiple units of measure for each product: you can buy in tons and sell in kgs, for example. The conversion between each category is made automatically (so long as you have set up the conversion rate in the product form first).

Managing double units of measure

The whole management of stock can be carried out with double units of measure (UOM and UOS – for Unit of Sale). For example an agro-food company can stock and sell ham by piece but buy and value it by weight. There's no direct relationship between these two units so a weighing operation has to be done.

This functionality is crucial in the agro-food industry, and can be equally important in fabrication, chemicals and many other industries.

Now create a new product:

1. Go to the *Products → Products* menu and click **New**.

2. Create a product – type `Titanium Alloy Radiator` in the **Name** field.

3. Click the **Search** icon to the right of the **Category** field to select the **Radiators** category.

4. The **Product Type** field should stay as `Stockable Product` its default value. The fields **Procure Method**, **Supply Method**, **Default UOM**, and **Purchase UOM** should also stay at their default values: in fact every other field in this tab remains untouched.

Figure 3.11: *Product Form*

5. Click on the **Prices & Suppliers** tab and enter `57.50` into the **Cost Price** field and `132.50` into the **Sale Price** field.

6. Click the **Accounting** tab, then click **Save** and observe that **Accounting Properties** here remain empty. When product transactions occur, the Income and Expense accounts that you've just defined in the Product Category are used by the Product unless an account is specified here, directly in the product, to override that.

7. Once the product is saved it changes to a non-editable state. If you had entered data incorrectly or left a required field blank, the form would have stayed editable and you'd need to click from tab to tab to find a field colored red, with an error message below it, that would have to be correctly filled in.

3.5.6 Stock locations

Click *Stock Management → Stock Locations Structure* to see the hierarchy of stock locations. These locations have been defined by the minimal default data loaded when the database was created. You'll use this default structure in this example.

Open ERP has three predefined top-level location types , `Physical Locations` and `Partner Locations` that act as their names suggest, and `Virtual Locations` that are used by Open ERP for its own purposes.

1. From the **Main Menu** click on *Stock Management → Configuration → Locations* to reach a list view of the locations (not the tree view).

2. Click on the name of a location, such as `Physical Locations/Tiny SPRL` to open a descriptive form view. Each location has a **Location type** and a **Parent Location** that defines the hierarchical structure. An **Inventory Account** can also be assigned to a location. While you're here you should change the location's name to Ambitious Plumbing Enterprises, since it was named before you changed the company name.

3. From the *Main Menu* click *Stock Management → Configuration → Warehouses* to view a list of warehouses. There's only the one at the moment, which should also be renamed from `Tiny SPRL` to `Ambitious Plumbing Enterprises`.

> **Valuation of stock**
>
> If you want real-time stock valuation that tracks stock movements you must assign an account to each stock location. As product items are added to and taken from each location Open ERP generates an account entry for that location defined by the configuration of the product being moved – and a stock valuation based (in the current versions of Open ERP) on either **Cost Price** or **Average Price**.
>
> For example, if you assign an account to the Supplier location you'll be able see the value of stock that you've taken from the supplier. Its contents can be valued in your accounts and it can manage inventory on consignment.

A Warehouse contains an input location, a stock location and an output location for sold products. You can associate a warehouse with a partner to give the warehouse an address. That doesn't have to be your own company (although it can be): you can easily specify another partner who may be holding stock on your behalf.

Location Structure

Each warehouse is composed of three locations **Location Input**, **Location Output**, and **Location Stock**. Your available stock is given by the contents of the **Location Stock** and its child locations.

So the **Location Input** can be placed as a child of the **Location Stock**, which means that when **Location Stock** is interrogated for product quantities, it also takes account of the contents of the **Location Input**. **Location Input** could be used as a goods-in QC location. The **Location Output** must never be placed as a child of **Location Stock**, since items in **Location Output**, which can be considered to be packed ready for customer shipment, should not be thought of as available for sale elsewhere.

In the default configuration, Open ERP uses the same `Stock` location for both Input and Output because it is easier to understand when you're starting out.

3.5.7 Setting up a chart of accounts

You can set up a chart of accounts during the creation of a database, but for this exercise you'll start with the minimal chart that you created (just a handful of required accounts without hierarchy, tax or subtotals).

A number of account charts have been predefined for Open ERP, some of which meet the needs of national authorities (the number of those created for Open ERP is growing as various contributors create and freely publish them). You can take one of those without changing it if it's suitable, or you can take anything as your starting point and design a complete chart of accounts to meet your exact needs, including accounts for inventory, asset depreciation, equity and taxation.

You can also run multiple charts of accounts in parallel – so you can put all of your transaction accounts into several charts, with different arrangements for taxation and depreciation, aggregated differently for various needs.

Before you can use any chart of accounts for anything you need to specify a Fiscal Year. This defines the different time periods available for accounting transactions. An initial Fiscal Year was created during the database setup so you don't need to do any more on this.

Click *Financial Management → Charts → Charts of Accounts* and then click **Open Charts** to open a new **Account charts** form where you define exactly what you want to see. Click **Open Charts** to accept the defaults and see a hierarchical structure of the accounts.

3.5.8 Make a backup of the database

If you know the super-administrator password, make a backup of your database using the procedure described at the very end of *Installation and Initial Setup*. Then restore it to a new database: `testing`.

This operation enables you to test the new configuration on `testing` so that you can be sure everything works as designed. Then if the tests are successful you can make a new database from `openerp_ch03`, perhaps called `live` or `production`, for your real work.

From here on, connect to this new testing database logged in as admin if you can. If you have to make corrections, do that on openerp_ch03 and copy it to a new testing database to continue checking it.

Or you can just continue working with the openerp_ch03 database to get through this chapter. You can recreate openerp_ch03 quite quickly if something goes wrong and you can't recover from it but, again, you'd need to know your super administrator password for that.

3.6 Testing a Purchase-Sale workflow

To familiarize yourself with the system workflow you'll test a purchase-sale workflow in two phases.

The first consists of product purchase, which requires the following operations:

1. Place a purchase order with Plumbing Component Suppliers for 10 Titanium Alloy Radiators at a unit price of 60.00.

2. Receive these products at your Goods In.

3. Generate a purchase invoice.

4. Pay your supplier.

Following this, you'll sell some of these products, using this sequence:

1. Receive a sales order for 6 Titanium Alloy Radiators from Smith and Sons, sold at a unit price of 130.00.

2. Despatch the products.

3. Invoice the customer.

4. Receive the payment.

3.6.1 Purchase Order

To place a Purchase Order with your supplier, use the menu *Purchase Management → New Purchase Order* for a new Purchase Order form.

Complete the following field:

- **Partner** : Plumbing Component Suppliers.

As you complete the **Partner** field, Open ERP automatically completes the **Address** field and the **Price List** field from information it takes out of the Partner record. Then click on the **Save Parent Record.** icon to the right of the **Order Line** field. This automatically saves the body of the **Purchase Order**, and changes to a **Create New Record.** icon. Click that to open the **Purchase Order Line** window.

Enter the following information

- **Product** : Titanium Alloy Radiator - type in part of this name then click the **Search** icon at the end of the line to complete it,

When you've selected a product on the product line, Open ERP automatically completes the following fields from information it finds in the Product record:

- **Product UOM** : the unit of measure for this product,

- **Description** : the detailed description of the product,

- **Scheduled date** : based on the product lead time,

- **Unit price** : the unit price of the product,

- **Analytic account** : if any account is specified then it will appear on the order line (it's not in this example),

- **Taxes** : applicable taxes defined in the partner, if specified, otherwise in the product, if specified (there aren't any in this example).

You can edit any of these fields to suit the requirements of the purchase order at the time of entry. Change the:

- **Quantity** : 10,

- **Unit Price** to 56.00.

Save the order line and close the **Purchase Order Line** window by clicking the **Close** button. You can then confirm the whole one-line order by clicking **Save**, which makes the form non-editable.

It's now in a state of Request for Quotation, so click **Confirm Purchase Order**, which corresponds to an approval from a manager or from Accounts within your own company and moves the order into Confirmedstate. Finally click **Approved by Supplier** to indicate the supplier's acknowledgment of the order. The order becomes Approved .

If you click the **Delivery & Invoices** tab you'll see the delivery **Destination** is your own company's Stock location and that the invoice was created from the order and is SI: PO001. It's not entirely obvious at this stage, but the invoice is in a draft state so it can be edited and, crucially, has no accounting impact yet: it's just ready for your accounting group to activate it.

3.6.2 Receiving Goods

After confirming the order you'd wait for the delivery of the products from your supplier. Typically this would be somebody in Stores, who would:

1. Open the menu *Stock Management → Incoming Products → Packings to Process* using the expand/collapse icon.

From the Purchase Order

You could have clicked the **Packing** link to the right of the Purchase Order to reach the same screen, but this would confuse the purchasing role with the stores role. That link is very useful during testing and training, however.

2. When the **Packing** window appears, select the name of the entry in the list (PACK1 to display the Packing List itself – you'd usually do a search for the supplier name or order number in a list that was larger than this – then click **Validate** to load the **Make Packing** form.

3. Click **Make Picking** to indicate that you're receiving the whole quantity of 10 units.

At this point you've accepted 10 units into your company, in a location that you've already seen.

To check actual stock levels, use the menu *Stock Management → Location Structure*, find Stockin the hierarchy under **Physical Locations**, using the expand/collapse controls to make your way through the tree and click it. You'll next get a **View Stock of Products** screen, where you just click **Open Products** to select everything that the system knows.

You'll see that **Products: Stock** shows everything in the Stocklocation (and below it) with **Real stock** (the actual quantity recorded) and **Future stock** (the quantities expected in future when all receipts and despatches have been made) – both 10 in this case.

Alternatively you could have clicked the Ambitious Plumbing Enterprisesline to highlight it (the line, not the Ambitious Plumbing Enterprisestext itself), and then click the **Lots by Location** button in the **Reports** to the top right of the form. You'll see that you've now got 10 pieces of Titanium Alloy Radiatorin the location Stockand also in the location Ambitious Plumbing Enterprises, its parent as shown in the figure *List of products and their stock levels*. If you explore further you'll also see you have −10 pieces in the Partner Location Suppliers.

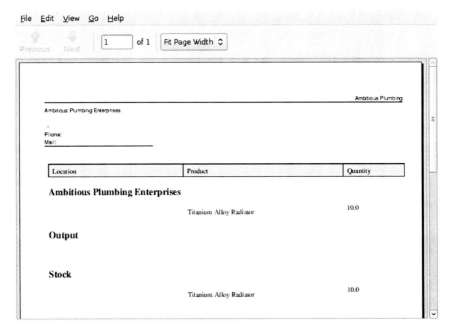

Figure 3.12: *List of products and their stock levels*

Traceability in double-entry

Open ERP operates a double-entry stock transfer scheme similar to double-entry accounting. Because of this you can carry out various analyses of stock levels in your warehouse, along with the corresponding levels in Partner Location at your Supplier. The double-entry system, analogous to that of accounting, enables you to keep track of stock movements quite easily, and to resolve any errors that occur.

3.6.3 Control of purchase invoices

When you've received an invoice from your supplier (which would usually be sent to your Accounts department) go to the menu *Financial Management → Invoices → Supplier Invoices → Draft Supplier Invoices* to open a list of supplier invoices waiting for receipt. These invoices enable your Accounts Department to match the the price and quantities ordered against the price and quantities on the supplier's invoice (and since it's not uncommon to receive an invoice showing details more favourable to the supplier than those agreed at the time of purchase, this is a useful function).

In this example, you created an invoice automatically when you confirmed the supplier's Purchase Order. That's because the **Invoicing Control** field on the order was set to `From Order`(the default option). Other options enable you to create invoices at the time of receiving goods or manually. The initial state of an invoice is `Draft`.

Now click the invoice for your order `PO001` to display its contents. You can compare the goods that you've recorded there with the invoice received from your supplier. If there's a difference it's possible to change the order lines to, for example, add a delivery charge. Click **Validate** to confirm the invoice and put it into the `Open` state.

Accounting entries are generated automatically once the invoice is validated. To see the effects on your chart of accounts, use the menu *Financial Management → Charts → Chart of Accounts*,then click **Open Charts** at the **Account charts** page to see that you have a debit of `560.00` in the `Purchases` account and a credit of `560.00` in the `Payable` account.

3.6.4 Paying the supplier

Select the menu *Financial Management → Invoices → Supplier Invoices → Unpaid Supplier Invoices* for a list of supplier invoices that haven't yet been paid. Click the `PO001` text itself to open the invoice in read-only mode. In practice you'd search for the invoice by order number or, more generally, for invoices nearing their payment date.

Click **Pay Invoice** in the toolbar to the right of the form, which opens a **Pay invoice** window with a description of the payment. Type `Pay Supplier` in the **Entry Name** field, and select `Bank Journal` in the **Journal/Payment Mode** field. Then click **Full Payment** to the top left of the form, which carries out the payment action within Open ERP and returns you to the invoice. Although this invoice is still in the **Unpaid Invoices** screen, you can see it is actually paid because the **Paid/Reconciled** box is now checked and the **State** is now `Done`.

Payment of an invoice

The method described here is for companies that don't use their accounting system to pay bills – just to record them. If you're using the `account` module fully other, more efficient, methods let you manage payments, such as entering account statements, reconciling paperwork, using tools for preparing payments, interfacing with banks.

You can monitor the accounting impact of paying the invoice through the chart of accounts available from the menu *Financial Management → Charts → Chart of Accounts*. Open ERP automatically creates accounting entries from the payment and can reconcile the payment to the invoice. You now have a new transaction that has debited the `Payable` account with `560.00` and credited the `Cash` account.

If you look in *Financial Management → Reporting → Journals* you'll see both accounting transactions, one in each of the `Purchase` Journal and `Bank` Journal in `Draft` state.

3.6.5 From Sales Proposal to Sales Order

In Open ERP, sales proposals and sales orders are managed using documents that are based on the same common functionality as purchase orders, so you'll recognize the following documents in general but see changes to their detail and to their workflows. To create a new sales proposal, use the menu *Sales Management → Sales Orders → New Quotation* which creates a new order in a state of `Quotation`, then:

1. Select the **Customer** `Smith and Offspring`. This has the effect of automatically completing several other fields: **Ordering Contact**, **Invoice Address**, **Shipping Address**, and the **Pricelist** `Default Sale Pricelist`. They're all only defaults so these fields can be modified as you need.

2. Click the **Save parent record.** icon to the right of the **Sales Order Lines** field. It saves the main order form and becomes a new **Create new record.** icon. Click that to open a **Sales Order Lines** window.

3. Select the product `Titanium Alloy Radiator` Although the **Product** field isn't itself required, it's used by Open ERP to select the specific product so that several other fields can be automatically completed on the order line of the proposal, such as **Description**, **Product UoM**, **Unit Price**, **Procure Method**, **Delivery Delay**, and **Taxes**.

4. Change the **Quantity** to 6 and the **Unit Price** to `130.00`Then click **Save** and the line appears on the quotation form. A blank order line form reappears so that you can enter another line, but it's enough now just to click **Close** to return to the order form.

5. On the **Other data** tab of this Sales Order select a **Packing Policy** of `Complete Delivery` and **Shipping Policy** of `Invoice on Order After Delivery` from their dropdown menu lists.

6. Return to the first tab **Sale Order** and validate the document by clicking guilabel:*Confirm Order* which calculates prices and the changes the order's state from `Quotation` to `In Progress`as shown in screenshot *Sales Order Form*. If you were in negotiation with the prospective customer you'd keep clicking **Compute** and **Save** keeping the document in `Quotation` state for as long as necessary.

7. In the last tab of the order, **History** you can see the **Packing List** that's been created and you'll be able to see any invoices that relate to this order when they're generated.

Figure 3.13: *Sales Order Form*

From the **Main Menu** click *Products → Products* to display a list of products: just the one, `Titanium Alloy Radiator` , currently exists in this example. Its **Real Stock** still shows `10.00` but its **Virtual Stock** now shows `4.00` to reflect the new future requirement of 6 units for despatch.

3.6.6 Preparing goods for despatch to customers

The stores manager selects the menu *Stock Management → Outgoing Products → Confirmed Packing Awaiting Availability* to get a list of orders to despatch. In this example there's only one, `PACK2` , so click the text to open the **Confirmed Packing Waiting Availability** form.

Running Schedulers

At the moment your Sales Order is waiting for products to be reserved to fulfil it. A stock reservation activity takes place periodically to calculate the needs, which also takes customer priorities into account. The calculation can be started from the menu *Manufacturing → Compute All Schedulers*. Running this automatically reserves products.

If you don't want to have to work out your stock needs but have a lean workflow you can install the `mrp_jit` (Just In Time) module.

Although Open ERP has automatically been made aware that items on this order will need to be despatched, it has not yet assigned any specific items from any location to fulfil it. It's ready to move `6.00 Titanium`

`Alloy Radiators` from the **Stock** location to the **Customers** location, so start this process by clicking **Check Availability**. The **Move** line has now changed from the `Confirmed` state to the `Available` state.

Then click the **Packing Done** button to reach the **Make Packing** window, where you click the **Make Picking** button to transfer the 6 radiators to the customer.

To analyze stock movements that you've made during these operations use *Stock Management → Locations Structure* to see that your stocks have reduced to 4 radiators and the generic `Customers` location has a level of 6 radiators.

3.6.7 Invoicing Goods

Use the menu *Financial Management → Invoices → Customer Invoices → Draft Customer Invoices* to open a list of Sales invoices generated by Open ERP. These are in the `Draft` state, which means that they don't yet have any presence in the accounting system. You'll find a draft invoice has been created for the order `SO001` once you have despatched the goods because you'd selected `Invoice on Order After Delivery`.

Once you confirm an invoice, Open ERP assigns it a unique number, and all of the corresponding accounting entries are generated. So open the invoice and click **Create** to do that and move the invoice into an `Open` state with a number of `2009/001`.

You can send your customer the invoice for payment at this stage. Click **Invoices** from the **Reports** section of the toolbar at the right of the form to get a PDF document that can be printed or emailed to the customer.

You can also attach the PDF document to the Open ERP invoice record. Save the PDF somewhere convenient on your PC (such as on your desktop). Then click the **Add an attachment to this resource** button to the top right of the invoice form (it looks like a clipboard). Browse to the file you just saved (`record.pdf` if you didn't change its name) from the **Attachments** dialog box that pops up, and **Close** the dialog box. This gives you a permanent non-editable record of your invoice on the Open ERP system.

Review your chart of accounts to check the impact of these activities on your accounting. You'll see the new revenue line from the invoice.

3.6.8 Customer Payment

Registering an invoice payment by a customer is essentially the same as the process of paying a supplier. From the menu *Financial Management → Invoices → Customer Invoices → Unpaid Customer Invoices*, click the name of the invoice that you want to mark as paid, or just check its checkbox in the list:

1. Use the **Pay Invoice** button in the **Action** section of the toolbar at the right to open a window that enables you to register the payment.

2. Select the **Entry Name** and type `Got paid by customer` and select the **Journal** to be `Bank Journal`.

3. Click **Full Payment**. The invoice is then marked as paid, with its **Paid/Reconciled** box checked as you can see if you select it again *Invoice Form*.

Check your Chart of Accounts as before to see that you now have a healthy bank balance in the `Cash` account.

Figure 3.14: *Invoice Form*

Part II

Sales and Purchasing

One of the most necessary business process is selling goods and services and, for goods and materials, their purchase.

The objective of this part of the book is to detail the core elements of Open ERP's sales management (in the chapter *Management of Sales*) and purchasing management (in the chapter *Purchasing Management*), and some of the many options that support those processes.

Management of Sales 4

This chapter describes Open ERP's sales management, following the complete sales order process from quotation to customer order, including the management of deliveries and of invoicing. It doesn't look at customer relations and pre-sales, which are handled by the CRM (Customer Relationship Management) modules described in an earlier part of the book.

It also describes the management of carriers, margin control and reporting, and price management and the handling of various types of sales discount campaign.

For this chapter you should start with a fresh database that includes demonstration data, with `sale` and its dependencies installed and no particular chart of accounts configured.

4.1 Sales Quotations

In Open ERP a quotation and an order are handled by the same underlying object, but in different states. You can consider an order to be a quotation that has evolved because it has been confirmed by the customer. Or, conversely, that a quotation is an order that hasn't yet been validated or cancelled. All of the orders and quotations in the system can be reached using the menu *Sales Management → Orders*.

4.1.1 Entering Quotation details

To enter details of a new quotations you can use the menu *Sales Management → Orders → New Quotation*. Open ERP then opens a new window so that you can enter data into new blank quotation form.

Some information is automatically completed by the system:

- an internal reference for the quotation or order,

- the sale point that the order will be delivered from,

- the order date.

You can modify any of that information before validating the quotation. The customer reference is shown in the header of the order. This optional field if for the customer's own reference number – if the customer doesn't supply one then just leave it empty.

You then enter all the data about the order in the **Sale Order** tab. Start by entering the customer name, selecting the correct customer from the list of customers in the system. You can create a new customer on the fly at this stage if necessary – press <F1> in the empty **Customer** field to do that.

Once the customer name has been selected, different fields of the order become completed automatically, based on the configuration of the partner form for that customer:

Figure 4.1: *Data entry for a new quotation*

- **Order Address** : person handling the order at the customer. By default, Open ERP proposes the Contact Address at the selected partner.

- **Delivery Address** : address used on the delivery order. By default, Open ERP proposes the Delivery address from the partner form. If nothing is defined in that slot, it uses the default address instead.

- **Invoice Address** : address used to send the invoice to the customer. By default, Open ERP proposes the address labelled **Invoice** from the partner form. If nothing is defined there, it uses the default address instead.

- **Price List** : will determine both the currency of the quotation and the price that will be used for each product.

- **Payment Conditions** : shows the payment method that the customer will follow, for example 50% on order, 50% on delivery.

- **Delivery Method** : for example Post - Express Mail.

You can modify any of these fields on the order as you go.

You can also set an analytic account for your order. This account will be used during invoicing to generate accounting entries corresponding to the invoice automatically. This is extremely useful for assigning revenues to the project or case specified by this order.

Analytic Accounts

If you're managing by task, the analytic account to be selected is the one that corresponds to the project for the order. The sale carried out by the order can be allocated to the project so that profitability calculations can be made.

Once the information has been entered, you can enter data for the order lines. To do that, create a new order line as shown in the figure *Entering a new customer order line*:

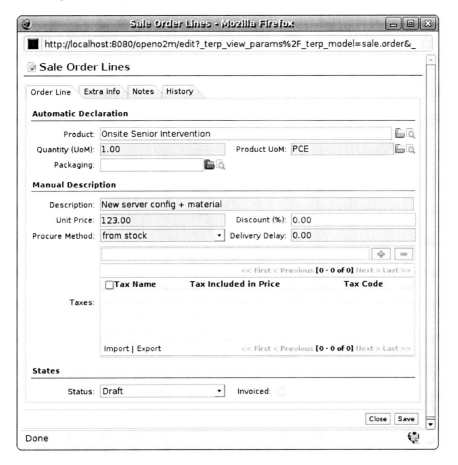

Figure 4.2: *Entering a new customer order line*

First of all select the product that is to be sold to the customer. Open ERP shows some useful information in the list of products to help you during your sale:

- **Real stock** : physically present in your warehouses. This value depends on the sale point selected in the order header. Different sale points can be linked to different warehouses, giving different stock levels, or can use the same warehouse.

- **Virtual stock** : shows a salesperson the quantity that can be sold, taking into account both stock reserved for other orders and amounts that could arrive in the short term.

- **Customer Price** : (May not be shown, depending on the installed modules). depends on the conditions attached to the customer, calculated on the list price. This is the price that's proposed by default in the customer quotation, unless it's been modified by the salesperson.

- **List Price** : the base sale price for the given product. It provides a base for the salesperson to be able to judge whether to offer a discount to the customer, and how much any discount should be.

- **Cost Price** : shows the cost price of the product. If the salesperson sells at less than this amount, then the company loses money.

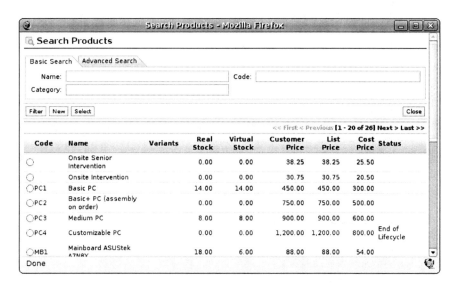

Figure 4.3: *Selecting a product in a Sales Order*

When the product that's to be sold to the customer has been selected, Open ERP automatically completes all the other required fields: price, unit of measure, description, discount, lead times, applicable taxes, default packaging and the product description. All of this information comes from the product form.

 Visible Discount

If a discounted price is taken from a price list then by default that figure is shown as the sale price to the customer. He'll see a discount of 0% along with unit price that is different from the list price. If you install the module `product_visible_discount` from addons-extra you can configure whether you want to make the discount explicitly visible on an order form as a percentage difference from the list price, or just show a reduced unit price as it does by default.

In the form, the selected product is presented in the language of the user so that he can see what he's selling. The description of the product sold can also be expressed in the customer's language. The translation to the customer's language is used on the quotation or order when it's printed.

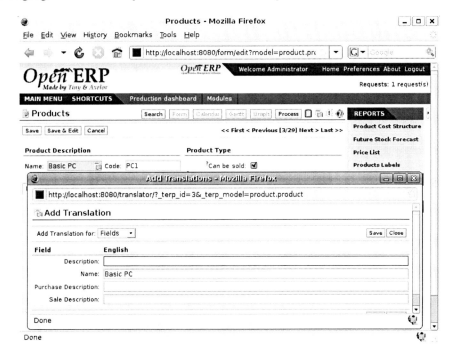

Figure 4.4: *Sale of a product in a partner language that differs from the user language*

 One-off Sales

If a product's only sold to a customer once, you don't have to enter data into a complete new product form just for that sale. You can manually complete all the information in the order without putting it into a product: description, price, quantity, lead time, taxes. In this case Open ERP won't generate a delivery note because the product isn't held in stock.

When all of the products are entered, you can print the quotation and send it to the customer. To do this, click on the report **Quotation / Order** in the **REPORTS** links to the right. Open ERP opens the quotation in PDF to enable to you to see it before printing.

You can then confirm the quotation to move it on to an order if the order is confirmed by the customer, or just cancel the window without confirming the order to leave it in quotation state. To find all of the current quotations, you can use the menu *Sales Management → Orders → My Orders → My Quotations*.

To follow the process for your order, you can click on the process view from the order form. Open ERP shows you an interactive process view of that order. For more information about its use, look at *Process*.

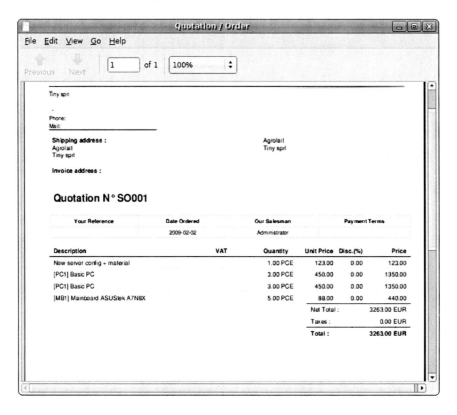

Figure 4.5: *Printing a customer quotation*

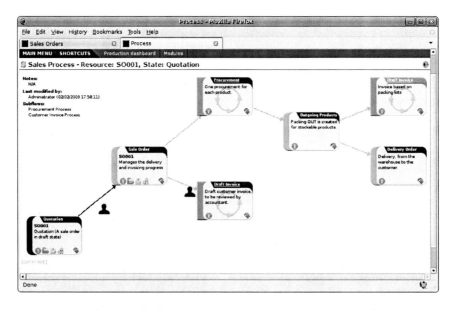

Figure 4.6: *Process view from following a customer order*

4.2 Management of Packaging

Products can be managed in several different packaged forms. For example if you sell batteries you can define the following packages for a given battery product:

- by Piece: a battery

- Blister pack: a pack of 4 batteries

- Pack of 100 blisters: 400 batteries

- Palette, containing 40 packs for a total of 16,000 batteries.

Open ERP's packaging management enables you to sell the same product in several different forms. The salesperson could sell, separately, one battery or a palette of batteries. In the order, you can select the default packaging type as a function of the quantities ordered.

For example, if the customer wants to buy 30,000 batteries, the salesperson can select the package `palette`. Open ERP will then propose the sale of 32,000 batteries, which corresponds to two palettes. Or the salesperson can select 75 packs.

The available packages are defined in the product form, in the **Packaging** tab. The first item on the list is the one that will be used by default.

Once a package has been defined on the order, Open ERP will throw up an alert if the ordered quantities don't correspond to the proposed packages. The quantity must be a multiple of the field **Quantity by Package** defined on the packaging form.

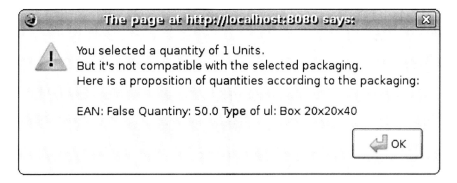

Figure 4.7: *Alert on the quantities sold compared with the packaging*

Don't confuse the management of packaging with the management of multiple units of measure. The Units of Measure are used to manage the stock differently in its different units. With packages, the stock is always managed by individual item but information about the package to use is supplied to the storesperson along with that item.

Even if the effects are the same, the printed documents will be different. The two following operations have the same effect on stock movement levels but will be printed differently on the sales order and the packing order:

- 32,000 batteries, delivered on two palettes,

- 2 palettes of batteries, with no information about packaging.

If the customer wants to order a palette and 10 packs, the salesperson can put two order lines on the sales order using the same product but different units of measure.

4.2.1 Example Packing and different products

It's sometimes more useful to define different products than to define several possible packages for the same product. A case of beer in a supermarket is a good example. A case holds 24 bottles, plus the empty case itself. The customer can buy bottles by the piece or a case of 24 bottles at one go.

You could define two packages for the product `Bottle of beer`: `PCE` and `case`. But this representation doesn't let you manage the stock and price of empty cases. So you might instead prefer a Bill of Materials for the sale, defining and using three different products:

- the empty case for the beer,

- the bottle of beer,

- the case of 24 bottles of beer.

You also define the bill of materials below which determines the make-up of the case of 24 beers:

- Case of 24 bottles of beer: 1 unit,

- Bottle of beer: 24 units,

- Empty case of beer: 1 unit.

Each of these three products has a different price. The products `Bottle of beer` and `Empty case of beer` have a stock level that needs to be managed. The `Case of 24 bottles of beer` has no stock because, if you sell the product, Open ERP automatically moves the stock in two lines, one for the empty case and the other for the 24 individual bottles of beer. For more information on bills of material for sale, see chapter *Manufacturing*.

4.3 Management of Alerts

To manage alerts on products or partners, you can install the `warning` module. Once that is installed, you will be able to configure a series of alerts on the partners or products by setting parameters in the new **Warnings** tab on each of the forms.

You can activate alerts for a series of events. For each alert you should enter a message that will be attached to the person setting off the event. The different available events on the partner form are:

- Entering a customer order for the partner,

Figure 4.8: *Management of alerts on partners*

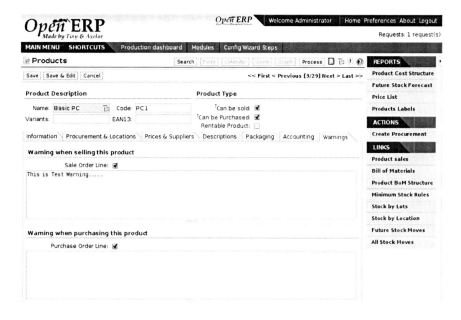

Figure 4.9: *Management of alerts on products*

- Entering a supplier order for the partner,

- Sending a delivery to the partner (or receiving an item),

- Invoicing a partner.

The alerts that can be configured on a product form are:

- The sale of that product,

- The purchase of that product.

For example, if you enter an alert for the invoicing of a customer, for an accountant entering an invoice for that customer, the alert message will be attached as shown in the figure *Alert from invoicing a customer*:

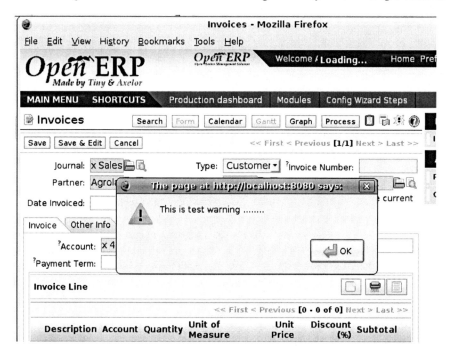

Figure 4.10: *Alert from invoicing a customer*

4.4 Control of deliveries and invoicing

4.4.1 Configuration of orders

Depending on the configuration of the order, several different possible consequences can follow. Three fields determine the future behaviour of an order:

- **Packing Policy** : Partial Delivery or Complete Delivery,

- **Shipping Policy** : `Shipping & Manual Invoice`, `Payment Before Delivery`, `Invoice on Order After Delivery`, and `Invoice from the Packing`,

- **Invoice on** : `Ordered Quantities` or `Delivered Quantities`.

> **Simplified view**
>
> If you work in the `Simplified View` mode, only the **Shipping Policy** field is visible in the second tab on the order. To get to the `Extended View` mode, assign the group **Usability – Extended View** to the current user.

4.4.2 Packing mode

The packing mode determines the way that the storesperson will do the packing. If the order is put into **Partial Delivery** mode, the packing order will appear in the list of things for the storesperson to do as soon as any of the products on the order is available. To get the list of items to be done you can use the menu *Stock Management → Outgoing Products → Available Packing*.

The storesperson will then be able to make a partial delivery of the quantities actually available and do a second packing operation later when the remaining products are available in stock.

If the packing mode is **Complete Delivery**, the packing list won't appear in the list of packings to do until all of the products are available in stock. This way there will only be a single delivery for any given order.

If the storesperson wants, the delivery mode can be modified on each packing list even after the order has been confirmed.

In the case of invoicing on the basis of packing, the cost of delivering the products will be calculated on the basis of multiple deliveries. This risks incurring a higher cost because of each delivery. If invoicing is on the basis of the orders, the customer will only be invoiced once for the whole delivery, even if the delivery of several items has already been made.

4.5 Management of Carriers

To manage deliveries in Open ERP, install the `delivery` module. (If you have installed the `profile_manufacturing` profile this is installed by default during configuration of the database.) This module enables you to manage:

- the different carriers with whom you work,

- the different possible modes of transport,

- cost calculation and invoicing of each delivery,

- the modes of transport and their tariffs.

Once the `delivery` module has been installed, the first thing to do is to configure the different modes of delivery accepted by your company. To do that use the menu *Stock Management → Configuration → Delivery → Delivery Method*.

For each delivery mode, you should define the following elements:

- Name of the delivery mode,

- The partner associated with the transport (which can be yourselves),

- The associated product.

For example you can create the following modes:

Table 4.1: Example Delivery Modes

Delivery Mode	Partner	Associated Product
Express Track	Mail Office	Express Track Delivery
Priority Courier	Mail Office	Courier Express Delivery
EFG Standard	EFG Inc	Delivery EFG
EFG Express	EFG Inc	Delivery EFG Express

Information about the invoicing of transport (such as accounts, applicable taxes) are entered in the product linked to the delivery mode. Ideally the product should be configured as **Product Type** `Service` and **Procure Method** `Make to Stock`.

You can use the same product for several delivery modes. This simplifies the configuration but you won't be able to separate out your sales figures by delivery mode.

4.5.1 Tariff grids

Unlike ordinary products, delivery prices aren't given by pricelists but by delivery grids, designed specifically for this purpose. For each delivery mode, you enter one or several tariff grids. Each grid is used for a given region/destination.

For example, for the postal tariffs for Priority Courier, you generally define the three tariff grids for Mail Office:

- Courier National,

- Courier Europe,

- Courier Outside Europe.

To define a new delivery grid, use the menu *Stock Management → Configuration → Deliveries → Delivery Pricelist*. You then give a name to your delivery grid and define the region for which the tariffs in the grid will be applicable. To do this, use the second tab **Destination**. There you can set:

- A list of countries (for UK or Europe, for example),

- A list of states,

- A range of post codes (for Paris you might have 75000 – 75900).

You must then set the rules for calculating the price of transport in the first tab **Grid definition**. A rule must first of all have a name. Then set the condition for which this rule is applicable, for example `Weight < 0.5kg`.

 Weights

Weights are expressed in kilograms. You can define a number with a decimal point or comma, so that to set 500g you'd put 0.5 in the weight rule.

Then set the sale price and the cost price. The price can be expressed in different ways:

- a fixed price,
- a variable price, as a function of weight, or volume, or weight x volume or price.

For example, mailing within France using 2008 tariffs would be defined as shown in the table.

Table 4.2: Example Tariff Rules

Rule Title	Condition	Price	Type of Price
S	Weight < 3 kg	6.9	Fixed
M	Weight < 5 kg	7.82	Fixed
L	Weight < 6 kg	8.53	Fixed
XL	Weight < 7 kg	9.87	Fixed

You can also define rules that depend on the total amount on the order. For example to offer fixed price delivery if the order is more than 150 USD, add the following rule:

Table 4.3: Additional Tariff Rule

Rule Title	Condition	Price	Type of Price
Franked > 150 USD	Price > 150 USD	10	Fixed

4.5.2 Using delivery modes

Once the delivery modes and their tariffs have been defined you can use them in a Sales Order. There are two methods for doing that in Open ERP.

- Delivery based on order quantities,
- Delivery based on deliverd quantities.

4.5.3 Delivery based on order quantities

To add the delivery charges on the quotation, use the action **Delivery Costs** available to the right of the form. A dialog box opens, asking you to select a delivery mode from one of the preconfigured available ones.

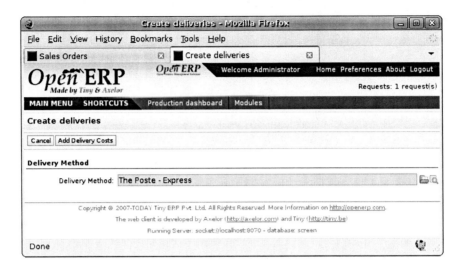

Figure 4.11: *Adding a delivery charge to an order*

Once the delivery mode has been selected, Open ERP automatically adds a line on the draft order with the amount calculated by the delivery function. This technique enables you to calculate the delivery charge based on the order and then, separately, how the products will really be delivered to the customer.

If you want to calculate the exact delivery charges depending on the actual deliveries you must use invoicing based on deliveries.

4.5.4 Delivery based on the packed items

To invoice the delivery on the basis of items packed you set the delivery mode in the **Delivery method** field on the second tab of the order, **Other data**. Don't add delivery lines to the Sales Order but to the Invoices after they have been generated for the delivered items.

For this to work properly, your order must be set to the state **Invoice from the Packing**. You can then confirm the order and validate the delivery.

When the manager has generated the invoices corresponding to the deliveries carried out, Open ERP automatically adds a line on each invoice corresponding to the delivery charge, calculated on the basis of the items actually sent.

4.6 Margin Control

It's important to keep good control of margins in every company. Even if you have a good level of sales it won't guarantee company profitability if margins aren't high enough. Open ERP provides a number of systems for monitoring margins. The main ones are:

- Margins on a sales order,
- Margins by product,

- Margins by project,

- Using price lists.

4.6.1 Margins on sales orders

If you want to check your margins on sales orders you can install the `sale_margin` module from `addons-extra`. This will add margins calculated on each order line and on the order total.

Figure 4.12: *An order with the module sale_margin*

The margin on each line is defined as the quantity sold multiplied by the sale price for the customer less the cost price of the products. By default, products are managed using standard price in Open ERP (cost price fixed manually and reviewed once per year). You can change that to `Average Weighted Price`, meaning that the product cost fluctuates with purchases from suppliers. After product receipt you can add fixed costs, such as delivery costs, in the cost of each product. Open ERP supports a third method of updating the cost price of products using the module `product_extended`, also in `addons-extra` at the time of writing. This adds a button to the product form which lets you automatically recalculate the cost price for the selected products. The cost price is calculated from the raw materials and the operations carried out (if the products have been manufactured internally so that you have set their costs).

4.6.2 Margins by product

To track margins by product, install the module `product_margin`. Once the module is installed you can see the margins by product by using the menu *Products → Reporting → Margins by Product*.

When you've clicked on the menu, Open ERP asks for an analysis period and the state of invoices. If no period is given, Open ERP will calculate margins on all of the operations without restriction. By default, however, Open ERP proposes a period of the last 12 months for analysis.

You can also filter the analysis on certain types of invoice:

- All invoices, including draft invoices not yet validated,

- All open and/or paid invoices,

- Paid invoices only.

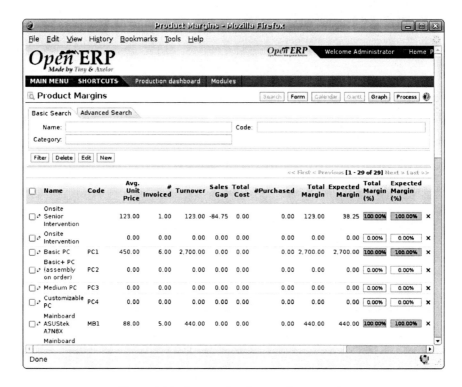

Figure 4.13: *Screen showing product margins*

You then get a margin analysis table. The following fields are given by product for sales:

- **Avg. Unit Price** : the average unit sale price,

- **Catalog Price** : the list price based on this product,

- **# Invoiced** : the number of sold products that have been invoiced,

- **Sales Gap** : the difference between the revenue calculated from list price and volume, and the actual sales,

- **Turnover** : the actual sales revenue for the product selected,

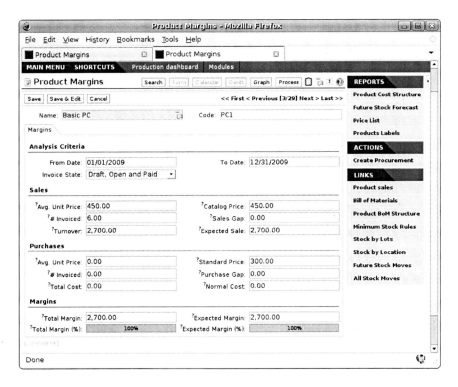

Figure 4.14: *Detail of margins for a given product*

- **Expected Sales** : the number of products sold multiplied by the list price.

The following fields are given by product for purchases:

- **Avg. Unit price** : the average unit purchase price,

- **Standard price** : the standard cost price of the product for the company,

- **# Invoiced** : the number of purchased products,

- **Purchase gap** : the difference between the total actual cost and the standard cost multiplied by the number of units purchased,

- **Total cost** : the total cost of purchases for the product under consideration,

- **Normal cost** : the number of products sold multiplied by the standard cost price.

The following fields are given by product for margins:

- **Total Margin**,

- **Expected Margin**,

- **Total Margin in percent**,

- **Expected Margin in percent**.

4.6.3 Margins by Project

To manage margins by project you must install the analytical accounts with management by task. Use of these accounts is described in *Analytic Accounts (which can be found in a companion volume to this book and in the online book)*. Install the module `account_analytic_analysis` and all of its dependencies. This module adds a tab on the analytic account form to handle the different margins in an analytic account representing a project or a case, and several new reports on those accounts.

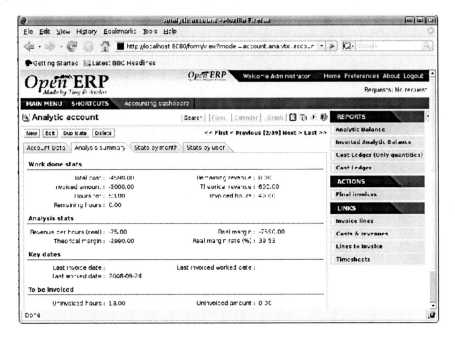

Figure 4.15: *Detail of margins for a case*

Start by opening a project's analytic account through the *Project Management → Financial Project Management → Analytic Accounts → All Analytic Accounts* and selecting one of them. In the new analytic account **Analysis summary** tab you'll find the following information:

- The total costs for the analytic account,

- The total amount of invoiced sales,

- The number of hours worked,

- The number of hours remaining to be worked,

- The remaining income,

- The theoretical income (hours worked multipled by their sale price),

- The number of hours invoiced,

- The real income per hour,

- The real margin,

- The theoretical margin taking into account everything yet to be invoiced,

- The real margin rate in percent,

- The last invoicing date,

- The last worked hours,

- The number of hours remaining to be invoiced,

- The amount remaining to be invoiced.

For detailed information on the analytic account you can use any of the several reports available in the toolbar to the right.

4.7 Price management policies

Some companies are notorious for their complicated pricelists. Many forms of price variation are used, such as end-of-year refunds, discounts, changes of terms and conditions with time, various prepayments, cascaded rebates, seasonal promotions, and progressive price reductions.

Rebate, Refund, Reduction

In some accounting jurisdictions you have to differentiate between the three following terms:

- Rebate: reimbursement to the client, usually at the end of the year, that depends on the quantity of goods purchased over a period.

- Refund: reduction on the order line or invoice line if a certain quantity of goods is purchased at one time or is sold in a framework of a promotional activity.

- Reduction: A one-off reduction resulting from a quality defect or a variation in a product's conformance to a specification.

Intelligent price management is difficult, because it requires you to integrate several conditions from clients and suppliers to create estimates quickly or to invoice automatically. But if you have an efficient price management mechanism you can often keep margins raised and respond quickly to changes in market conditions. A good price management system gives you scope for varying any and all of the relevant factors when you're negotiating a contract.

To help you work most effectively, Open ERP's pricelist principles are extremely powerful yet are based on simple and generic rules. You can develop both sales pricelists and purchase pricelists for products capable of accommodating conditions such as the date period, the quantity requested and the type of product.

> **Don't confuse the different price specifications**
>
> Don't confuse the sale price with the base price of the product. In Open ERP's basic configuration the sale price is the list price set on the product form but a customer can be given a different sale price depending on the conditions.

It's the same for purchase price and standard cost. Purchase price is your suppliers' selling price, which changes in response to different criteria such as quantities, dates, and supplier. This is automatically set by the accounting system. You'll find that the two prices have been set by default to the same for all products with the demonstration data, which can be a source of confusion. You're free to set the standard cost to something different.

Each pricelist is calculated from defined policies, so you'll have as many sales pricelists as active sales policies in the company. For example a company that sells products through three sales channels could create the following price lists:

1. Main distribution:

    - pricelist for Walbury,
    - pricelist for TesMart,

2. Postal Sales.

3. Walk-in customers.

A single pricelist can exist in several versions, only one of which is permitted to be active at a given time. These versions let you set different prices at different points in time. So the pricelist for walk-in customers could have five different versions, for example: Autumn, Summer, Summer Sales, Winter, Spring. Direct customers will see prices that change with the seasons.

Each pricelist is expressed in a single currency. If your company sells products in several currencies you'll have to create as many pricelists as you have currencies.

The prices on a pricelist can depend on another list, which means that you don't have to repeat the definition of all conditions for each product. So a pricelist in USD can be based on a pricelist in EUR. If the currency conversion rates between EUR and USD change, or the EUR prices change, the USD rates can be **automatically** adjusted.

4.7.1 Creating pricelists

To define a pricelist use the menu *Products → Pricelists → Pricelists* .

For each list you should define:

- a **Name** for the list,
- a **Type** of list: Sale for customers or Purchase for suppliers,
- the **Currency** in which the prices are expressed.

Customer Price

If you install the module `edi` (in `addons-extra` at the time of writing) a third type of list appears – the **Customer Price** - which defines the price displayed for the end user. This doesn't have to be the same as your selling price to an intermediary or distributor.

Pricelist versions

Once the list is defined you must provide it with at least one version. To do that use the menu *Products → Pricelists → Pricelist Versions*. The version contains all of the rules that enable you to calculate a price for a product and a given quantity.

So set the **Name** of this associated version. If the list only has a single version you can use the same name for the pricelist and the version. In the **Pricelist** field select the pricelist you created.

Then set the **Start date** and **End date** of this version. The fields are both optional: if you don't set any dates the version will be permanently active. Only one version may be active at any one point, so bear this in mind when creating them. Use the **Active** field in the versions to activate or disable a pricelist version.

Automatically updating the sale pricelist

You can make any sale pricelist depend on one of the other pricelists. So you could make your sale pricelist depend on your supplier's purchase pricelist, to which you add a margin. The prices are automatically calculated as a function of the purchase price and need no further manual adjustment.

Rules for calculating price

A pricelist version is made up of a set of rules that apply to the product base prices.

You define the conditions for a rule in the first part of the definition screen labeled **Rules Test Match**. The rule applies to the **Product** or **Product Template** and/or the named **Product Category**. If a rule is applied to a category then it is automatically applied to all of its subcategories too (using the tree structure for product categories).

If you set a minimum quantity in **Min. Quantity** the rule will only apply to a quantity the same as or larger than that set. This lets you set reduced rates in steps that depend on the quantities ordered.

Several rules can be applied to an order. Open ERP evaluates these rules in sequence to select which to apply to the specified price calculation. If several rules are valid only the first in sequence is used for the calculation. The **Sequence** field determines the order, starting with the lowest number and working up.

Once a rule has been selected, the system has to determine how to calculate the price from the rule. This operation is based on the criteria set out in the lower part of the form, labeled **Price Computation**.

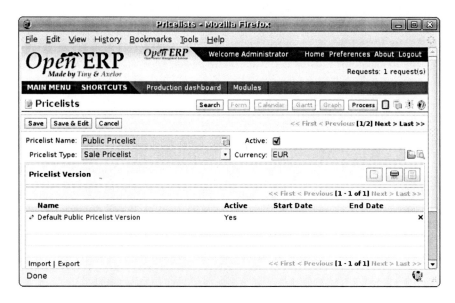

Figure 4.16: *Detail of a rule in a pricelist version*

The first field you have to complete is labeled **Based on**. Set the mode for partner price calculation, choosing between:

- the **List Price** set in the product file,

- the **Standard Cost** set in the product file,

- an **Other Pricelist** given in the field **If Other Pricelist**,

- the price that varies as a function of a supplier defined in the **Partner section of the product form**.

Several other criteria can be considered and added to the list, as you'll see in the following section.

Next, various operations can be applied to the base price to calculate the sales or purchase price for the partner at the specified quantities. To calculate it you apply the formula shown on the form: `Price = Base Price x (1 - Field1) + Field2`.

The first field, **Field1**, defines a discount. Set it to 0.20 for a discount of 20% from the base price. If your price is based on standard cost, you can set -0.15 to get a 15% price uplift compared with the standard costs.

Field2 sets a fixed supplement to the price, expressed in the currency of the pricelist. This amount is just added (or subtracted, if negative) to the amount calculated with the **Field1** discount.

Then you can specify a rounding method. The rounding calculation is carried out to the nearest number. For example if you set 0.05 in this example, a price of 45.66 will be rounded to 45.65, and 14,567 rounded to 100 will give a price of 14,600.

Swiss special situation

In Switzerland, the smallest monetary unit is 5 cents. There aren't any 1 or 2 cent coins. So you set Open ERP's rounding to 0.05 to round everything in a Swiss franc pricelist.

The supplement from **Field2** is applied before the rounding calculation, which enables some interesting effects. For example if you want all your prices to end in 9.99, set your rounding to 10 and your supplement to -0.01 in **Field2**.

Minimum and Maximum margins enable you to guarantee a given margin over the base price. A margin of 10 USD enables you to stop the discount from returning less than that margin. If you put 0 into this field, no effect is taken into account.

Once the pricelist is defined you can assign it to a partner. To do this, find a Partner and select its **Properties** tab. You can then change the **Purchase Pricelist** and the **Sale Pricelist** that's loaded by default for the partner.

4.7.2 Case of using pricelists

Take the case of an IT systems trading company, for which the following product categories have been configured:

All products

1. Accessories

   • Printers
   • Scanners
   • Keyboards and Mice

2. Computers

   • Portables
   • Large-screen portables
   • Computers
   • Office Computers
   • Professional Computers

In addition, the products presented in the table below are defined in the currency of the installed chart of accounts.

TABLE

Table 4.4: Examples of products with their different prices

Product	List Price	Standard Price	Default supplier price
Acclo Portable	1,200	887	893
Toshibishi Portable	1,340	920	920
Berrel Keyboard	100	50	50
Office Computer	1,400	1,000	1,000

Default pricelists

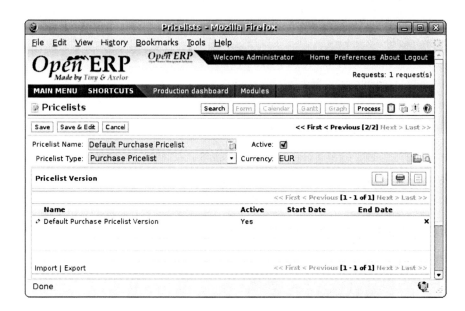

Figure 4.17: *Default pricelist after installing Open ERP*

When you install the software two pricelists are created by default: one for sales and one for purchases. These each contain only one pricelist version and only one line in that version.

The price for sales defined in the Default Public Pricelist is set by default to the Public Price of the product in the product file, which is the Sale Price in the Product file.

The price for purchases defined in the Default Purchase Pricelist is set by default in the same way to the Standard Cost of the product in the product file.

Example of a trading company

Take the case of a trading company, where the sale price for resellers can be defined like this:

- For portable computers, the sale price is calculated from the list price of the supplier Acclo, with a supplement of 23% on the cost of purchase.

- For all other products the sale price is given by the standard cost in the product file, on which 31% is added. The price must end in `.99`.

- The sale price of Berrel keyboards is fixed at 60 for a minimum quantity of 5 keyboards purchased. Otherwise it uses the rule above.

- Assume that the Acclo pricelist is defined in Open ERP. The pricelist for resellers and the pricelist version then contains three lines:

  1. `Acclo` line:
     - **Product Category** : `Portables`,
     - **Based on** : `Other pricelist`,
     - **Pricelist if other** : `Acclo pricelist`,
     - **Field1** : `-0.23`,
     - **Priority** : `1`.

  2. `Berrel Keyboard` line:
     - **Product Template** : `Berrel Keyboard`,
     - **Min. Quantity** : `5`,
     - **Field1** : `1.0`,
     - **Field2** : `60`,
     - **Priority** : `2`.

  3. `Other products` line:
     - **Based on:** `Standard Price`,
     - **Field1** : `-0.31`,
     - **Field2** : `-0.01`,
     - **Rounding** : `1.0`.
     - **Priority** : `3`.

It's important that the priority of the second rule is set below the priority of the third in this example. If it were the other way round the third rule would always be applied because a quantity of 5 is always greater than a quantity of 1 for all products.

Also note that to fix a price of 60 for the 5 Berrel Keyboards, the formula `Price = Base Price x (1 - 1.0) + 60` has been used.

Establishing customer contract conditions

The trading company can now set specific conditions to a customer, such as the company TinAtwo, who might have signed a valid contract with the following conditions:

- For Toshibishi portables, TinAtwo benefits from a discount of 5% of resale price.

- For all other products, the resale conditions are unchanged.

The list price for TinAtwo, called `TinAtwo contract`, contains two rules:

1. `Toshibishi portable`:

   - **Product** : `Toshibishi Portable`,
   - **Based on** : `Other pricelist`,
   - **Pricelist if other** : `Reseller pricelist`,
   - **Field1** : `0.05`,
   - **Priority** : `1`.

2. `Other Products`:

   - **Product** :
   - **Based on** : `Other pricelist`,
   - **Pricelist if other** : `Reseller pricelist`,
   - **Priority** : `2`.

Once this list has been entered you should look for the partner form for TinAtwo again. Click the **Properties** tab to set the **Sale List Price** field to *TinAtwo Contract*. If the contract is only valid for one year, don't forget to set the **Start Date** and **End Date** fields in the **Price List Version**.

Then when salespeople prepare an estimate for TinAtwo the prices proposed will automatically be calculated from the contract conditions.

4.7.3 Different bases for price calculation

Open ERP's flexibility enables you to make prices that depend not only on prices on the product form, but in addition to the two predefined ones – Cost Price and Public Price.

To do this use the menu *Products → Definitions → Price Types*. Create a new entry for the new price type. Enter the field name, the field on the product form that this type of price corresponds to and the currency that will be expressed in this field. The operation works just as well on new fields added to the product form to meet specific developments.

Once this operation has been carried out you can make pricelists depend on this new price type.

Then, adding the weight and/or volume field, the price of a product by piece can vary by its weight and/or volume. This is different from defining a price by weight – in that case the default unit of measure is weight and not piece.

4.7.4 Pricelists and managing currencies

If your trading company wants to start a product catalog in a new currency you can handle this several ways:

- Enter the prices in a new independent pricelist and maintain the lists in the two currencies separately,

- Create a field in the product form for this new currency and make the new pricelist depend on this field: prices are then maintained separately but in the product file,

- Create a new pricelist for the second currency and make it depend on another pricelist or on the product price: the conversion between the currencies will then be done automatically at the prevailing currency conversion rate.

4.8 Rebates at the end of a campaign

If you want to provide discounts on an order, use the pricelist system in Open ERP. But it's better to work with end-of-campaign rebates or year-end rebates. In this case the customer pays a certain price for the whole of the campaign or the year and a rebate is returned to him at the end of the campaign that depends on the sales he's made throughout the year.

4.8.1 Example: Using returns for the end of a campaign

Take the case of a contract negotiations with a wholesaler. To get the best selling price, the wholesaler will ask you for a good deal and will sign up to a certain volume of orders over the year.

You can then propose a price based on the volume that the wholesaler agrees to sell. But then you don't have any control over his orders. If at the end of the year the wholesaler hasn't taken the agreed volumes then you can't do anything. At most you can review his terms for the following year.

Rebates at the end of a campaign can help you avoid this sort of problem. You can propose a contract where the price is dependent on the usual wholesaler's terms. You can propose a rebate grid which will be assigned at the end of the year as a function of the actual sales made. Install the `discount_campaign` module (in `addons-extra` at the time of writing) to generate rebates at the end of the campaign. Once the modules have been installed you can configure your campaign using the menu *Sales Management → Configuration → Discount campaign*.

> **Year-end rebate**
>
> Most companies use the term *year-end rebate*, where rebates are applied at the end of the year. But if you're using rebates at the end of a campaign, this would only actually be the case if the campaign lasts exactly one year.

A campaign must have a name, a start date, and an end date. After entering this information, you should describe the lines of the campaign. Each line can be applied to a product or a category of products. Then set the quantity of products sold from which the discount is applied, and the amount of the rebate as a percentage of the actual sales volume.

When you've defined the campaign you can active it by clicking the **Open** button. The figure *Configuring a discount campaign for computers* shows a campaign with a rebate on computers which is between 10% and 20% depending on the sales volume.

Once the campaign has been defined you can assign a given campaign to various partners. To do that set a **Discount Campaign** in the second tab **Sales and Purchases** of the partner form.

Finally at the end of the campaign you should close it and Open ERP will automatically generate invoices or credit notes for your partner associated with this campaign. Open ERP opens credit notes in the `Draft` state that you can modify before validating them. To calculate the amount on the credit note, Open ERP uses all of the invoices sent out during the period of the campaign as its basis.

You can also reach all of the draft credit notes using the menu *Financial Management → Invoices → Customer Refunds*.

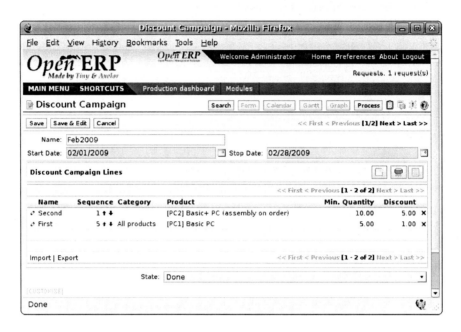

Figure 4.18: *Configuring a year-end rebate*

Figure 4.19: *Configuring a discount campaign for computers*

4.9 Open orders

In some industries, customers commonly place orders for a certain volume of product and ask for regular deliveries from an order up to the total amount on it. This principle, called open orders, is managed by the `sale_delivery` module in Open ERP.

Open ERP handles open orders easily. An open order is an order for a certain quantity of products but whose deliveries are planned for various dates over a period of time.

To do that you must install the `sale_delivery` module (in `addons-extra` at the time of writing). A Sales Order is entered as a normal order but you also set the total quantity that will be delivered on each order line.

Then you can use the new tab **Deliveries** on the order to plan the quantities sold and enter your delivery planning there.

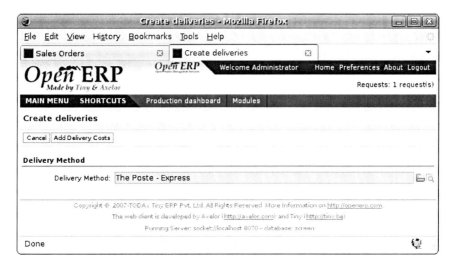

Figure 4.20: *Managing open orders, planning forecasts*

In the order lines, Open ERP shows you the quantity planned in addition to the quantity sold so you can verify that the quantities sold equal the quantities to be delivered. When you confirm the order, Open ERP no longer generates a single delivery order but plans scheduled despatches.

Invoicing Mode

If you work with Open Orders, you should set the order into the mode **Invoice from the Packing**. Then the storesperson will be able to replan and change the quantities of the forecast deliveries in the system.

4.10 Layout templates

The `sale_layout` module enables you to have a more elaborate template than the standard order forms. For example you could put the following in the order lines:

- a horizontal separator line,
- titles and subtitles,
- subtotals at the end of the section,
- comments,
- a page break.

This enables you to lay out a more elaborate professional-looking quotation page. There's also the module `account_invoice_layout` which gives you the same functionality for invoice templates.

The two figures *Template for an invoice in Open ERP using the account_invoice_layout module* and *The resulting printed invoice* show an invoice template in Open ERP and the resulting printed invoice.

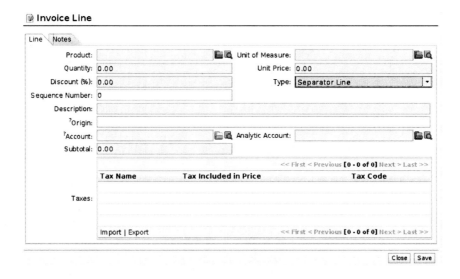

Figure 4.21: *Template for an invoice in Open ERP using the account_invoice_layout module*

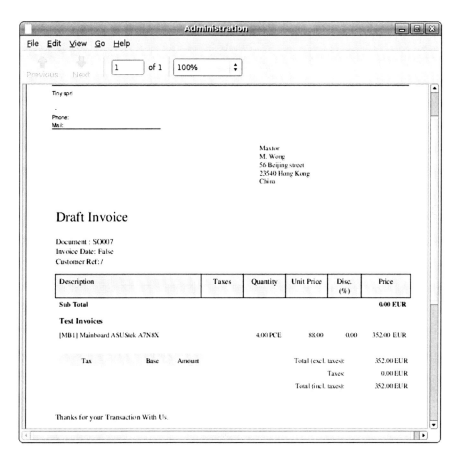

Figure 4.22: *The resulting printed invoice*

Purchasing Management 5

In the preceding chapters you saw how to use customer invoices and delivery notes in Open ERP. This chapter is about the management of purchases, the process ahead of these two operations. You'll now see how Open ERP handles and simplifies this and the control of purchases from suppliers.

For this chapter you should start with a fresh database that includes demonstration data, with `sale` and its dependencies installed (which indirectly depends on, and installs, the `purchase` module) and no particular chart of accounts configured.

5.1 All the elements of a complete workflow

The supplier order is the document that lets you manage price negotiations, control supplier invoices, handle goods receipts and synchronize all of these documents.

Start by looking at the following order workflow:

1. Price request to the supplier,

2. Confirmation of purchase,

3. Receipt and control of products,

4. Control of invoicing.

5.1.1 Setting up your database

To set a system up for these examples, create a new database with demonstration data in it, and select the **Minimal Profile** when you log in as the *admin* user. You can enter your own company details when asked, or just select the default of **Tiny SPRL** if you want. Then install the `purchase` module, which installs several other modules as dependencies. Continue the remainder of this chapter logged in as the admin user.

5.1.2 Price request from the supplier

To enter data for a new supplier price request, use the menu *Purchase Management → New Purchase Order*. Open ERP opens a blank purchase form that you use for requesting prices from a supplier. This is shown in the figure *Data entry for a supplier order*. If the price request came from an automatic procurement created by Open ERP you'll find a reference to the document that generated the request in the **Origin** field.

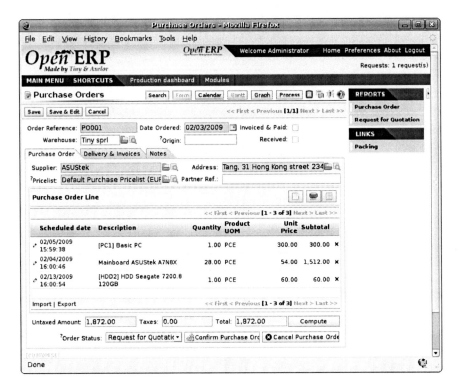

Figure 5.1: *Data entry for a supplier order*

Managing Alerts

If you install the `warning` module you will be able to define alerts that appear when the purchaser enters a price request or order. You can set alerts on the product and on the supplier.

The internal reference, the date, and the warehouse that the products should be delivered to are completed automatically by Open ERP but you can change these values if you need. Select a supplier. Once a supplier has been selected, Open ERP automatically completes the contact address for the supplier. The pricelist is also completed when you select the supplier. This should bring in all of the conditions that you've negotiated with the supplier for a given period.

Supplier Selection

Searching for a supplier is limited to all of the partners in the system that have the **Supplier** checkbox checked. If you don't find your supplier it might be worth checking the whole list of all partners to make sure that the supplier hasn't been partially entered into the system.

Once the main body of the purchase order has been completed you can enter the product lines.

Figure 5.2: *Order line on a supplier order*

When you've completed the product, Open ERP automatically completes the other fields on the form:

- **Unit of Measure**, taken from the **Purchase UoM** field on the product form,

- The **Description** of the product in the supplier's language,

- **Scheduled date**, calculated from the order date and the lead time

- **Unit price**, provided by the supplier pricelist,

- **Taxes, taken from the information on the product form and partner form,** depending on the rules seen in *Financial Analysis*.

Product wording and code

When you enter supplier names on the product form, you can set a name and a product code for each individual supplier. If you do that, Open ERP will then use those details in place of your own internal product names for that selected supplier.

If you work with management by case you can also set the analytic account that should be used to report all the purchase costs. The costs will then be reported at the receipt of the supplier invoice.

Management by case

Analytic accounts can be very useful for all companies that manage costs by case, by site, by project or by folder. To work with several analytic axes you should install the module `purchase_analytic_plans`.

For that the analytic account is automatically selected as a function of the partner, the date, the products or the user, you can install the module `account_analytic_default` (which is installed automatically as a dependency of `purchase_analytic_plans`, since the latter depends on it).

In the second tab of the product line you can enter a note that will be attached when the order confirmation or price quotation is printed. This note can be predefined on the product form to automatically appear on each order for that product. For example you can put "Don't forget to send by express delivery as specified in our contract reference 1234."

Once the document has been completed, you can print it as a price estimate to send to the supplier. You can set a note for the attention of the supplier in the form's third tab.

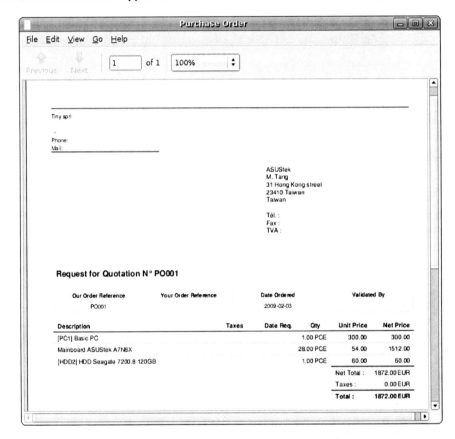

Figure 5.3: *Printing the supplier price quotation*

Then leave the document in the `Draft` state. When you receive a response from the supplier, use the menu *Purchase Management → Purchase Orders → Requests for Quotation*. Select the order and complete its details.

When you want to approve the order, use the button **Confirm Purchase Order**. The price request then passes into the `Confirmed` state. No further changes are possible. To approve it for purchase click the button **Approved by Supplier**.

Approval Receipt

You can confirm the order but not approve it straightaway. Do this when you want to approve the order after you've received an order acknowledgement from the supplier. This gives you an intermediate state for all orders waiting validation from the supplier using the menu *Purchase Management → Purchase Orders → Purchase Orders Awaiting Approval.*

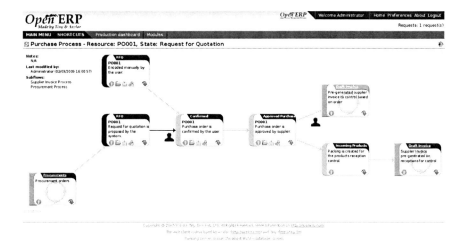

Figure 5.4: *Supplier order process*

Supplier Approval

If you want to automate the data entry stage at goods receipt, install the module `purchase_approve`. This will automatically approve all the orders that have been confirmed.

5.1.3 Goods receipt

Once the order has been approved, Open ERP automatically prepares the goods receipt order in the draft state for you. To get a list of the products you're waiting for from your suppliers, use the menu *Stock Management → Incoming Products → Packings to process.*

Purchasing Services

If you buy services from your supplier, Open ERP doesn't generate a goods receipt note. There's no service receipt equivalent to a goods receipt.

Select the document that corresponds to the item that you're receiving. Usually the goods receipt note is found by making a search on the order reference or the supplier name. You can then confirm the receipt of the products.

As you saw in *Logistics and Stock Management*, if you receive only part of the order, Open ERP manages the remainder of that order. A second receipt note is then automatically created for the goods not received. You can cancel it if you think that you will never receive the remaining products.

After receiving the goods, Open ERP will show you which orders are open and the state of their receipt and invoicing if you return to the list of orders.

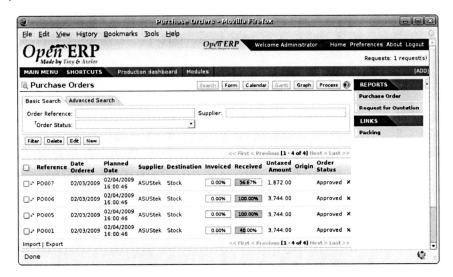

Figure 5.5: *List of open orders, and their receipt and invoice status*

5.1.4 Control of invoicing

To control supplier invoicing, Open ERP provides three systems as standard, which can differ order by order:

- Invoicing based on quantities ordered,

- Invoicing based on quantities received,

- Manual Invoicing.

The mode of invoicing control is set in the second tab of the purchase order in the field **Invoicing Control**.

Default value

A company generally uses a single invoicing control method for all of its invoices. So you're advised to go and set a default value in the **Invoicing Control** field after installation.

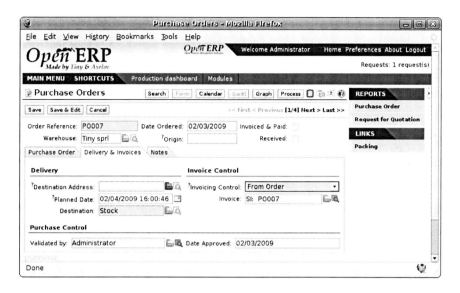

Figure 5.6: *Supplier order, invoice control*

5.1.5 Control based on orders

If you selected your invoicing control based on orders, Open ERP will automatically generate a supplier invoice in the draft state when the order is confirmed. You can obtain a list of invoices waiting using the menu *Financial Management → Invoices → Supplier Invoices → Draft Supplier Invoices*.

When you receive a paper invoice from your supplier, all you need to do is validate the invoice pre- generated by the system. Don't forget to check the price and the quantities. When the invoice is confirmed the accounting entries represent the cost of purchase and are automatically entered into the system.

The supplier order is then automatically set as `Paid` when you pay the supplier invoice.

This method of controlling invoices is often used in service companies, because the invoiced amounts correspond to the ordered amounts. In logistics by contrast you most often work with invoicing controlled by goods receipt.

5.1.6 Control based on goods receipt

To control your supplier invoices based on goods receipt, set the field **Invoicing Control** on the second tab of the order to **From Picking**.

In this case no invoice, draft state or any other, is generated by the order. On the goods receipt note, the field **Invoicing Control** is set to **To be Invoiced**.

The storesperson can then receive different orders. If he wants to generate the draft invoice for a goods receipt, he can click the action **Create Invoice**. Open ERP asks you then for the journal for this invoice. It then opens that or the generated invoices (in the case of creating invoices for several receipts at one time) which enables you to modify it before confirming it.

This approach is useful when you receive the invoice at the same time as the item from the supplier. Usually invoices are sent by post some days later. In this case, the storesperson leaves the item unchanged without generating an invoice. Then once per day or once per week the accountant will create the draft invoices based on all the receipts for the day. To do that he uses the menu *Stock Management → Incoming Products → Generate Draft Invoices on Receptions*. He clicks on the action to generate all draft invoices from the list of receipts that haven't yet been invoiced. At that point, the accountant can decide if he wants to generate an invoice per item or group all items for the same partner into the same invoice.

Invoices are then handled just like those controlled from `On Order`. Once the invoice arrives at the accounting service he just compares it with the invoices waiting to control what the supplier invoices you.

> **Delivery Charges**
>
> To manage delivery charges, install the module `purchase_delivery` (which was in `addons-extra` at the time of writing). This will automatically add delivery changes to the creation of the draft invoice as a function of the products delivered or ordered.

5.1.7 Tenders

To manage tenders, you should use the module `purchase_tender` (which was in `addons-extra` at the time of writing). This lets you create several supplier price reqests for a single supply requirement. Once the module is installed, Open ERP adds a new *Purchase Tenders* menu in *Purchase management*. You can then define the new tenders.

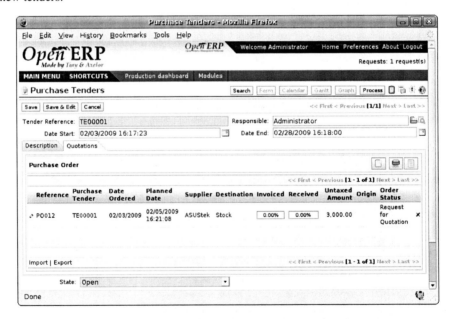

Figure 5.7: *Defining a tender*

To enter data for a new tender, use the menu *Purchase Management → Purchase Tenders → New Purchase*

Tenders. Open ERP then opens a new blank tender form. The reference number is set by default and you can enter information about your tender in the other fields.

If you want to enter a supplier's response to your tender request, add a new draft purchase order into the list on the **Quotation** tab of your tender document. If you want to revise a supplier price in response to negotiations, edit any appropriate Purchase Order that you've left in the draft state and link that to the tender.

In the general list of purchase orders, Open ERP shows, in the new second column **Purchase Tender**, if the order has a tender reference.

When one of the orders about a tender is confirmed, all of the other orders are automatically cancelled by Open ERP. That enables you to accept just one order for a particular tender.

5.1.8 Price revisions

Open ERP supports several methods of calculating and automatically updating product costs:

- Standard price: manually fixed, and

- Standard price: revalued automatically and periodically,

- Weighted average: updated at each receipt to the warehouse.

This cost is used to value your stock and represents your product costs. Included in that cost is everything directly related to the received cost. You could include such elements as:

- supplier price,

- delivery charges,

- manufacturing costs,

- storage charges.

5.1.9 Standard Price

The mode of price management for the product is shown in the third tab **Prices & Suppliers** on the product form. On each individual product you can select if you want to work in Standard Price or on weighted Average Price.

Simplified view

If you work in the Simplified View mode you won't see the field that lets you manage the price calculation mode for a product. In that case the default value is standard price.

The Standard Price setting means that the product cost is fixed manually for each product in the field **Cost Price**. This is usually revalued once a year based on the average of purchase costs or manufacturing costs.

You usually use standard costs to manage products where the price hardly changes over the course of the year. For example the standard cost could be used to manage books, or the cost of bread.

Those costs that can be fixed for the whole year bring certain advantages:

- you can base the sale price on the product cost and then work with margins rather than a fixed price per product,

- accounting is simplified because there's a direct relationship between the value of stock and the number of items received.

To get and automated periodic revaluation of the standard price you can use the module product_extended (from addons-extra at the time of writing). This adds an action on the product form enabling you to set a date on all the selected products. Open ERP then recalculates the price of the products as a function of the cost of raw materials and the manufacturing operations given in the routing.

5.1.10 Weighted average

Working with Standard Prices does not lend itself well to the management of the cost price of products when the prices change a lot with the state of the market. This is case for many commodities and energy.

In this case you'd want Open ERP to automatically set the price in response to each goods receipt movement into the warehouse. The deliveries (exit from stock) have no impact on the product price.

Calculating the price

At each goods receipt the product price is recalculated using the following accounting formula: $NP = (OP * QS + PP * QR) / (QS + QR)$, where the following notation is used:

- NP: New Price,

- OP: Old Price,

- QS: Quantity actually in stock,

- PP: Price Paid for the quantity received,

- QR: Quantity received.

If the products are managed as a weighted average, Open ERP will open a window that lets you specify the price of the product received at each goods receipt. The purchase price is by default set from the purchase order, but you can change the price to add the cost of delivery to the various received products, for example.

Once the receipt has been confirmed, the price is automatically recalculated and entered on the product form.

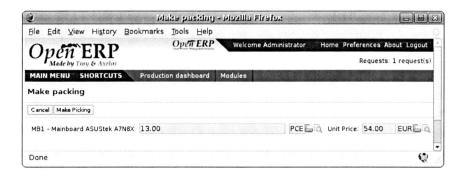

Figure 5.8: *Goods receipt of products managed in weighted average*

5.2 Analyis of purchases

5.2.1 Elementary statistics

To get statistics about your purchases you can install the modules `report_purchase` and `product_margin`.

The first, `report_purchase`, will add two new reports in your purchase menu, analysis of purchases by month and by product, and analysing product by month and by product category. To use these reports use the menu *Purchase Management → Reporting → This month → Purchases by product*.

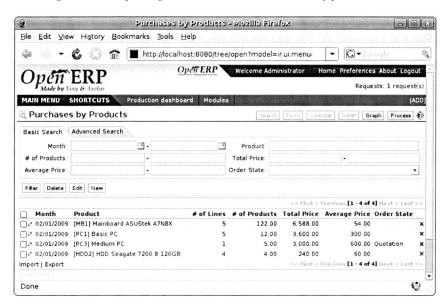

Figure 5.9: *Analysis of purchases over the month by product*

This analysis is carried out on supplier orders and not on invoices or the quantities actually received. To get an analysis by product, use the module `product_margin`. The function of this module is described in detail in the chapter *Management of Sales*.

To analyze the received quantities, you can use the statistical modules in Stock Management.

5.3 Supplier relationship management

To manage supplier relations, you should install the `crm_configuration` module. You will then be able to manage supplier complaints and integrate them with your emails and document management.

Once you've installed the `crm` module, check the checkbox by the **Complaints** option during configuration. Open ERP will then create a menu in your working database for managing supplier complaints.

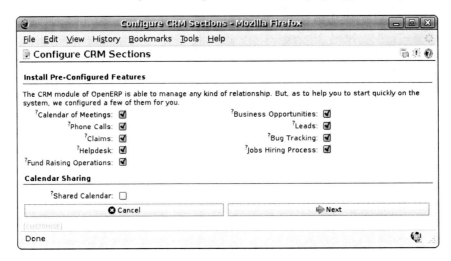

Figure 5.10: *Selection of the management of complaints in the CRM installation*

Once the module is installed you can use the menu *CRM & SRM → After Sales Service → Complaints → New Supplier Complaint*.

The CRM module has many reports predefined. You can analyse:

- the number and the severity of the complaints by supplier or user,

- the response time of your suppliers to your requests,

- the supplier problems by type.

5.4 Analytic accounts

To manage purchases by project you should use the analytic accounts. You can set an analytic account on each line of a supplier order. The analytic costs linked to this purchase will be managed by Open ERP from the goods receipt and confirmation of the supplier invoice. The `hr_timesheet_invoice` module lets

Figure 5.11: *Data entry screen for a supplier complaint*

you reinvoice the analytic costs automatically using parameters in the analytic accounts such as sale pricelist, associated partner company, and maximum amount.

So you can put an invoice order with a defined invoice workflow in place based on the analytic accounts. If you're working `Make to Order`, the workflow will be:

1. Customer Order,

2. Procurement order on Supplier,

3. Receive invoice and goods from the supplier,

4. Delivery and invoicing to the customer.

When re-invoicing based on costs you'd get the following workflow:

1. Enter the customer contract conditions from the analytic accounts,

2. Purchase raw materials and write the services performed into the timesheets,

3. Receive the supplier invoice and the products,

4. Invoice these costs to the customer.

Analytic multiplans

If you want several analysis plans you should install the module `purchase_analytic_plans`. These let you split a line on a supplier purchase order into several accounts and analytic plans. Look back at *Analytic Accounts (which can be found in a companion volume to this book and in the online book)* for more information on the use of analytic accounts.

Part III

Stock and Manufacturing

This part of the book concentrates on physical materials - the handling of stock and the transformation of materials by assembly and manufacture.

Stocks are the physical embodiment of their product specification, "things" rather than datasheets. So they need to be stored and moved between locations, and tracked in sets and individually. They have a size, a weight, and a cost. Open ERP manages all of this in some rather useful and unique ways, as described in the chapter *Logistics and Stock Management*.

Manufacture, described in detail in the chapter *Manufacturing*, is the transformation of materials and components, perhaps using measurable resources, into other products and services, adding value to your company on the way.

chapter
5-7

Logistics and Stock Management 6

Open ERP's stock management is at once very simple, flexible and complete. It's based on the concept of double entry that revolutionized accounting. The system can be described by Lavoisier's maxim "nothing lost, everything changed" or, better, "everything moved". In Open ERP you don't talk of disappearance, consumption or loss of products: instead you speak only of stock moves from one place to another.

Just as in accounting, the Open ERP system manages counterparts to each of its main operations such as receipts from suppliers, deliveries to customers, profits and losses from inventory, and consumption of raw materials. Stock movements are always made from one location to another. To satisfy the need for a counterpart to each stock movement, the software supports different types of stock location:

- Physical stock locations,

- Partner locations,

- Virtual counterparts such as production and inventory.

Physical locations represent warehouses and their hierarchical structure. These are generally the locations that are managed by traditional stock management systems.

Partner locations represent your customers' and suppliers' stocks. To reconcile them with your accounts, these stores play the role of third-party accounts. Reception from a supplier can be shown by the movement of goods from a partner location to a physical location in your own company. As you see, supplier locations usually show negative stocks and customer locations usually show positive stocks.

Virtual counterparts for production are used in manufacturing operations. Manufacturing is characterized by the consumption of raw materials and the production of finished products. Virtual locations are used for the counterparts of these two operations.

Inventory locations are counterparts of the stock operations that represent your company's profits and losses in terms of your stocks.

The figure *Stores location structure when Open ERP has just been installed* shows the initial configuration of the stores locations when the software is installed.

Hierarchical stock locations

In Open ERP locations are structured hierarchically. You can structure your locations as a tree, dependent on a parent-child relationship. This gives you more detailed levels of analysis of your stock operations and the organization of your warehouses.

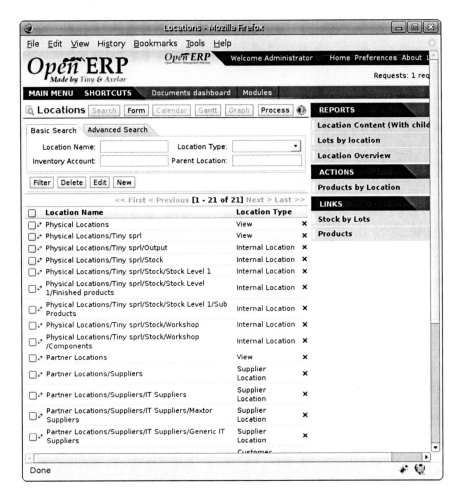

Figure 6.1: *Stores location structure when Open ERP has just been installed*

Locations and Warehouses

In Open ERP **warehouses** represent your places of physical stock. A warehouse can be structured into several locations at multiple levels. Locations are used to manage all types of storage place, such as at the customer and production counterparts.

For this chapter you should start with a fresh database that includes demo data, with `stock` and its dependencies installed and no particular chart of accounts configured.

6.1 Understanding double-entry stock management

To illustrate this concept of stock management, see how stock moves are generated by the following operations:

- Receiving products from a supplier,
- Delivery to a customer,
- Inventory operation for lost materials,
- Manufacturing.

The structure of stock locations is shown by the figure *Stores location structure when Open ERP has just been installed*. Stocks are assumed to be totally empty and no operation is in progress nor planned.

If you order '30 bicycles' from a supplier, Open ERP will then do the following operations after the receipt of the products:

Table 6.1: Stock Move operation from Suppliers to Stock

Location	Products
Partner Locations > Suppliers > Suppliers	-30 bicycles
Physical Locations > Tiny SPRL > Stock	+30 bicycles

If you deliver 2 bicycles to a European customer you will get the following transactions for the delivery:

Table 6.2: Stock Move operation from Stock to European Customers

Location	Products
Physical Locations > Tiny SPRL > Stock	-2 bicycles
Partner Locations > Customers > European Customers	+2 bicycles

When the two operations are complete you'll then get the following stock in each location:

Table 6.3: Resulting stock situation

Location	Products
Partner Locations > Suppliers > Suppliers	-30 bicycles
Physical Locations > Tiny SPRL > Stock	+28 bicycles
Partner Locations > Customers > European Customers	+2 bicycles

So you can see that the sum of the stocks of a product in all the locations in Open ERP is always zero. In accounting you'd say that the sum of the debits is equal to the sum of the credits.

Partner locations (customers and suppliers) aren't located under your company in the hierarchical structure, so their contents are not considered as part of your own stock. So if you look just at the physical locations inside your own company those two bicycles are no longer in your company. They're not in your own physical stock but it's still very useful to see them in your customer's stock because that helps when you carry out detailed stock management analysis.

Accounts

In managing stock, a gap between the data in the software and real quantities in stock is difficult to avoid. Double-entry stock management gives twice as many opportunities to find an error. If you forget two items of stock this error will automatically be reflected in the counterpart's location.

You can make a comparison with accounting, where you'll easily find an error because you can look for an anomaly in an account or in the counterparts: if there's not enough in a bank account then that's probably because someone's forgotten to enter a customer's invoice payment. You always know that the sum of debits must equal the sum of the credits in both accounting and Open ERP's stock management.

In accounting, all documents lead to accounting entries that form the basis of management accounting. If you create invoices or code in statements of account, for example, the results of the operations are accounting entries on accounts. And it's the same for stock management in Open ERP. All stock operations are carried out as simple stock moves. Whether you pack items, or manufacture them, or carry out a stock inventory operation, stock moves are carried out every time.

You've seen a fairly simple example of goods receipt and product delivery, but some operations are less obvious – a stock inventory operation, for example. An inventory operation is carried out when you compare the stock shown in software with real stock numbers counted in the stores. In Open ERP, with its double-entry stock management, you'd use stock moves for this inventory operation. That helps you manage your stock traceability. If there are 26 Bicycles in real stock but Open ERP shows 28 in the system. You then have to reduce the number in Open ERP to 26. This reduction of 2 units is considered as a loss or destruction of products and the correction is carried out as in the following operation:

Table 6.4: Inventory operation to adjust stock

Location	Products
Physical Locations > Tiny SPRL > Stock	-2 bicycles
Virtual Locations > Inventory Loss	+2 bicycles

The product stock under consideration then becomes:

Table 6.5: Real and counterpart stocks when operations are completed

Location	Products
Partner Locations > Suppliers > Suppliers	-30 bicycles
Physical Locations > Tiny SPRL > Stock	+26 bicycles
Partner Locations > Customers > European Customers	+2 bicycles
Virtual Locations > Inventory Loss	+2 bicycles

This example shows one of the great advantages of this approach in terms of performance analysis. After a few months, you can just make a stock valuation of the location `Virtual Locations > Inventory Loss` to give you the value of the company's stock losses in the given period.

Now see how the following manufacturing operation is structured in Open ERP. To make a bicycle you need two wheels and a frame. This means that there should be a reduction of two wheels and a frame from real stock and the addition of a bicycle there. The consumption / production is formalized by moving products out of and into physical stock. The stock operations for this are as follows:

Table 6.6: Stock situation resulting from manufacture

Location	Products	Step
Virtual Locations > Default Production	+2 Wheels	Consumption of raw materials
Physical Locations > Tiny SPRL > Stock	-2 Wheels	Consumption of raw materials
Virtual Locations > Default Production	+1 Frame	Consumption of raw materials
Physical Locations > Tiny SPRL > Stock	-1 Frame	Consumption of raw materials
Virtual Locations > Default Production	-1 Bicycle	Manufacture of finished products
Physical Locations > Tiny SPRL > Stock	+1 Bicycle	Manufacture of finished products

So you've now got the outcome you need from the consumption of raw materials and the manufacture of finished products.

Assessing created value

You might already have noticed a useful effect of this approach: if you do a stock valuation in the `Default Production` location you get a statement of value created by your company (as a negative amount). Stock valuation in any given location is calculated by multiplying quantities of products in stock by their cost. In this case the raw material value is deducted from the finished product value.

6.2 Complete workflow from supplier to customer

Now you'll follow a practical example by adapting stock management operations. In order you'll see:

- defining a new product,

- initial setting of inventory,

- receiving products from a supplier,

- delivering to a customer,

- analysis of the state of stock.

6.2.1 Defining a new product

To start, define the following product:

Table 6.7: Product Definition

Field	Value
Name	Central Heating Type 1
Code	CCT1
Product Type	Stockable Product
Supply Method	Buy

Use the menu *Products → Products*, then click **New** to define a new product.

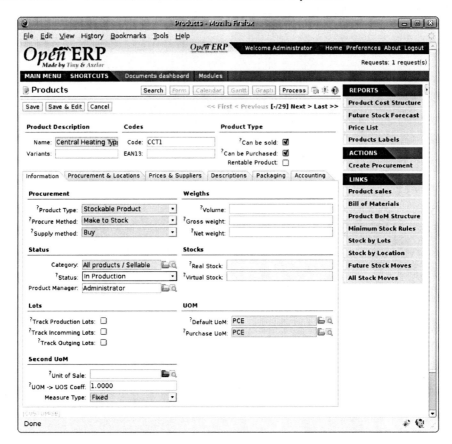

Figure 6.2: *Definition of a new product*

Three fields are important for stock management when you're configuring a new product:

- **Product Type**,

- **Procure Method**,

- **Supply Method**.

6.2.2 Product Types

The product type indicates if the product is handled in stock management and if Open ERP manages its procurement. The three distinct product types are:

- **Stockable Product** : this product is used in stock management and its replenishment is more or less automated as defined by the rules established in the system. Examples, a bicycle, a computer or a central heating system.

- **Consumable** : handled in stock management, you can receive it, deliver it and make it. But its stock level isn't managed by the system. Open ERP assumes that you've got sufficient levels in stock at all time, so it doesn't restock it automatically. Example, nails.

- **Service** : doesn't appear in the various stock operations. Example, a consulting service.

6.2.3 Procure Methods – Make to Stock and Make to Order

The procure method determines how the product will be replenished:

- **Make to Stock** : your customers are supplied from available stock. You procure a set quantity of each product when its stock is too low. Example, a classic distributor.

- **Make to Order** : when a customer order is confirmed, you then procure or manufacture the products for this order. A customer order 'Make to Order' won't modify stock in the medium term because you restock with the exact amount that was ordered. Example, computers from a large supplier assembled on demand.

You find a mix of these two modes used for the different final and intermediate products in most industries. The procurement method shown on the product form is a default value for the order, enabling the salesperson to choose the best mode for fulfilling a particular order by varying the sales order parameters as needed.

The figures *Change in stock for a product managed as Make to Stock* and *Change in stock for a product managed as Make to Order* show the change of stock levels for one product managed Make to Order and another managed Make to Stock. The two figures are taken from Open ERP's **Future Stock Forecast** report, available from the product form.

> **Logistical Methods**
>
> The **Make to Stock** logistical approach is usually used for high volumes and when the demand is seasonal or otherwise easy to forecast. The **Make to Order** approach is used for products that are measured, or very costly to stock or have a short re-stocking time.

6.2.4 Supply Methods

Open ERP supports two supply methods:

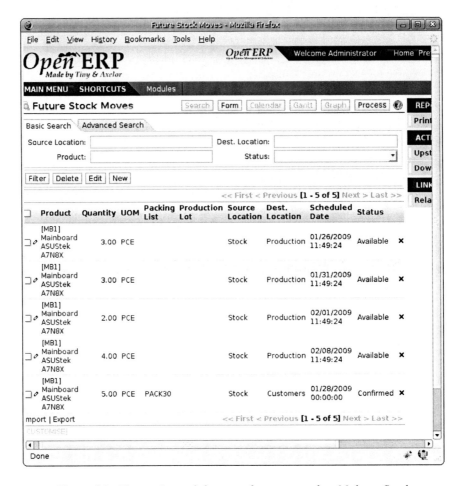

Figure 6.3: *Change in stock for a product managed as Make to Stock*

- Produce: when the product or service is supplied from internal resources,

- Buy: when the product is bought from a supplier.

These are just the default settings used by the system during automated replenishment. The same product can be either manufactured internally or bought from a supplier.

These three fields (**Supply Method**, **Procurem Method**, **Product Type**) determine the system's behaviour when a product is required. The system will generate different documents depending on the configuration of these three fields when satisfying an order, a price quotation to a supplier or a manufacturing order.

Open ERP manages both stockable products and services. A service bought from a supplier in **Make to Order** mode, will generate a subcontract order from the supplier in question.

Figure *Workflow for automatic procurement, dependent on the configuration of the product* illustrates different cases for automatic procurement.

The table below shows all possible cases for the figure *Workflow for automatic procurement, dependent on the configuration of the product*.

Figure 6.4: *Change in stock for a product managed as Make to Order*

Table 6.8: Consequences of Procurement Methods Make to Stock and Make To Order

Procurement Method	Produce	Buy
MTS	Wait for availability	Wait for availability
MTO	Production Order	Supplier Order

Table 6.9: Consequences of Procurement Methods when using Services

Procurement Method	Produce	Buy
MTS	/	/
MTO	Create task	Subcontract

You'll see the automated management processes for procurement in detail further on in this chapter.

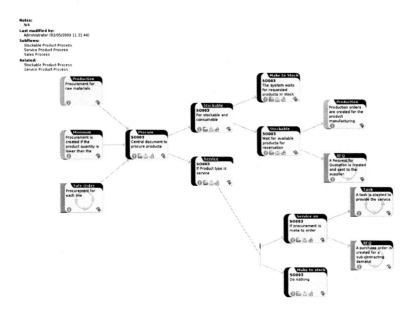

Figure 6.5: *Workflow for automatic procurement, dependent on the configuration of the product*

6.2.5 Units of Measure

Open ERP supports several units of measure. Quantities of the same product can be expressed in several units of measure at once. For example you can buy grain by the tonne and resell it by kg. You just have to make sure that all the units of measure used for a product are in the same units of measure category.

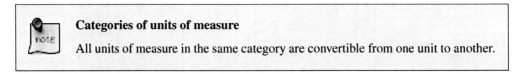

Categories of units of measure

All units of measure in the same category are convertible from one unit to another.

The table below shows some examples of units of measure and their category. The factor is used to convert from one unit of measure to another as long as they are in the same category.

Table 6.10: Example Units of Measure

UoM	Category	Factor
Kg	Weight	1
Gram	Weight	1000
Tonne	Weight	0.01
Hour	Working time	8
Day	Working time	1
Half-day	Working time	2
Item	Unit	1
100 Items	Unit	0.01

Depending on the table above you have 1Kg = 1000g = 0.001 Tonnes. A product in the `Weight` category could be expressed in Kg, Tonnes or Grammes. You can't express them in hours or pieces.

Use the menu *Products → Configuration → Units of Measure → Units of Measure* to define a new unit of measure.

In the definition of a Unit of Measure, you have a **Rounding precision** factor which shows how amounts are rounded after the conversion. A value of 1 gives rounding to the level of one unit. 0.01 gives rounding to one hundredth.

Secondary Units

Open ERP supports double units of measure. When you use this, the whole of the stock management system is encoded in two units that don't have a real link between them.

This is very useful in the agro-food industry, for example: you sell ham by the piece but invoice by the Kg. A weighing operation is needed before invoicing the customer.

To activate the management options for double units of measure, assign the group **Useability / Product UoS View** to your user.

In this case the same product can be expressed in two units of measure belonging to different categories. You can then distinguish between the unit of stock management (the piece) and the unit of invoicing or sale (kg).

In the product form you can then set one unit of measure for sales and stock management, and one unit of measure for purchases.

These units are given suggested titles. For each operation on a product you can use another unit of measure, as long as it can be found in the same category as the two units already defined. If you use another unit of measure, Open ERP automatically handles the conversion of prices and quantities.

So if you have 430 Kg of carrots at 5.30 EUR/Kg, Open ERP will automatically make the conversion if you want to sell in tonnes – 0.43 tonnes at 5300 EUR / tonne. If you had set a rounding factor of 0.1 for the **tonne** unit of measure then Open ERP will tell you that you have only 0.4 tonnes available.

6.3 Stocks

In the product form you can find a report that will give you the stock levels of the various different products in any selected location. If you haven't selected any location, Open ERP calculates stocks for all of the physical locations.

Availability of stock

Depending on whether you look at the product from a customer order or from the menu of a product form you can get different values for stock availability. If you use the product menu you get the stock in all of the physical stock locations. Looking at the product from the order you will only see the report of the warehouse selected in the order.

The two fields are:

- **Real Stock** : quantity physical present in your warehouse,
- **Virtual Stock** : calculated this way: real stock – outgoing + incoming.

Virtual Stock

Virtual stock is very useful because it shows what the salespeople can sell. If it's more than real stock it's because products will be coming in and if it's smaller than real stock then it's because certain products are reserved for other sales orders or works orders.

Detail of future stock

To get more detail about future stock, you can click **Future Stock Forecast** to the right of the product form to get the report *Printout of forecast stock levels* below. Open ERP shows a graph of the change of stock in the days to come, varying as a function of purchase orders, confirmed production and sales orders.

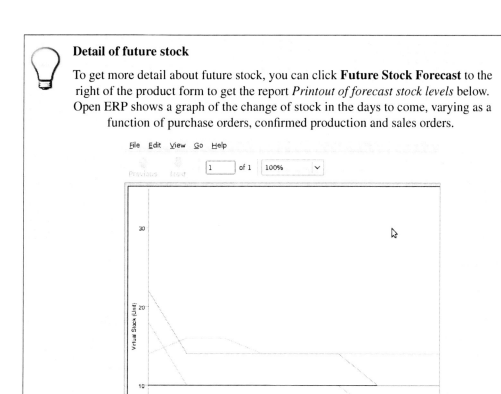

Figure 6.6: *Printout of forecast stock levels*

6.3.1 Lead times and locations

The tab **Procurement & Locations** contains information about different lead times and locations. Three lead time figures are available:

- **Customer Lead Time** : lead time promised to the customer, expressed in number of days between the order and the deliver to the customer,

- **Manufacturing Lead Time** : lead time, in days, between a production order and the end of production of the finished product,

- **Warranty (months)** : length of time in months for the warranty for the delivered products.

Warranty

The warranty period is used in the management of repairs and after-sales service. You can find more information on this subject in *Manufacturing*.

Fields in the section **Storage Localisation** are given for information – they don't have any impact on the management of stock.

Counterpart locations are automatically proposed by the system but the different values can be modified. You'll find counterpart locations for:

- **Procurement,**

- **Production,**

- **Inventory**.

A procurement location is a temporary location for stock moves that haven't yet been finalized by the scheduler. When the system doesn't yet know if procurement is to be done by a purchase or production, Open ERP uses the counterpart location **Procurement**. You'll find there everything that hasn't yet been planned by the system. The quantities of product in this location cancel each other out.

6.3.2 Initial Inventory

Once a product has been defined, use an initial inventory operation to put actual current quantities into the system by location for the products in stock. Use the menu *Stock Management → Periodical Inventory → New Periodical Inventory* for this.

Give a name (for example `Initial Inventory` or `Lost Product XYZ`) and a date for each inventory operation. You can then enter data about the quantities available for each product by location. Start by showing the location, for example `Stock`, and then select the product. Open ERP automatically completes the actual quantity actually available for that product in the location shown. You can then change that value to correct the value in stock.

Enter data for a single line in your inventory:

- **Location** : Stock,

- **Product** : PC1 Computers,

- **Quantity** : 23 Units.

Figure 6.7: *Defining a new inventory operation*

Periodical Inventory

You are usually legally required to do a stock check of all your products at least once a year. As well as doing a complete annual stock check, Open ERP also supports the method of periodical inventory.

That means you can check the stock levels of a proportion of your products every so often. This system is accepted in France as long as you can guarantee that all of your products have been counted at least once per year. To do this, use the report *Stock Management → Reporting → Dates of Inventories*.

This gives you the last inventory date by product.

You can do this the same way for all products and all locations, so you only carry out small inventory operations through the year rather than a single large stock check at one point in the year (which usually turns out to be at an inconvenient time).

When your inventory operation is finished you can confirm it using the button to the bottom right of the form. Open ERP will then automatically create the stock moves to close the gaps, as mentioned at the start of this chapter. You can verify the moves generated using the second tab of the inventory operation form.

The correct levels of your product are now in your stock locations. A simple way of verifying this is to reopen the product form to see the quantities available in stock.

6.3.3 Receipt of a supplier order

Supplier goods receipt forms are automatically prepared by Open ERP by the purchase management process. You'll find a list of all the awaited receipts in the menu *Stock Management → Incoming Goods → Packing to Process*. Use the order number or the supplier name to find the right goods receipt form for confirmation of a goods in. This approach enables you to control quantities received by referring to the quantities ordered.

Figure 6.8: *List of items waiting*

You can also do goods-in data entry manually if there's no order, using the same menu *Stock Management → Incoming Goods → New Reception Packing*.

A new goods-in data entry form then opens. Enter the supplier data in the **Partner** field and you can type in the reference number from your supplier in the field **Origin**. You should then enter data about the products received in the lines.

The source location is already completed by default because of your supplier selection. You should then give the destination location where you will place the products. For example, enter `Stock`. At this stage you can set a lot number for traceability (this function will be described later in this chapter, so leave this field empty for the moment).

Once the form has been completed you can confirm the receipt of all the products at the same time using the **Process Now** button. If you want to enter data for a goods receipt that you're still waiting for click the button **Process Later**.

Figure 6.9: *Form for entering goods received from a supplier order*

The products then arrive in stock and should reflect the quantities shown on the product form.

In the goods receipt form, the field **Invoicing Control** lets you influence the way you send invoices to suppliers. If this is set to `To be invoiced` a supplier invoice will now be generated automatically in the draft state, based on the goods received. Your accountant then has to confirm this pre-invoicing once the supplier's invoice is received. This enables you to verify that the invoiced quantities correspond to the quantities received.

6.3.4 Customer delivery

Everything about goods receipt can also be done manually for a customer delivery. But this time, use the automated product delivery processes based on customer orders. Install the `sale` module so that you can proceed further in this section of the chapter.

Now create a new customer order from the menu *Sales Management → Sales Orders → New Quotation*. Enter the following data in this order:

- **Shop** : Tiny SPRL

- **Customer** : Agrolait

- **Order Line** :

  - **Product** : PC1 Computer,
  - **Quantity** : 3 PCE
  - **Procurement Method** : from stock.

You've seen already that Open ERP shows you the available product stock when you've selected list mode. The real stock is equal to the virtual stock because you've nothing to deliver to customers and you're not waiting for any of these products to be received into stock. The salesperson then has all the information needed to take orders efficiently.

Then confirm the quotation to convert it to an order. If you return to the product form you'll see the virtual stock is now smaller than the real stock. That happens because three products have been reserved by the order that you created, so they can't be sold to another customer.

Start the scheduler through the menu *Manufacturing → Compute All Schedulers*. Its functionality will be detailed in *Manufacturing*. This manages the reservation of products and places orders based on the dates promised to customers, and the various internal lead times and priorities.

Just in Time

Install the module `mrp_jit` to schedule each order in real time after it's been confirmed. This means that you don't have to start the scheduler or wait for its periodical start time.

You can now look at the the list of deliveries waiting to be carried out using the menu *Stock Management → Outgoing Products → Available Packings*. You find a line there for your order representing the items to be sent. Double-click the line to see the detail of the items proposed by Open ERP.

Figure 6.10: *Entering an order for three computers*

States

Open ERP distinguishes between the states **Confirmed** and **Assigned**.

You say that an item is **Confirmed** when it's needed but the available stock is insufficient. You say that an item is **Assigned** when it's available in stock and the storesperson reserves it: the necessary products have been reserved for this specific operation.

You can confirm a customer delivery using the **Confirm** button. A window then opens where you can enter the quantities actually delivered. If you enter a value less than the forecast one, Open ERP automatically generates a partial delivery notes and a new order for the remaining items. For this exercise, just confirm all the products.

If you return to the list of current orders you will see that your order has now been marked as delivered (done). A progress indicator from 0% to 100% is shown by each order so that the salesperson can follow the progress of their orders at a glance.

Figure 6.11: *Items on a customer order*

Negative Stock

Stock Management is very flexible so that it can be more effective. For example if you forget to enter products at goods in, this won't prevent you from sending them to customers. In Open ERP you can force all operations manually using the button **Force assignment**. In this case your stocks risk falling negative. You should monitor all stocks for negative levels and carry out an inventory correction when that happens.

6.3.5 Analysing stock

Now look at the effect of these operations on stock management. There are several ways of viewing stocks:

- from the product form,
- from the locations,
- from the orders.

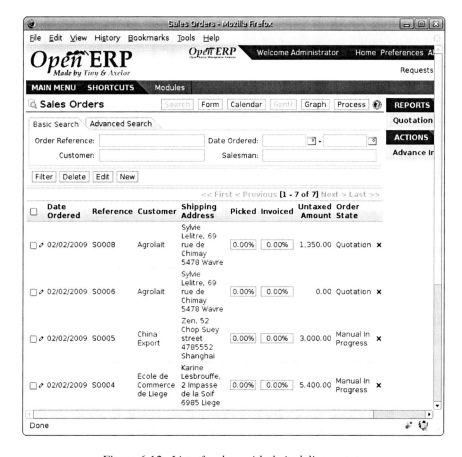

Figure 6.12: *List of orders with their delivery state*

Start by opening the product form from the menu *Products → Products* and looking at the list of items. You'll immediately see the following information about the products:

- **Real Stock**,

- **Virtual Stock**.

If you want more information you can use the actions to the right of the form. If you click the report **Future Stock Forecast**, Open ERP opens a graphical view of the stock levels for the selected products changing with time over the days and weeks to come. The value at the left of the graph is the real stock (today) and the value at the right is the virtual stock (stock in the short term future).

To get the stock levels by location use the button **Stock by Location**. Open ERP then gives you the stock of this product split out over all the possible locations. If you only want to see the physical locations in your company just filter this list using the Location Type **Internal Locations**. By default, physical locations are already colored red to distinguish them better. Consolidate locations (the sum of several locations, following the hierarchical structure) are colored blue.

You can get more detail about all the stock moves from the product form. You'll then see each move from a source location to a destination location. Everything that influences stock levels corresponds to a stock move.

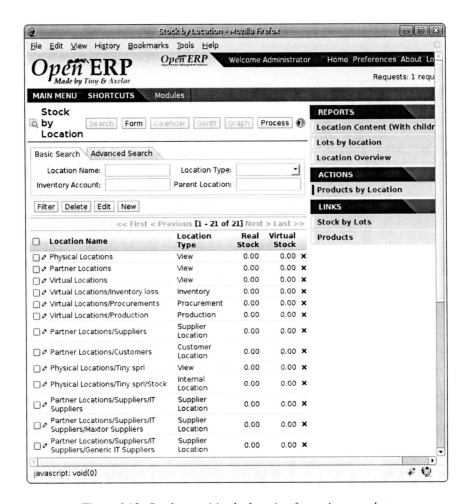

Figure 6.13: *Stock quantities by location for a given product*

You could also look at the stocks available in a location using the menu *Stock Management → Stock Locations Structure*. You can then use the structure shortcuts at the and the location tree in the main window. Click a location to look at the stocks by product. A location containing child locations shows the consolidated contents for all of its child locations.

You should now check the product quantities for various locations to familiarize yourself with this double-entry stock management system. You should look at:

- supplier locations to see how goods receipts are linked,

- customer locations to see how packing notes are linked,

- inventory locations to see the accumulated losses and profits,

- production locations to see the value created for the company.

Also look at how the real and virtual stocks depend on the location selected. If you enter a supplier location:

- the real stock shows all of the product receipts coming from this type of supplier,

- the virtual stock takes into account the quantities expected from these suppliers (+ real stock + quantities expected from these suppliers). It's the same scheme for customer locations and production locations.

6.4 Logistics Configuration

In this section you'll see how to configure stock management to match your company's needs. Open ERP can handle many different situations by configuring it to behave as required.

6.4.1 Stock locations

You've seen in the preceding sections that the whole of stock management is built on a concept of stock locations. Locations are structured hierarchically to account for the subdivision of a warehouse into sections, aisles, and/or cupboards. The hierarchical view also enables you to structure virtual locations such as production counterparts. That gives you a finer level of analysis.

Use the menu *Stock Management → Configuration → Locations* then click **New** to define new locations.

You should then give a name to your stock location. Now look at location types and localization.

6.4.2 Location types

The location must have one of the following types:

- View: shows that the location is only an organizational node for the hierarchical structure, and can't be involved in stock moves itself. The view type is not usually made into a leaf node in a structure – it usually has children.

- Customer: destination for products sent to customers,

- Supplier: source of products received from suppliers,

- Internal: locations for your own stock,

- Inventory: the counterpart for inventory operations used to correct stock levels,

- Production: the counterpart for production operations; receipt of raw material and sending finished products,

- Procurement: the counterpart for procurement operations when you don't yet know the source (supplier or production). Products in this location should be zero after the scheduler run completes.

You can have several locations of the same type. In that case your product, supplier and warehouse configurations determine the location that's to be used for any given operation.

The counterparts for procurement, inventory and production operations are given by the locations shown on the product form. The counterparts of reception and delivery operations are given by the locations shown on the partner form. The choice of stock location is given by the configuration of the warehouse, linked to a Shop.

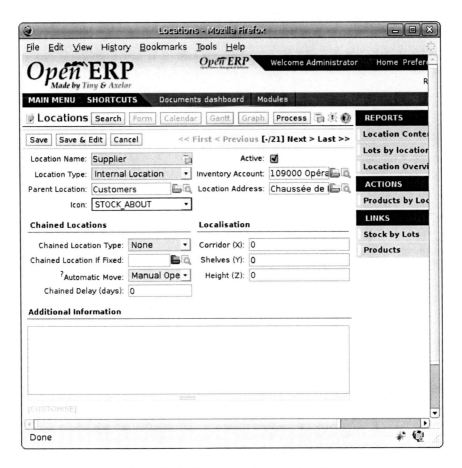

Figure 6.14: *Definition of a stock location*

6.4.3 Localization

Each location can be given an address. That enables you to create a location for a customer or a supplier, for example. You can then give it the address of that customer or supplier. You should indicate to Open ERP on the partner form that it should use this location rather than the default location given to partner deliveries.

> **Subcontracting production**
>
> You'll see in the chapter, *Manufacturing*, that it is possible to assign a location to a manufacturing workcenter. If this location is at a supplier's you must give it an address so that Open ERP can prepare a delivery order for the supplier and a receive operation for the manufactured goods.
>
> Creating a location specifically for a partner is also a simple solution for handled consigned stocks in Open ERP.

Figure 6.15: *Definition of stock locations on the product form*

 Consigned Stock

Consigned stock is stock that is owned by you (valued in your accounts) but is physically stocked by your supplier. Or, conversely, it could be stock owned by your customer (not valued by you) but stocked in your company.

To enable you to consolidate easily at a higher level, the location definition is hierarchical. This structure is given by the field **Parent location**. That also enables you to manage complex cases of product localization. For example, you could imagine the following scenario.

Example Structure for two warehouses

A company has a warehouse in Paris and in Bordeaux. For some orders you must deliver the products from Paris, and for others from Bordeaux. But you should also specify a fictitious warehouse that Open ERP uses to calculate if it should deliver products from Paris or from Bordeaux.

To do this in Open ERP, you'd create a third warehouse 'France' which consolidates the warehouses in Paris

---

Figure 6.16: *Definition of stock locations on the partner form*

and Bordeaux. You create the following physical locations:

- Company
    - Output
        * Warehouses France
            · Warehouse Paris
            · Warehouse Bordeaux

Open ERP will then deliver the goods from the warehouse that has the ordered product in stock. When products are available in several warehouses, Open ERP will select the nearest warehouse. To formalize the notion of distance between warehouses you should use the geographic co-ordinates (X, Y, Z) of the different stores to enable Open ERP to search for the nearest goods.

The same co-ordinates could also be used to structure the shelves, aisles and interior rooms in a warehouse.

6.4.4 Accounting valuation in real time

If you have experience of managing with traditional software you'll know the problem of getting useful indicators. If you ask your accountant for a stock valuation or the value added by production he'll give you a figure. If you ask for the same figure from your stores manager you'll get an entirely different amount. You have no idea who's right!

In Open ERP the management of stock is completely integrated with the accounts, to give strong coherence between the two systems. The double-entry structure of locations enables a very precise correspondence between stocks and accounts.

Each stock movement also generates a corresponding accounting entry in an accounting journal to ensure that the two systems can stay in permanent synchronization.

To do that, set up a general account for each location that should be valued in your accounts. If a product goes to one location or another and the accounts are different in the two locations, Open ERP automatically generates the corresponding accounting entries in the accounts, in the stock journal.

If a stock move will go from a location without an account to a location where an account has been assigned (for example goods receipt from a supplier order), Open ERP generates an accounting entry using the properties defined in the product form for the counterpart. You can use different accounts per location or link several location to the same account, depending on the level of analysis needed.

You use this system for managing consigned stocks:

- a supplier location that is valued in your own accounts or,

- a location in your own company that isn't valued in your accounts.

6.4.5 Linked locations

Locations in Open ERP can be linked between each other to define paths followed by products. So you can then define rules such as: all products that enter the warehouse must automatically be sent to quality control. The warehouse and quality control are represented by two different locations.

Then when a product arrives in a location, Open ERP can automatically suggest that you send the product to another linked location. Three link modes are available:

- Manual,

- Automatic,

- Automatic without steps.

The manual mode will create an internal move order to the linked location once products arrive in the source locations. This order will wait for a confirmation of the move by a user. This enables you to have a list of moves to do, proposed by the system and confirmed by the storesperson.

Product Logistics

The module `stock_location` lets you generate paths to follow, not just at the level of locations but also at the level of products. It then enables you to manage default locations for a given product or to refer to the products as a function of operations such as quality control, supplier receipt, and after-sales service.

A more detailed explanation of this module, with examples, is given at the end of this chapter.

The automatic mode will do the same but won't wait for a confirmation from the user. Products will automatically be sent to the linked location without any intervening manual operation to do. This corresponds to the case where, for simplicity, you delete a step in the process so the end user can set off the process automatically.

The `automatic without steps` mode won't include the additional stock move but will change the destination move transparently to assign the linked the location. You could then assign a destination location to which you send all the products that arrive in your warehouse. The storesperson will modify the goods receipt note.

If there is a linkage to do, the field **Type of linked location** lets the destination location be determined. If the field is set to 'customer', the location is given by the properties of the partner form. If the field is set to `fixed`, the destination location is given by the field **Location if link is fixed**.

Some operations take a certain time between order and execution. To account for this lead time, you can set a value in days in the field **Link lead time**. Then the extra move (automatic or not) will be carried out several days after the original move. If you use the mode `automatic without steps`, the lead time is inserted directly into the initial order. In this way you can add security lead times at certain control points in the warehouse.

6.4.6 Case of structuring locations

You'll see in the next part that linking locations lets you manage a whole series of complex cases in managing production efficiently:

- handling multiple operations for a customer order,
- tracking import and export by sea transport,
- managing a production chain in detail,
- managing rented products,
- managing consigned products.

To show these concepts, five cases of structuring and configuring these locations are given below. Many other configurations are possible depending on needs.

6.4.7 Handling customer orders

Customer orders are usually handled in one of two ways:

- item note (or preparation order), confirmed when the item is ready to send,

- delivery order (or freight note), confirmed when the transporter has delivered the item to a customer.

You use the following stock move in Open ERP to simulate these operations:

- Packing Note: Stock > Output,

- Delivery Order: Output > Customer.

The first operation is automatically generated by the customer order. The second is then generated by the stock management by showing that the `Output` location is linked to the `Customer` location. That then gives the two operations waiting. If the `Output` location isn't situated beneath the stock location you then have to move the item from stock to the place that the item is prepared.

Some companies don't want to work in two steps, because it just seems like extra work to have to confirm a delivery note in the system. You can then set the link mode to 'Automatic' to make Open ERP automatically confirm the second step. It's then assumed the all the items have automatically been delivered to the customer.

6.4.8 Linked Production

The `stock_location` module enables you to manage the linkages by product in addition to doing that by location. You can then create a location structure that represents your production chain by product.

The location structure looks like this:

- Stock
    - Level 1
    - Level 2
        * Link 1
            · Operation 1
            · Operation 2
            · Operation 3
            · Operation 4

You can then set the locations a product or a routing must go through on the relevant form. All products that enter the production chain will automatically follow the predetermined path.

To improve your logistics, you'll see further on in this chapter how you can put minimum stock rules onto different locations to guarantee security stocks for assembly operators. Reports on the state of stocks in different locations will rapidly show you the bottlenecks in your production chain.

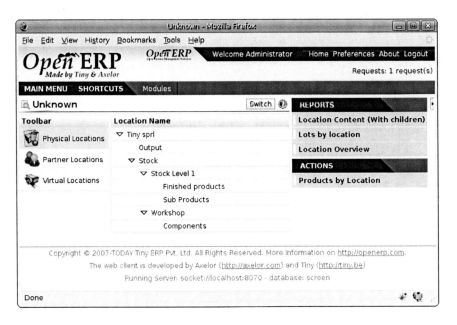

Figure 6.17: *Logistics for a given product*

6.5 Import / Export

Managing import / export with foreign companies can sometimes be very complex. Between a departure port and destination company, products can get stopped for several weeks at sea or somewhere in the numerous transportation stages and customs. To manage such deliveries efficiently it's important to:

- know where your products are,
- know when they're likely to arrive at their destination,
- know your value in transit,
- follow the development of the different steps.

Linked locations in Open ERP enable this all to be managed rather elegantly. You can use a structure like this:

- Suppliers
    - European Suppliers
    - Chinese Suppliers
- In transit
    - Shanghai Port
    - Pacific Ocean
    - San Francisco Port
    - San Francisco Customs

6.5.1 Stock

The transit location are linked between themselves with a manual confirmation step. The internal stock move is validated at each port and customs arrival. Open ERP prepares all the linked moves automatically.

> **Intrastat**
>
> Companies that do import / export should install the module `report_intrastat`. This enables them to prepare the reports needed to declare product exports.

You can use the lead times between different locations to account for real delays. Your lead times and stock forecasts are calculated by Open ERP to estimate the arrival of incoming products so that you can respond to a customer's needs as precisely as possible.

You can also value the products in transit in your account depending on the chosen stock location configuration.

6.5.2 Rental locations

You can manage rental locations in Open ERP very simply using the same system of linked locations. Using the module `stock_location` you can set a return date for rental items sent to customer location after a certain rental period.

Then the set of real and virtual stocks is maintained daily in real time. The different operations such as delivery and receipt after a few days are automatically suggested by Open ERP which simplifies the work of data entry.

You then have the product list found in the customer locations and your own stock in your stock location. The list of goods receipts waiting is automatically generated by Open ERP using the location links.

The same principle is used for internal stock to generate the quality control for certain products.

6.5.3 Consigned Products

The principle of linked locations is used to manage consigned products. You can specify that certain products should be returned to you a certain number of days after they have been delivered to customers.

When the products have been delivered Open ERP automatically creates goods receipts for the consigned product. The specified date is obviously approximate but enables you to forecast returns.

6.6 Warehouses

Warehouses are designed for physical locations from which you can deliver to the customer and to which you receive raw materials. Then when you buy products from a supplier you should take account of which Warehouse you use for this purchase. This also enables the end user to not have to choose from a list of locations but simply a real warehouses.

Use the menu *Stock Management* → *Configuration* → *Warehouses* then click **New** to configure a new warehouse.

A warehouse is defined by a link between three locations:

- The **Location Stock** field shows the place of products available for delivery to a customer direct from this warehouse. Availability is given by all the products in that location and any child locations.

- The **Location Input** field shows where ordered products are received from a supplier to that warehouse. It can be the same as the stock location if, for example, you want to do a quality control operation on your incoming raw materials.

- The **Location Output** field (called Output in the demonstration database) is designed as a buffer zone in which you store all the items that have been picked but not yet delivered to a customer. You're strongly advised not to put this location within the stock hierarchy but instead at a level higher or the same.

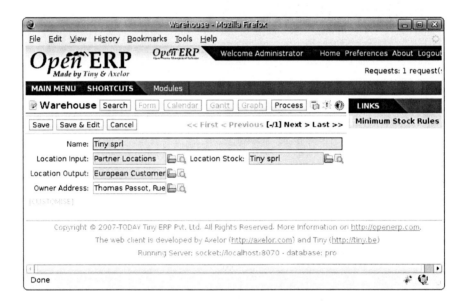

Figure 6.18: *Warehouse parameters*

You can also set an address for the warehouse. This address should ideally be an address for your company. Once the warehouse has been defined it can be used in:

- Minimum stock rules,

- Supplier orders,

- Customer orders (using the definition of a point of sale, which is linked to a warehouse).

6.6.1 Automatic procurement

Several methods of automatically procuring products can be carried out by Open ERP:

- the workflow used by products that have the procurement mode **Make to Order**,

- using minimum stock rules for **Make to Stock** products,

- using the master production schedule for **Make to Stock** products.

The two last methods are described below.

6.6.2 Minimum stock rules

To automatically make stock replenishment proposals, you can use minimum stock rules. To do this use the menu *Stock Management → Automatic Procurements → Minimum Stock Rules*.

The rule is the following: if the virtual stock for the given location is lower than the minimum stock indicated in the rule, the system will automatically propose a procurement to increase the level of virtual stock to the maximum level given in the rule.

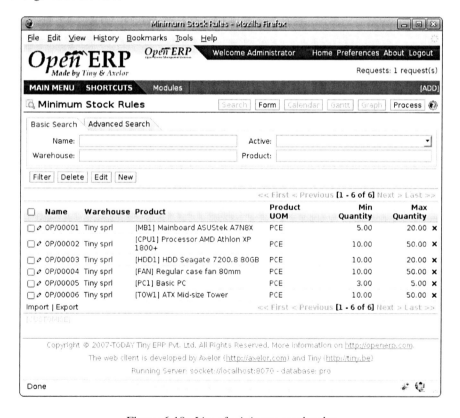

Figure 6.19: *List of minimum stock rules*

Conflict resolution

You may find that draft production or procurement orders don't happen correctly. That can happen if the system is badly configured (for example if you've forgotten to set the supplier on a product).

To check this, look at the list of procurements in the exception state in the menu *Stock Management → Automatic Procurements → Exceptions Procurements*. More detail on handling these exceptions is given in *Manufacturing*.

It's important to underline that the rule is based on virtual quantities and not just on real quantities. It then takes account of the calculation of orders and receipts to come.

Take the following example:

- Products in stock: 15

- Products ordered but not delivered: 5

- Products in manfacture: 2

The rules defined are:

- Minimum stock: 13

- Maximum stock: 25.

Once the rules have been properly configured the purchasing manager only needs to look at the list of orders for confirmation with the supplier using the menu *Purchase Management → Purchase Orders → Requests for Quotation*.

Note that the procurement doesn't require that you buy from a supplier. If the product has a **Supply method** of Produce the scheduler will generate a production order and not a supplier order.

You can also set multiple quantities in the minimum stock rules. If you set a multiple quantity of 3 the system will propose procurement of 15 pieces not the 13 it really needs. In this case it automatically rounds the quantity upwards.

In a minimum stock rule, when you indicate a warehouse it suggests a stock location by default in that warehouse. You can change that location by default when the scheduler completes, by location and not by warehouse.

6.7 Scheduling

The master production plan, sometimes called the MPS (Master Production Schedule), enables you to generate forecasts for incoming and outgoing material. It's based on forecasts of inputs and outputs by the logistics manager.

MPS, Procurement and Production

Open ERP distinguishes between Production, Purchase and Production.

Production is manufacture, Purchase is the acquisition of goods from another party, and Procurement is either or both of those. So it would be better to call the MPS the Master Procurement Schedule. Which Open ERP does!

Product trading

Also called the Production Plan, this tool is also very useful for traded products which aren't manufactured. You can then use it for stock management with purchased and manufactured products.

To be able to use the production plan, you must install the `stock_planning` module. This can be found amongst Open ERP's `addons-extra` rather in the main set of `addons`. (Beware! One reason it is not in the core of Open ERP at the time of writing could be because some screens have no navigation controls, so you can't always easily get back to the main Open ERP system).

6.7.1 Sales Forecasts

The first thing to do to work with a production plan is to define the periods for stock management. Some companies plan daily, others weekly or monthly.

Stock Management interval

The interval chosen for managing stock in the production plan will depend on the length of your production cycle. You generally work daily, weekly or monthly.

If your products take several days to assemble it's preferable to have a weekly plan. If your manufacturing cycles are several months you can work with a monthly plan.

To do this use the menu *Sales Management → Configuration → Create Sales Periods*. A window appears enabling you to automatically define the next periods that will be provided for stock management.

Salespeople can then enter their sales forecasts by product and by period using the menu *Sales Management → Sales Forecasts → My Sales Forecasts*. The forecasts can be made by quantity or by value. For a forecast by amount Open ERP automatically calculates for you the quantity equivalent to the estimated amount. This can be modified manually as needed before completion.

6.7.2 Production Plan

The manager responsible for logistics then plans receipts (manufacturing or purchases) and outgoings (consumption or customer deliveries) by period. To do this use the menu *Stock Management → Planning → Master Procurement Schedule*.

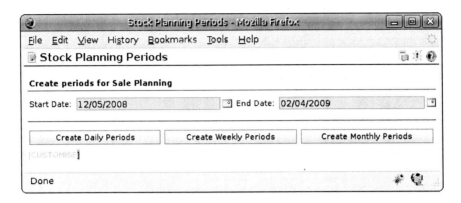

Figure 6.20: *Defining periods for stock management*

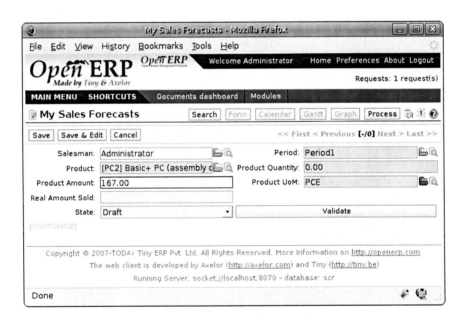

Figure 6.21: *Sales Forecast to help create a master production plan*

For each period and product Open ERP gives you the following information:

- stock estimated at the end of the period, calculated as stock in the following period less total estimated outgoings plus total estimated inputs,

- closed entries, coming from production or confirmed purchases,

- forecast inputs for the period, calculated using the incoming entries less the closing amounts,

- planned inputs entered manually by the logistics manager,

- closed outgoings which are the consumption of manufacturing waiting and deliveries to be made to customers,

- forecast outgoings, calculated from the planned outgoings, less the closing amounts,

- planned outgoings, manually entered by the logistics manager,

- sales forecasts, which represent the sum of forecasts made by the salespeople.

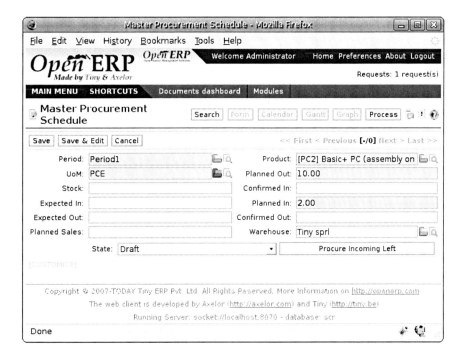

Figure 6.22: *The master production schedule (MPS)*

The production plan then enables the logistics manager to play with the forecast income and outgoings and test the impact on the future stock for the product under consideration. It enables you for example to check that the stock doesn't fall below a certain level for the product under consideration.

You can also open the production plan for past periods. In this case Open ERP shows you the real stock moves, by period for forecast reports.

If you don't have automated procurement rules for a product you can start procurement at any time based on the estimates of the production plan. To do this press the button **Procure Incoming Left** (i.e. remaining) on the **Master Procurement Schedule**. Open ERP plans procurement for an amount equal to the entries forecast.

6.8 Management of lots and traceability

The double-entry management in Open ERP enables you to run very advanced traceability. All operations are formalized in terms of stock moves, so it's very simple to search for the cause of any gaps in stock moves.

 Upstream and downstream traceability

Upstream traceability runs from the raw materials received from the supplier and follows the chain to the finished products delivered to customers. (Note that the name is confusing - this would often be considered a downstream direction. Think of it as **Where Used**.)

Downstream traceability follows the product in the other direction, from customer to the different suppliers of raw material. (Note that the name is confusing - this would often be considered an upstream direction. Think of it as **Where Supplied**.)

6.8.1 Stock Moves

Use the menu *Stock Management → Traceability → Low Level → Stock Moves* to track past stock transactions for a product or a given location. All the operations are available. You can filter on the various fields to retrieve the operations about an order, or a production activity, or a source location, or any given destination.

Each stock move is in a given state. The different possible states are:

- Draft : the move has so far had no effect in the system. The transaction hasn't yet been confirmed,

- Confirmed : the move will be done, so it will be counted in the calculations of virtual stock. But you don't know whether it will be done without problem because the products have been reserved for the move,

- Validated : the move will be done and the necessary raw material have been reserved for the transaction,

- Done : the stock move has been done, and entered into the calculations of real stock,

- Waiting : in the case of transactions From Order , this state shows that the stock move is blocked waiting for the end of another move,

- Cancelled : the stock move wasn't carried out, so there's no accounting for it in either real stock or virtual stock.

Delivery orders, goods receipts and internal picking lists are just documents that group a set of stock moves. You can also consult the history of these documents using the menu *Stock Management → Traceability → Low level → Packing*.

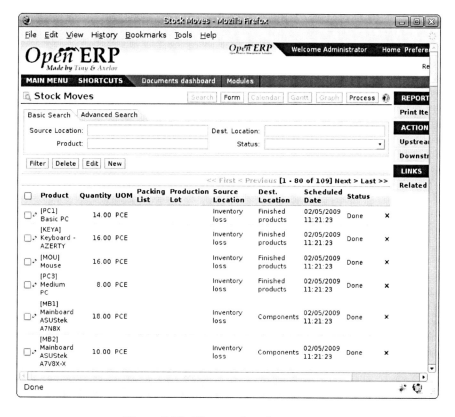

Figure 6.23: *History of stock movements*

6.8.2 Lots

Open ERP can also manage product lots. Two lot types are defined:

- Production lots (batch numbers) are represented by a unique product or an assembly of identical products leaving the same production area. They are usually identified by bar codes stuck on the products. The batch can be marked with a supplier number or your own company numbers.

- Tracking numbers are logistical lots for identifying the container for a set of products. This corresponds, for example, to the pallet numbers on which several different products are stocked.

These lots can be encoded onto all stock moves and, specifically, on goods-in lines, internal moves and product deliveries.

To enter the lot number in an operation you can use an existing lot number or create a new lot. A production lot (batch number) is used for a single product. A tracking number can be used several times for different products, so you can mix different products on a pallet or in a box.

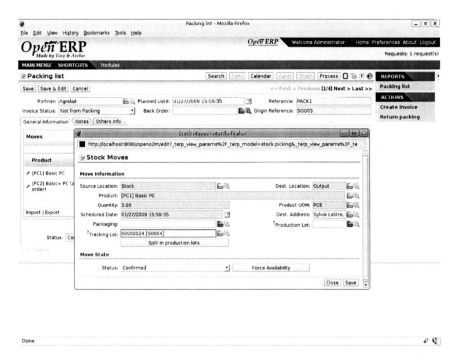

Figure 6.24: *Entering a line for production receipt*

Simplified View

In the Simplified View the tracking numbers can't be seen: the field is hidden. To get to Extended View mode, assign the group **Usability – Extended View** to the current user.

You can also specify on the product form the operations in which a lot number is required. You can then compel the user to set a lot number for manufacturing operations, goods receipt, or customer packing.

You don't have to encode the lot number one by one to assign a unique lot number to a set of several items. You only need to take a stock move for several products line and click the button **Split in Production Lots**. You can then give a lot number prefix (if you want) and Open ERP will complete the prefix in the wizard with a continuing sequence number. This sequence number might correspond to a set of pre-printed barcodes that you stick on each product.

6.8.3 Traceability

If you code in the lot numbers for stock moves as described above you can then investigate the traceability of any given lot number. To do this use the menu *Stock Management → Traceability → Production Lots*, or *Stock Management → Traceability → Tracking Lots*.

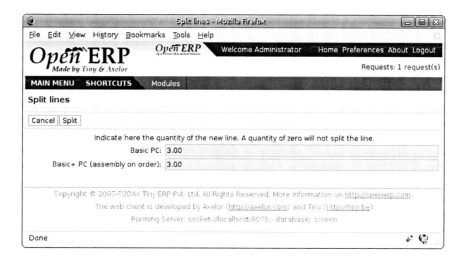

Figure 6.25: *Splitting a lot into uniquely identified parts*

Product Shortcuts

From the product form, the toolbar to the right offers useful information:

- **Minimum stock rules**,
- **Stocks by location**,
- **Sales detail**,
- **Stocks by lot**,
- **Bills of Materials**.

Search for a particular lot using the filters for the lot number, the date or the product. Once you can see the form about this lot several actions are possible:

- **Traceability upstream** : from supplier through to customers,
- **Traceability downstream** : from customer back to suppliers,
- Stock in all the physical and virtual locations.

Finally, on a lot, you can enter data on all the operations that have been done on the product. That forms a useful history of the pre-sales operations.

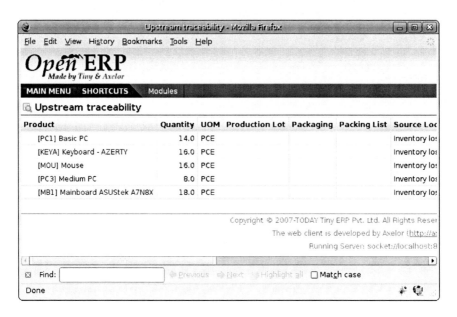

Figure 6.26: *Tracing upstream in Make to Order*

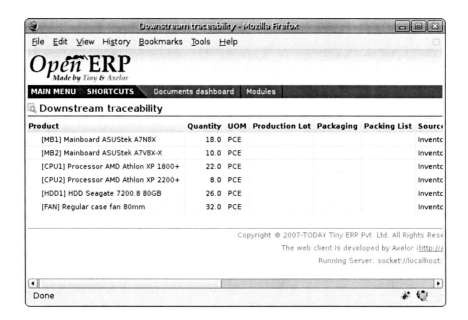

Figure 6.27: *Tracing downstream in Make to Stock*

6.9 Management by Journal

You can manage stock through journals in the same way as you can manage your accounts through journals. This approach has the great advantage of being able to define journals in various ways as you need them to meet your company's needs.

For example, a large company may want to organize deliveries by department or warehouse. You can then create a journal and a manager for each department. The different users can then work in a journal as a function of their position in the company. That enables you to structure your information better.

A company that does a lot of transport can organize its journals by delivery vehicle. The different delivery orders will then be assigned to a journal representing a particular vehicle. Then if the vehicle has left the company you can confirm all the orders that are found in the journal all at the same time.

6.9.1 The different journals

Install the module `sale_journal` to work with journals. This adds three new concepts to Open ERP:

- Invoicing journals,

- Order journals,

- Delivery journals.

Invoicing journals are used to assign purchase orders and/or delivery order to a given invoicing journal. Everything in the journal can be invoiced in one go, and you can control the amounts by journal. For example you can create the following journals: daily invoicing, end-of-week invoicing, and end-of-month invoicing. It's also possible to show the invoicing journal by default in the partner form.

Order journals look like orders and are automatically transferred to orders for the corresponding items. These enable you to classify the orders in various ways, such as by department, by salesperson, or by type. Then if a salesperson looks at her own journals after an order she can easily see the work on current items compared with her own orders.

Default Values

To enter all the orders in their own order journal, a salesperson can use the default values that are entered in the fields when creating orders.

Finally the delivery journals are used to post each item into a delivery journal. For example you can create journals dated according to customer delivery dates (such as Monday's deliveries, or afternoon deliveries) or these journals could represent the day's work for delivery vehicles (such as truck1, truck2).

6.9.2 Using the journals

You'll now see how to use the journals to organize your stock management in practice. After installing the module `sale_journal` look at the list of partners. In the tab **Sales and Purchases** on any of them you'll now see the field **Invoicing Method**.

Figure 6.28: *Partner form in invoicing mode*

You can create a new **Invoicing Journal** on a partner on the fly. You can show if the invoices should be grouped or not after you have generated them in the journal. Create a second invoicing journal `End-of-Month Invoicing` which you can assign to another partner.

Then enter the data for some orders for these two partners. After entering this order data, the field **Invoicing Mode** is completed automatically from the partner settings. Put these orders into the Invoicing Mode based on items in the second tab.

Look at the assembly notes about these orders in the field **Invoicing Mode** is automatically shown there. Then confirm the different orders in the list.

At the end of the day, the invoicing supervisor can put the list by journal. To do this, use the menu *Stock Management → Sorted List → List to invoice*. Choose the invoicing journal and all the lists of orders to invoice then open in list view. It's then possible to automatically carry out invoicing by clicking the action **Invoice** (the gears symbol in the application client).

Figure 6.29: *Defining an invoicing journal*

 Confirming invoices

By default, invoices are generated in the draft state which enables you to modify them before sending them to the customer. But you can confirm all the invoices in one go by selecting them all from the list and doing the action 'Confirm draft invoices'.

At the end of the month the invoicing management does the same work but in the journal 'month-end invoicing'.

You can also enter a journal to confirm / cancel all the orders in one go. Then you can do several quotations and assign them in a journal and confirm or cancel them en masse at once.

6.10 Advanced elements of stock management

In this section you'll enter the details of management and control of stocks.

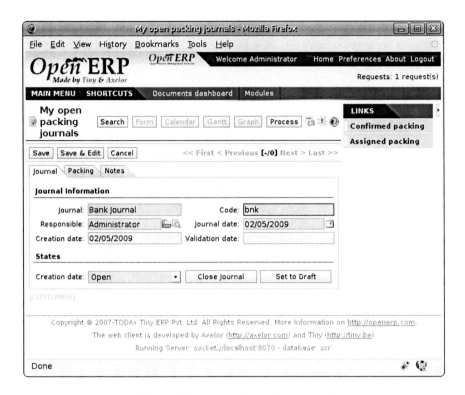

Figure 6.30: *View of an order journal*

6.10.1 Requirements Calculation / Scheduling

Requirements calculation is the calculation engine that plans, prioritizes and starts the automated procurement as a function of rules defined in the products.

Requirements Calculation

Requirements Calculation is often called Scheduling.

By default, it automatically starts once per day. You can also start it manually using the menu *Manufacturing → Start All Schedulers*. It then uses the parameters defined in the products, the suppliers, and the company to determine the priorities between the different product orders, deliveries and purchases from suppliers.

6.10.2 Just in Time

By default, scheduling starts automatically once a day. You should make this run happen overnight to ensure that the system doesn't slow down under a heavy load of scheduling when you're also trying to use it interactively yourselves.

To set the time it starts use the menu *Administration → Configuration → Scheduler → Scheduled Actions*. Select the rule called 'Run MRP Scheduler' and modify the date and time of the next execution. Some companies want to plan orders progressively as they are entered so they don't wait until procurement orders are planned the next day. Install the module `mrp_jit` to handle this. Once it's installed, each requirement (that could result in a Production or Purchase Order) will be planned in real time as soon as it's been confirmed.

Then if you make a customer order with a product that's `Make To Order` the quotation request to a supplier will be generated. ..tip :: Delivery from the supplier or to the customer

> The `sale_supplier_direct_delivery` module enables you to deliver the product directly from the supplier to the customer. At the time of writing this module is in `addons-extra`. The logic that the product follows is configured individually for each product and affects only those products marked `Make to Order`.

This mode is not always sensible. Each order is processed immediately it's been confirmed. So if an order is to be delivered in three months the scheduler will reserve goods in stock for each order once it's been confirmed. It would have been more sensible to leave these products available for other orders.

If a Purchase Order's **Invoicing Control** is configured `From Order`, the scheduler will immediately create the corresponding supplier quotation request. It would have been preferable to delay for several weeks if you could have used the lead time to group the purchase with other future orders.

So the negative effects of working with the Just in Time module are:

- Poor priority management between orders,
- Additional stocked products.

6.10.3 Planning

You've seen that most Open ERP documents can be changed in a planning view. It's the same for deliveries and goods receipts. You can put them into a calendar view at any time to plan your deliveries or goods receipts.

Planned dates on a packing order are put on each stock move line. Then if you have a packing order containing several products you don't have to have all of the lines on the order delivered on the same day. The minimum and maximum dates on a packing order show the earliest and latest dates on the stock move lines for the packing.

If you move a packing order in the calendar view, the planned date on the stock move lines will automatically be moved as a result.

6.10.4 Management of partial deliveries

Partial deliveries, sometimes called Back Orders, are generated automatically by Open ERP. When you confirm a customer delivery or the receipt of products from suppliers, Open ERP asks you to confirm the quantity delivered or received.

If you leave the quantities alone, Open ERP confirms and then closes the order for delivery or receipt. If you modify a quantity, Open ERP will automatically generate a second delivery or goods receipt document for the

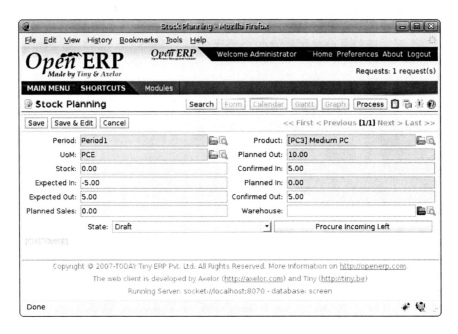

Figure 6.31: *Planning the deliveries of customer products*

remaining quantities. The first will be confirmed and the second will remain on the list of waiting deliveries (or receipts).

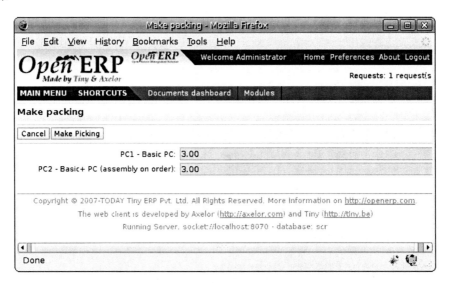

Figure 6.32: *Confirmation screen for delivered quantities*

When you open the list of current deliveries, you find the field **Partial delivery** which shows the reference number of the first delivery sent to the customer. That enables you to quickly find the deliveries for partial orders each day so that you can treat them as a priority.

6.10.5 Receiving supplier products

Open ERP supports three approaches to controlling data entry on products ordered from suppliers:

- Manual data entry,

- Using the goods receipt documents pre-generated by the system,

- Selecting from all the products waiting from the supplier, independently from goods receipt documents.

You can see how the configuration of the supplier order affects receipts in detail in *Purchasing Management*.

6.10.6 Manual data entry of goods receipt

To enter data about goods receipt manually you must use the menu *Stock Management → Goods Receipt → New items received*. Then enter the necessary data manually in the goods receipt form.

6.10.7 Confirming pre-generated goods receipt documents

If you use Supplier Orders in Open ERP, product receipts are automatically generated by the system when the purchase order is confirmed. You don't have to enter any date, just confirm that the quantities ordered match the quantities received.

In this case Open ERP generates a list of all products waiting to be received from the menu *Stock Management → Incoming Products → Packing to Process*.

Then you just look for the corresponding entry using the supplier name or order reference. Click it and confirm the quantities. If it shows you quantities that differ from the control form, Open ERP will automatically generate another receipt document that will be set open, waiting for the remaining deliveries. You can leave it open or cancel it if you know that products missed by your supplier will never be delivered.

6.10.8 Confirmation by selecting products waiting

The approach shown above is very useful if goods receipts correspond to the original orders. If your suppliers deliver items that don't necessarily coincide with the orders, however, it is easier to work by products received rather than by orders.

In this case you can manually create a new goods receipt using the menu *Stock Management → Incoming Products → New Reception Packing*. Instead of entering all the product lines manually you can click the button at the lower right **Products not received**. Open ERP then opens a list of all the goods waiting from that supplier and you can then automatically add some or all of them on your form. This method of data entry is very useful when you're entering goods received at one time from several orders.

6.10.9 Product routing

You should install the `stock_location` module if routing products to customers, from suppliers or in your warehouse is determined by the identity of the product itself.

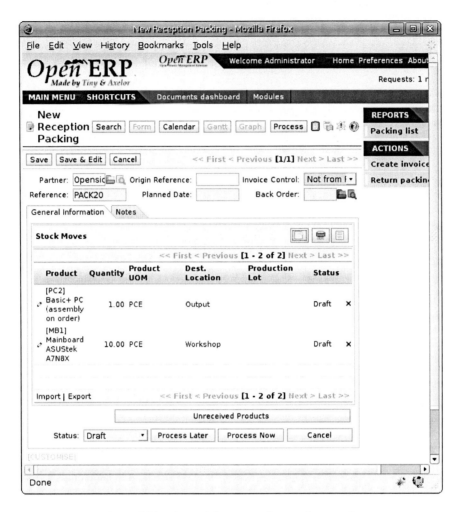

Figure 6.33: *Manual data entry for product receipt*

This will let you configure logistics rules individually for each product. For example, when a specific product arrives in stores it can automatically be sent to quality control. In this case it must be configured with rules on the product form. The fields that make up those rules are:

- **Source location** : the rule only applies if a product comes from this location,

- **Destination location** : the rule only applies if a product ends up in this location,

- **Type of move**: automatic, manual, automatic with no steps,

- **Lead time for move**,

- **Name of operations** : a free text field which will be included in the automatic stock move proposed by Open ERP.

You'll now see some examples of using these locations and logistics by product:

Figure 6.34: *List of items waiting for receipt*

- A rentable product,

- A product bought in China, following its freight by ship from port to port,

- A product that you want to send to quality control before putting it in stocks.

Example 1: A rentable product

A rentable product is just a product delivered to a customer that is expected to be returned in a few days time. When it has been delivered to the customer, Open ERP will generate a new goods receipt note with a forecast date at the end of the rental period. So you generate a list of goods pending receipt that you confirm when they are returned to your stores. To do this you should configure a product with the following rules:

Figure 6.35: *Managing the paths from one location to another in a product form*

Table 6.11: Example Product For Rental

Field	Value
Source location	Customer
Destination location	Stock
Type of Movement	Manual
Lead time	15 days
Operation	Product return

Then when the product is delivered to the customer, Open ERP automatically generates a goods receipt form in the draft state ready for returning it to Stock. This is due in 15 days time. With such a system your forecasts and stock graphs can always be correct in real time.

Example 2: Management of imports by sea

To manage products that follow a complex logistical import path by sea and then into customs, create as many 'Supplier' locations as there are steps, then create rules to move the product from one place to the other during the purchase.

Take a product that has been bought in China and delivered to you stores in Brussels, Belgium. Import by sea take around 7 weeks and must go through the following steps:

- Delivery from the supplier to the port of Shanghai: 2 days,

- Sea transport from Shanghai to the port of Anvers: 1 month,

- Customer at the port of Anvers: 2 weeks,

- Delivery by truck from the port of Anvers to your stores: 3 days.

You should track the movement of your goods and enter all the documents as each move is made so that you know where your goods are at any moment, and can estimate when they are likely to arrive in your stores. To do this, create all the locations for the intermediate steps:

- Shanghai Port,

- Anvers Port,

- Anvers Customs.

Finally, on the product form, create the following rule to show that when purchased, the goods don't arrive at your stores directly, but instead at the port of Shanghai. In this example the stores are configured to enter all the products in a location called 'Input'.

Table 6.12: Rule to move products automatically to Shanghai Port

Field	Value
Source location	Input
Destination location	Shanghai Port
Type of Movement	Automatic without steps
Lead time	2 days
Operation	Sending to Shanghai Port

Open ERP will then change the usual product receipt (which has them arriving in the Input location) to a delivery from this supplier to the external port. The move is automatically carried out because operations at this level are too labour-intensive to be done manually.

You then have to create a rule on the product form to move it from one location to another:

Table 6.13: Rule to move products manually from Shanghai Port to Anvers Port

Field	Value
Source location	Shanghai Port
Destination location	Anvers Port
Type of Movement	Manual
Lead time	30 days
Operation	Sending to Anvers Port by ship

Table 6.14: Rule to move products manually from Anvers Port to Anvers Customs

Field	Value
Source location	Anvers Port
Destination location	Anvers Customs
Type of Movement	Manual
Lead time	15 days
Operation	Customs at Anvers

Table 6.15: Rule to move products manually from Anvers Customs to Stock

Field	Value
Source location	Anvers Customs
Destination location	Stock
Type of Movement	Manual
Lead time	3 days
Operation	Truck transport into stock

Once the rules have been configured, Open ERP will automatically prepare all the documents needed for the internal stock movements of products from one location to another. These documents will be assigned one after another depending on the order defined in the rules definition.

When the company received notification of the arrival at a port or at customers, the corresponding move can be confirmed. You can then follow, using each location:

- where a given goods item can be found,

- quantities of goods awaiting customs,

- lead times for goods to get to stores,

- the value of stock in different locations.

Example 3: Quality Control

You can configure the system to put a given product in the Quality Control bay automatically when it arrives in your company. To do that you just configure a rule for the product to be placed in the Quality Control location rather than the Input location when the product is received from the supplier.

Table 6.16: Rule to move products manually from Input to Quality Control

Field	Value
Source location	Input
Destination location	Quality Control
Type of Movement	Manual
Lead time	0 days
Operation	Quality Control

Once this product has been received, Open ERP will then automatically manage the request for an internal movement to send it to the `Quality Control` location.

Manufacturing

The management of manufacturing described in this chapter covers planning, ordering, stocks and the manufacturing or assembly of products from raw materials and components. It also discusses consumption and production of products, as well as the necessary operations on machinery, tools or human resources.

The management of manufacturing in Open ERP is based on its stock management and, like it, is very flexible in both its operations and its financial control. It benefits particularly from the use of double-entry stock management for production orders. Manufacturing management is implemented by the `mrp` module. It is used for transforming all types of products:

- Assemblies of parts: composite products, soldered or welded products, assemblies, packs,

- Machined parts: machining, cutting, planing,

- Foundries: clamping, heating,

- Mixtures: mixing, chemical processes, distillation.

You'll work in two areas: on products in the first part of this chapter, and on operations in the second part. The management of products depends on the concept of classifications while the management of operations depends on routing and workcenters.

 Bills of Materials

Bills of Materials, or manufacturing specifications, go by different names depending on their application area, for example:

- Food: Recipes,

- Chemicals: Equations,

- Building: Plans.

For this chapter you should start with a fresh database that includes demo data, with `mrp` and its dependencies installed and no particular chart of accounts configured.

7.1 Management of production

Production Orders describe the operations that need to be carried out and the raw materials usage for each stage of production, You use specifications (bills of materials) to work out the raw material requirements and the manufacturing orders needed for the finished products.

Manufacturing has the following results:

- Stock reduction: consumption of raw materials,

- Stock increase: production of finished goods,

- Analytic costs: manufacturing operations,

- Added accounting value of stock: by the creation of value following the transformation of products.

7.2 Bills of Materials

7.2.1 Use of Bills of Materials

Bills of Materials are documents that describe the list of raw materials used to make a finished product. To illustrate the concept of specification you're going to work on a cabinet where the manufacturing plan is given by the figure *Plan of construction of a cabinet.*

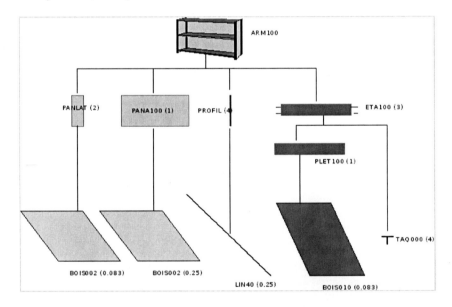

Figure 7.1: *Plan of construction of a cabinet*

The cabinet is assembled from raw materials and intermediate assemblies:

Table 7.1: Product Definitions before defining Bills of Materials

Product Code	Description
ARM100	Cabinet
PANLAT	Wooden Side Panel
PANA100	Rear Panel
PROFIL	Metal Strut
ETA100	Shelf
PLET100	Shelf Panel
BOIS002	Wood Panel
BOIS010	Wood Panel
TAQ000	Panel Pins
LIN040	Lintel

To describe how to assemble this cabinet, you define a bill of materials for each intermediate product and for the final cabinet assembly. These are given by the table below.

Table 7.2: Bill of Materials for 1 ARM100 Unit

Product Code	Quantity	Unit of Measure
PANLAT	2	Unit
PANA100	1	Unit
PROFIL	4	Unit
ETA100	3	Unit

Table 7.3: Bill of Materials for 1 ETA100 Unit

Product Code	Quantity	Unit of Measure
PLET100	1	Unit
TAQ000	4	Unit

Table 7.4: Bill of Materials for 1 PLET100 Unit

Product Code	Quantity	Unit of Measure
BOIS010	0.083	m2

Table 7.5: Bill of Materials for 1 PROFIL Unit

Product Code	Quantity	Unit of Measure
LIN40	0.25	m

Table 7.6: Bill of Materials for 1 PANA100 Unit

Product Code	Quantity	Unit of Measure
BOIS002	0.25	m2

Table 7.7: Bill of Materials for 1 PANLAT Unit

Product Code	Quantity	Unit of Measure
BOIS002	0.083	m2

The bills of materials are then used by the software to calculate the raw material needs based on the requirements of the finished products. Then if you want to manufacture 10 cabinets, the system can calculate what will be consumed:

Table 7.8: Total Quantities

Product Code	Quantity	Unit of Measure
BOIS002	2 * 0.083 + 0.25	m2
LIN040	1	m
BOIS002	0.083 * 3	m2
TAQ000	12	Unit

Bill of Materials

To see the bill of materials in tree view, use the menu *Manufacturing → Configuration → Bill of Materials → Bill of Materials Structure*.

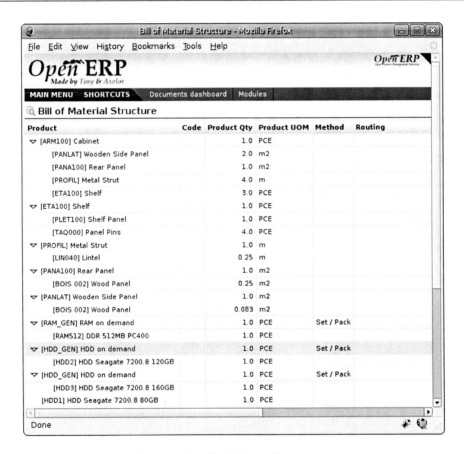

Figure 7.2: *Bill of Materials structure*

Use the menu *Manufacturing → Configuration → Bill of Materials → New Bill of Materials* to define a new bill of materials.

Figure 7.3: *Screen defining a Bill of Materials*

In the area below the bill of materials you should set the finished product, which will be manufactured or assembled. Once the product has been selected, Open ERP automatically completes the name of the bill of materials and the default Unit of Measure for this product.

The type of BoM (**BoM Type** : Phantom or Normal) and the **Routing** field will be described in more detail later in the chapter.

After this you can select the raw materials that are used in the manufacture of the finished product. The quantities are set out in a report based on the quantities of finished product and the quantities needed to produce them from the bill of materials. The second tab, **Revisions**, is used to set down all the changes made to the bill of materials. After each change you can specify a revision number and some notes on the modifications you carried out.

Simplified View

The Revisions tab is only visible if the user works in the Extended View mode (which means that the user must belong to the group `Usability / Extended View.`

Figure 7.4: *Revisions of a Bill of Materials*

In the third tab, **Properties**, you can put a free text reference to a plan, a sequence number that is used to determine the priorities between bills of materials, dates between which a bill of materials is valid, and values for rounding and product efficiency.

Rounding is used to set the smallest **Unit of Measure** for expressing the quantities of the selected product. So if you set the rounding to 1.00 you'll not be able to manufacture half a piece. The **Efficiency** of the product lets you indicate the percentage you lose during manufacture. This loss can be set for the finished product or for each raw materials line. The impact of this efficiency figure is to reserve more raw materials for manufacture than you'd otherwise use just from the Bill of Materials calculations.

The final part of the third tab lets you set some properties for the product's manufacturing processes. These will be detailed further on in the chapter in the section on configurable products.

7.3 Multi-level Bills of Materials

In Open ERP each line of a bill of materials may itself be a bill of materials. So you can define BoMs with several levels. Instead of defining several BoMs for the cabinet in the figure *Plan of construction of a cabinet* you could define the single bill of materials below:

Table 7.9: Single Bill of Materials for 1 ARM100 Unit

Product Code	Quantity	Unit of Measure
ARM100	1	Unit
PANLAT	2	Unit
BOIS002	0.166	m2
PANA100	1	Unit
BOIS002	0.25	m2
PROFIL	4	Unit
LIN040	1	m
ETA100	3	Unit
PLET100	3	Unit
BOIS010	0.249	m2
TAQ000	12	Unit

Open ERP behaves differently depending on whether the bill of materials is defined in several small BoMs each on a single level or in one BoM tree-structured on several levels.

So if you select a BoM using intermediate products that automatically generates production orders based on calculated requirements, Open ERP will propose manufacturing an intermediate product. To manufacture a cabinet, you'd create 6 production orders:

Table 7.10: Production Order

Product Code	Quantity	Unit of Measure
PLET100	3	Unit
BOIS010	0.25	m2

Table 7.11: Production Order

Product Code	Quantity	Unit of Measure
ETA100	3	Unit
PLET100	3	Unit
TAQ000	12	Unit

Table 7.12: Production Order

Product Code	Quantity	Unit of Measure
PROFIL	4	Unit
LIN040	1	m

Table 7.13: Production Order

Product Code	Quantity	Unit of Measure
PANA100	1	Unit
BOIS002	0.25	m2

Table 7.14: Production Order

Product Code	Quantity	Unit of Measure
PANA100	2	Unit
BOIS002	0.17	m2

Table 7.15: Production Order

Product Code	Quantity	Unit of Measure
ARM100	1	Unit
PANLAT	2	Unit
PANA100	1	Unit
PROFIL	4	Unit
ETA100	3	Unit

In the case where a single bill of materials is defined in multiple levels, a single manufacturing order will be generated for each cabinet, including all of the sub-BoMs. You'd then get the following production order:

Table 7.16: Single manufacture from a tree-structured BoM

Product Code	Quantity	Unit of Measure
ARM100	1	Unit
BOIS002	0.17	m2
BOIS002	0.25	m2
LIN040	1	m
BOIS010	0.25	m2
TAQ000	12	Unit

7.3.1 Phantom Bills of Materials

If a finished product is defined using intermediate products that are themselves defined using other BoMs, Open ERP will then propose the manufacture of each intermediate product. This will give several production orders. If you only want a single production order you can define a single BoM with several levels.

Sometimes, however, it is useful to define the intermediate product separately and not as part of a multi-level assembly even if you don't want separate production orders for intermediate products.

In the example, the intermediate product ETA100 is used in the manufacture of several different cabinets. So you'd want to define a unique BoM for it even if you didn't want any instances of this product to be built, nor wanted to re-write these elements in a series of different multi-level BoMs.

If you only want a single production order for the complete cabinet, and not one for the BoM itself, you can define the BoM line corresponding to product ETA100 in the cabinet's BoM as type **Phantom**. Then it will automatically put ETA100's BoM contents into the cabinet's production order even though it's been defined as multi-level.

This way of representing the assembly is very useful because it allows you to define reusable elements of the assembly and keep them isolated.

If you define the BoM for the ARM100 cabinet in the way shown by the table below, you'll get two production orders when the order is confirmed, as shown in the tables below that.

Table 7.17: Definition and use of phantom BoMs

Product Code	Quantity	Unit of Measure	Type of BoM
ARM100	1	Unit	normal
PANLAT	2	Unit	normal
PANA100	1	Unit	phantom
PROFIL	4	Unit	phantom
ETA100	3	Unit	phantom

Table 7.18: Production Order from phantom BoMs

Product Code	Quantity	Unit of Measure
ARM100	1	Unit
PANLAT	2	Unit
BOIS002	0.25	m2
LIN040	1	m
BOIS010	0.25	m2
TAQ000	12	Unit

Table 7.19: Production Order from normal BoM

Product Code	Quantity	Unit of Measure
PANLAT	2	Unit
BOIS002	0.17	m2

7.3.2 Assembly Bills of Materials

Sales Bills of Materials

In some software this is named a Sales Bill of Materials. In Open ERP the term assembly is used because the effect of the bill of materials is visible not only in sales but also elsewhere, for example in the intermediate manufactured products.

Assembly bills of materials enable you to define assemblies that will be sold directly. These could also be used in deliveries and stock management rather than just sold in isolation. For example if you deliver the cabinet in pieces for self-assembly, set the ARM100 BoM to type `Assembly`.

When a salesperson creates an order for an ARM100 product, Open ERP automatically changes the ARM100 from a set of components into an identifiable package for sending to a customer. Then it asks the storesperson to pack 2 PANLAT, 1 PANA100, 4 PROFIL, 3 ETA100. This is described as an ARM100 not just the individual delivered products.

Example: Large distributor

As an example of using these assemblies, take the case of a supermarket. In a supermarket, you can buy bottles of cola individually or in a pack of 6 bottles. The pack and the bottles are two different products and the barcodes used are also different.

But customers have the right to open a pack and extract some bottles to take them individually to the checkout. The supermarket can't track its stock in packs and bottles any more, but only individually in bottles.

So you can define a bill of materials for sale which defines a pack as an assembly of 6 bottles. Then when you've sold a pack, you can find a pack on the invoice or bill of sale but the associated stock operation will still be 6 bottles.

In the case of this assembly, this isn't a production order to transform the product. The transformation is done directly between the order and the set.

Assemblies and Purchases

The use of assemblies for selling to customers has been described here, but this functionality works just as well for purchases from suppliers.

So in the example of a supermarket, you can buy cola in packs and the storesperson will see a number of bottles at goods in reception.

7.3.3 Configurable Bills of Materials

In Open ERP you can define several bills of materials for the same product. In fact you can have several manufacturing methods or several approved raw materials for a given product. You'll see in the following section that the manufacturing procedure (the routing) is attached to the Bill of Materials, so the choice of bill of materials implicitly includes the operations to make it.

Once several bills of materials have been defined for a particular product you need to have a system to enable Open ERP to select one of them for use. By default the bill of materials with the lowest sequence number is selected by the system.

To gain more control over the process during the sale or procurement, you can use **properties**. The menu *Production Management → Configuration → Properties* enables you to define properties, which can be defined arbitrarily to help you select a bill of materials when you have a choice of BoMs.

Properties

Properties is a concept that enables the selection of a method for manufacturing a product. Properties define a common language between salespeople and technical people, letting the salespeople to have an influence on the manufacture of the products using non-technical language and the choices decided on by the technicians who define Bills of Materials.

For example you can define the properties and the following groups:

Table 7.20: Properties

Property Group	Property
Warranty	3 years
Warranty	1 year
Method of Manufacture	Serial
Method of Manufacture	Batch

Once the bills of materials have been defined you could associate the corresponding properties to them. Then when the salesperson goes to encode a product line he can attach the properties there. If the product must be manufactured, Open ERP will automatically choose the bill of materials that matches the defined properties in the order most closely.

Note the properties are only visible in the Bills of Materials and Sales Management if you're working in the Extended View mode. If you can't see it on your screen add the group `Useability / Extended View` to your user.

Example: Manufacturing in a batch or on a production line

As an example, take the manufacture of the cabinet presented above. You can imagine that the company has two methods of manufacturing this cabinet:

- Manually: staff assemble the cabinets one by one and cut the wood plank by plank. This approach is usually used to assembly prototypes. It gets you very rapid production, but at a high cost and only in small quantities.

- On a production line: staff use machines that are capable of cutting wood by bandsaw. This method is used for production runs of at least 50 items because the lead times using this method are quite lengthy. The delay to the start of production is much longer, yet the cost per unit is much lower in this volume.

You define two bills of materials for the same cabinet. To distinguish between them, you will define to properties in the same group: `manual assembly` and `production line assembly`. On the quotation, the salesperson can set the method of manufacture he wants on each order line, depending on the quantities and the lead time requested by the customer.

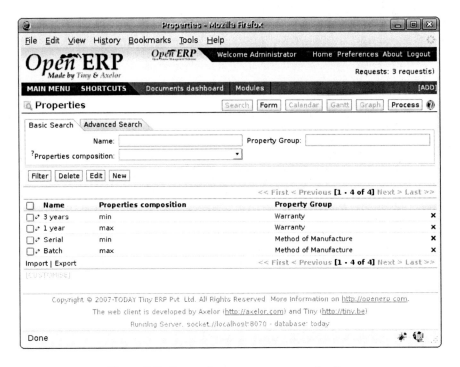

Figure 7.5: *Properties on a customer order line*

bills of materials and substitute products

In some software, you use the term `substitute` for this principle of configurable properties in a bill of materials.

By putting a bill of materials on its own line, you can also implement substitute products. You set the bill of materials to type `Assembly` to make the substitution transparent and to prevent Open ERP from proposing an intermediate production order.

7.4 Manufacturing

Once the bills of materials have been defined, Open ERP becomes capable of automatically deciding on the manufacturing route depending on the needs of the company.

Production orders can be proposed automatically by the system depending on several criteria described in the preceding chapter:

- Using the `Make to Order` rules,
- Using the `Order Point` rules,
- Using the Production plan.

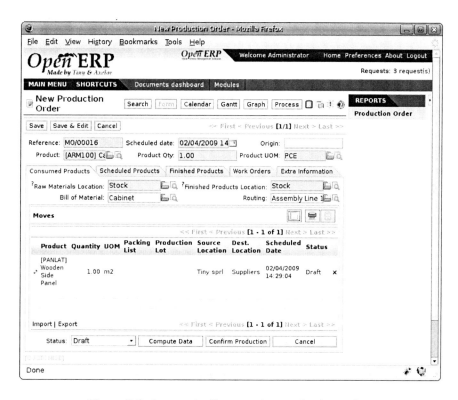

Figure 7.6: *Automatically proposing production orders*

Clearly it's also possible to start production manually. To do this you can use the menu *Manufacturing →
Production Orders → New Production Order*. If you haven't installed the Just-In-Time planning module
`mrp_jit`, you should start using Open ERP to schedule the Production Orders automatically using the various
system rules. To do this use the menu *Manufacturing → Compute All Schedulers*.

7.5 Workflow for complete production

To understand the usefulness and the functioning of the system you should test a complete workflow on the
new database installed with the demonstration data. In the order you can see:

- The creation of a customer order,

- The manufacturing workflow for an intermediate product,

- The manufacture of an ordered product,

- The delivery of products to a customer,

- Invoicing at the end of the month,

- Traceability for after-sales service.

Demonstration data

To follow the workflow shown below exactly, you should keep the same quantities as in the example and start from a new database. Then you won't run into exceptions that would result from a lack of stock.

This more advanced case of handling problems in procurement, will be sorted out later in the chapter.

7.5.1 The customer order

Begin by encoding a customer order. To do this, use the menu *Sales Management → Sales Orders -> New Quotation*. Enter the following information:

- **Customer** : Agrolait,

- **Shipping Policy** : Invoice from picklist (second tab),

- **Order Line** :

    - **Product** : PC2 – Basic PC (assemble on demand),

    - **Quantity (UoM)** : 1,

    - **Product UoM** : PCE,

    - **Procure method** : Make To Order.

Once the quotation has been entered you can confirm it immediately by clicking the button **Confirm Order** at the bottom to the right. Keep note of the order reference because this follows all through the process. Usually, in a new database, this will be SO007 . At this stage you can look at the process linked to your order using the **Process** button above and to the right of the form.

Start the requirements calculation using the menu *Manufacturing → Compute All Schedulers*.

7.5.2 Producing an Intermediate Product

To understand the implications of requirements calculation, you must know the configuration of the sold product. To do this, go to the form for product PC2 and click on the link **Bill of Materials** to the right. You get the scheme shown in *Composition of product PC2 in the demonstration data* which is the composition of the selected product.

Manufacturing the PC2 computer must be done in two steps:

1: Manufacture of the intermediate product: CPU_GEN

2: Manufacture of the finished product using that intermediate product: PC2

The manufacturing supervisor can then consult the product orders using the menu *Manufacturing → Production Orders → Production Orders To Start*. You then get a list of orders to start and the estimated start date to meet the ordered customer delivery date.

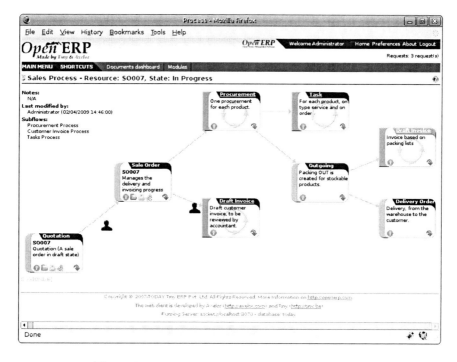

Figure 7.7: *Process for handling Sales Order SO007*

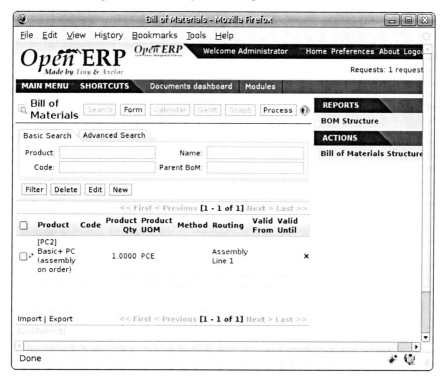

Figure 7.8: *Composition of product PC2 in the demonstration data*

Figure 7.9: *List of production orders*

You'll see the production order for CPU_GEN but not that for PC2 because that one depends on an intermediate product. Return to the production order for CPU_GEN and click below it. If there are several of them, select the one corresponding to your order using the reference that contains your order number (in this example SO007).

The system shows you that you must manufacture product CPU_GEN using the components: MB1, CPU1, FAN, RAM. You can then confirm the production twice:

Start of production: consumption of raw materials,

End of production: manufacture of finished product.

At this stage, you should click to edit the line for the product MB1 to enter a lot number for it. The lot number is usually shown the parent chart, so you should just copy that over. To do that put the cursor in the field **Production Lot** and press <F1> to create a new lot. Set a lot reference, for example: MB1345678 . The system may then show you a warning because this lot is not in stock, but you can ignore this message.

The production order must be in the closed state as shown in the figure *Production order after the different stages*.

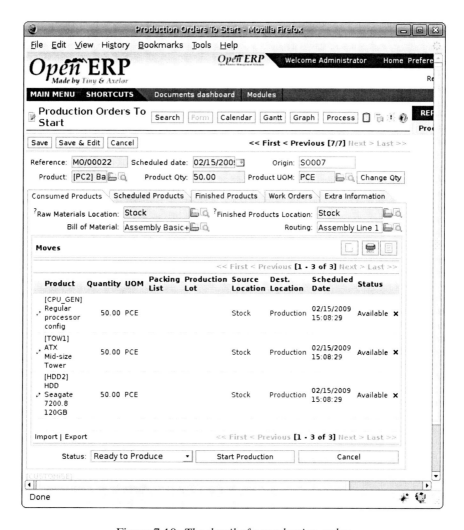

Figure 7.10: *The detail of a production order*

7.5.3 Manufacture of finished product

Having manufactured the intermediate product CPU_GEN, Open ERP then automatically proposes the manufacture of the computer PC2 using the order created earlier. So return to the menu for production orders to start *Manufacturing → Production Orders → Production Orders to start.*

You'll find computer PC2 which has been sold to the customer, as shown in the figure *List of production orders.*

Just as for product CPU_GEN, confirm the production order between two dates: start of production and end of production.

The product sold to the customer has now been manufactured and the raw materials have been consumed and taken out of stock.

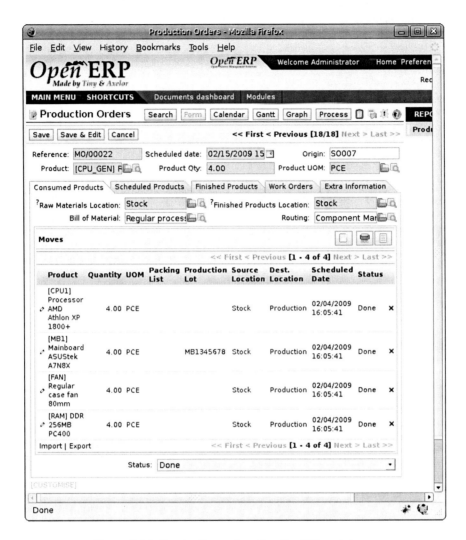

Figure 7.11: *Production order after the different stages*

Automatic Actions

As well as managing the use of materials and the production of stocks, manufacturing can have the following automatic effects which are detailed further on in the chapter:

- adding value to stock,

- generating operations for assembly staff,

- automatically creating analytical accounting entries.

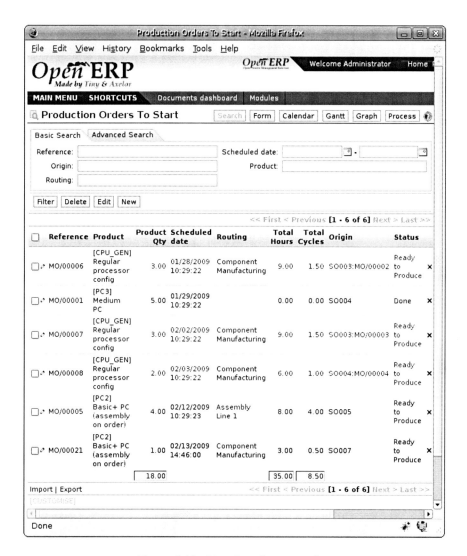

Figure 7.12: *List of production orders*

7.5.4 Delivery of product to the customer

When the products have been manufactured, the storesperson automatically finds the order in his list of items to do. To see the items waiting for delivery, use the menu *Stock Management → Outgoing Products → Available Packing*. You'll find lists of packing to be done, there, as shown in the figure *List of packing operations to be done*.

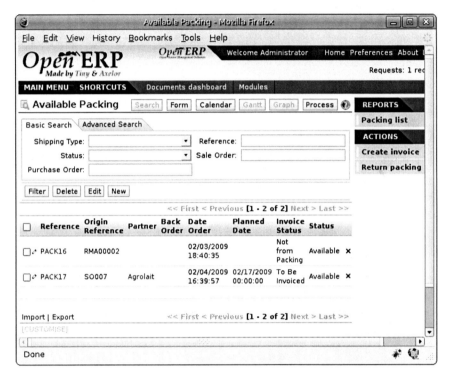

Figure 7.13: *List of packing operations to be done*

The packing orders are presented in priority order of despatch so the storesperson must begin with the orders at the top of the list. Confirm that your packing list has been created by looking for the customer name (Agrolait) or by its reference (SO007). Click on it and then click the button **Approve**.

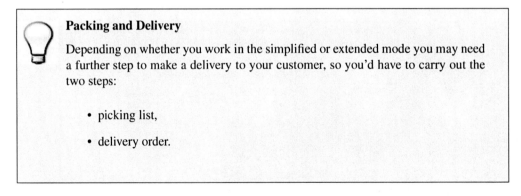

Packing and Delivery

Depending on whether you work in the simplified or extended mode you may need a further step to make a delivery to your customer, so you'd have to carry out the two steps:

- picking list,
- delivery order.

7.5.5 Invoicing at delivery

Periodically the administrator or an accountant can send invoices based on the deliveries that have been carried out. To do that, you can use the menu *Stock Management → Outgoing Products → Packing to Invoice → Packing by Invoice Method*. You then get a list of all the deliveries that have been made but haven't yet been invoiced.

So select some or all of the deliveries. Click on the action **Create Invoice**. Open ERP asks if you want to group the deliveries from the same partner into a single invoice or if you'd prefer to invoice for each delivery individually.

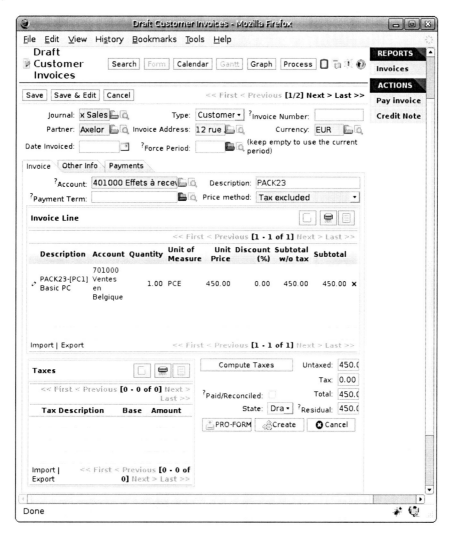

Figure 7.14: *Invoicing of deliveries*

Invoices are generated automatically in the `Draft` state by Open ERP. You can modify invoices before approving them finally.

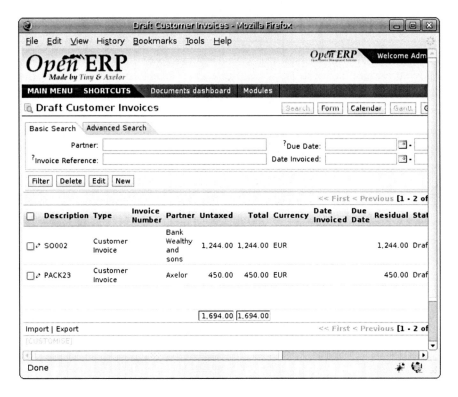

Figure 7.15: *List of invoices generated by the system based on deliveries*

Once you have reviewed the different invoices that were generated, you can confirm them one by one or all at once by using the available actions. Then print the invoices using the multiple print option and send them to your customers by post.

7.5.6 Traceability

Now suppose that the customer phones you to tell you about a production fault in a delivered product. You can consult the traceability through the whole manufacturing chain using the serial number indicated on the product MB1. To look through the detailed history, use the menu *Stock Management → Traceability → Production Lots*.

Find the product corresponding to the product or lot number. Once it's been found you can use traceability as described in the section *Management of lots and traceability* in the *Logistics and Stock Management* chapter.

7.6 Production order in detail

To open a Production Order, use the menu *Manufacturing → Production Orders → New Production Order*. You get a blank form for entering a new production order as shown in the figure *New production order*.

The production order follows the process given by the figure *Process for handling a production order*.

Figure 7.16: *New production order*

The date fields, priority and reference, are automatically completed when the form is first opened. Enter the product that you want to produce, and the quantity required. The **Product UOM** by default is completed automatically by Open ERP when the product is first created.

You then have to set two locations:

The location from which the required raw materials should be found, and

The location for depositing the finished products.

For simplicity, put the Stock location in both places. The field **Bill of Materials** will automatically be completed by Open ERP when you click the button **Compute Data**. You can then overwrite it with another BoM to specify something else to use for this specific manufacture.

The tabs **Planned Products** and **Work Orders** are also completed automatically when you click **Compute Data**. You'll find the raw materials there that are required for the production and the operations needed by the assembly staff.

If you want to start production, click the button **Confirm Production**, and Open ERP then automatically completes the **Moves** fields in the **Consumed Products** and **Finished Products** fields. The information in the **Consumed Products** tab can be changed if:

- you want to enter a serial number for raw materials,

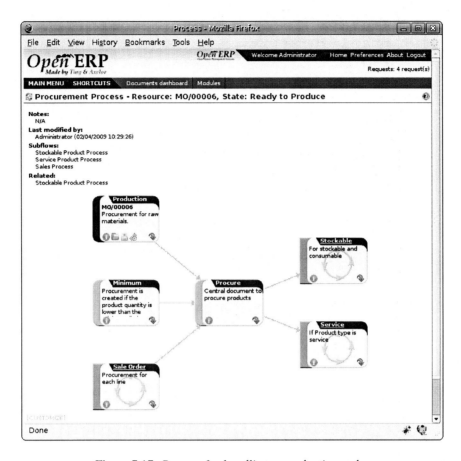

Figure 7.17: *Process for handling a production order*

• you want to change the quantities consumed (lost during production).

For traceability you can set lot numbers on the raw materials used, or on the finished products. To do this click on one of the lines of the first or the third tab. Note the **Production lot** and **Tracking lot** numbers.

Once the order is confirmed, you should force the reservation of materials using the **Force Reservation** button. This means that you don't have to wait for the scheduler to assign and reserve the raw materials from your stock for this production run. This shortcuts the procurement process.

If you don't want to change the priorities, just leave the production order in this state and the scheduler will create a plan based on the priority and your planned date.

To start the production of products, click **Start Production**. The raw materials are then consumed automatically from stock, which means that the draft (Waiting) movements become Done .

Once the production is complete, click **Production Finished**. The finished products are then moved into stock.

7.7 Scheduling

The requirements scheduler is the calculation engine which plans and prioritises production and purchasing automatically from the rules defined on these products. It's started once per day. You can also start it manually using the menu *Manufacturing → Compute All Schedulers*. This uses all the relevant parameters defined in the products, the suppliers and the company to determine the priorities between the different production orders, deliveries and supplier purchases.

You can set the starting time by modifying the corresponding action in the menu *Administration → Configuration → Scheduler → Scheduled Actions*. Modify the Run MRP Scheduler configuration document.

Figure 7.18: *Configuring the start time for calculating requirements*

Calculating requirements / scheduling

Scheduling only validates procurement confirmed but not started. These procurement reservations will themselves start production, tasks or purchases depending on the configuration of the requested product.

You take account of the priority of operations in starting reservations and procurement. The urgent requests, or those with a date in the past, or those with a date earlier than the others will be started first so that if there are not enough products in stock to satisfy all the requests, the most urgent will be produced first.

7.8 Calculation of lead times

All procurement operations (that is, the requirement for both production orders and purchase orders) are automatically calculated by the scheduler. But more than just creating each order, Open ERP plans the timing of each step. A planned date calculated by the system can be found on each order document.

To organize the whole chain of manufacturing and procurement, Open ERP bases everything on the delivery date promised to the customer. This is given by the date of the confirmation in the order and the lead times shown in each product line of the order. This lead time is itself proposed automatically in the field **Customer Lead Time** shown in the product form. This is the difference between the time on an order and that of the delivery.

To see a calculation of the lead times, take the example of the cabinet above. Suppose that the cabinet is assembled in two steps, using the two following bills of materials.

Table 7.21: Bill of Materials for 1 ARM100 Unit

Product Code	Quantity	Unit of Measure
PANLAT	2	Unit
BOIS002	0.25	m2
LIN040	1	m
BOIS010	0.25	m2
TAQ000	12	Unit

Table 7.22: Bill of Materials for 2 PANLAT Units

Product Code	Quantity	Unit of Measure
BOIS002	0.17	m2

The PANLAT is made from an order using the workflow shown. The BOIS02 is purchased on order and the other products are all found in stock. An order for the product ARM100 will then generate two production orders (ARM100 and PANLAT) then produce two purchase orders for the product BOIS02. Product BOIS02 is used in the production of both ARM100 and PANLAT. Set the lead times on the product forms to the following:

Table 7.23: Lead Times

Product Code	Customer Lead Time	Production Lead Time	Supplier Lead Time
ARM100	30 days	5 days	
PANLAT		10 days	
BOIS02			5 days

A customer order placed on the 1st January will set up the following operations and lead times:

- Delivery ARM100: 31 January (=1st January + 30 days),

- Manufacture ARM100: 26 January (=31 January – 5 days),

- Manufacture PANLAT: 16 January (=26 January – 10 days),

- Purchase BOIS02 (for ARM100): 21 January (=26 January – 5 days),

- Purchase BOIS02 (for PANLAT): 11 January (=16 January – 5 days).

In this example, Open ERP will propose placing two orders with the supplier of product BOIS002. Each of these orders can be for a different planned date. Before confirming these orders the purchasing manager could group these orders into single order.

7.8.1 Security days

The scheduler will plan all operations as a function of the time configured on the products. But it is also possible to configure these factors in the company. These factors are then global to the company, whatever the product concerned. In the description of the company, on the **Configuration** tab, you find the following parameters:

- Security days: number of days to deduct from a system order to cope with any problems of procurement,

- Purchase lead time: additional days to include for all purchase orders with this supplier,

- Production lead time: number of additional days needed for manufacturing.

- Period for calculating requirements: all the requests which are for procuring for a later date to the number of days which aren't calculated in the scheduler.

 Purchasing lead time

The security delay for purchases is the average time between the order generated by Open ERP and the real purchase time from the supplier by your purchasing department. This delay takes account of the order process in your company, including order negotiation time.

Take for example the following configuration:

- Security days: 2,

- Purchase Lead time: 3,

- Production Lead Time: 1.

The example above will then be given the following lead times:

- Delivery ARM100: 29 January (=1st January + 30 days – 2 days),

---

- Manufacture ARM100: 23 January (=29 January – 5 days – 1 day),

- Manufacture PANLAT: 12 January (=26 January – 10 days – 1 day),

- Purchase BOIS02 (for ARM100): 15 January (=26 January – 5 days – 3 days),

- Purchase BOIS02 (for PANLAT): 4 January (=12 January – 5 days – 3 days).

7.9 Operations

In the first part of this chapter, manufacturing management was handled in terms of products and materials. This section focuses on manufacturing operations. To manufacture or assemble products, as well as using raw materials and finished product you must also handle operations such as assembly, drilling wood, and cutting timber.

The different operations will have different impacts on the costs of manufacture and planning depending on the available workload.

7.9.1 Definition of concepts

To manage operations you should understand the following concepts

- Workcenters,

- Routing,

- Operations.

7.9.2 Workcenters

Workcenters represent units of product, capable of doing material transformation operations. You can distinguish three types of workcenter: machines, tools and human resources.

Workcenter

Workcenters are units of manufacture consisting of one or several people and/or machines that can be considered as a unit for the purposes of forecasting capacity and planning.

Use the menu *Manufacturing → Configuration → Workcenters* to define a new workcenter. You get a form as shown in the figure *Definition of a workcenter*.

A workcenter must have a name and a code. You then assign a type: machine, human resource, tool, and a description of operating hours or functionality. The figure *Working hours for a workcenter* represents the hours from Monday to Friday, from 09:00 to 17:00 with a break of an hour from 12:00.

Figure 7.19: *Definition of a workcenter*

You should show a description of the workcenter and its operations.

Once the database is encoded you should enter data about the production capacity of the workcenter. Depending on whether you have a machine or a person, a workcenter will be defined in cycles or hours. If it represents a set of machines and people you can use both cycles and hours at the same time.

A Cycle

A cycle corresponds to the time required to carry out an assembly operation. The user is free to determine which is the reference operation for a given workcenter. It must be represented by the cost and elapsed time of manufacture.

For example, for a printing workcenter, a cycle will be the printing of 1 page or of 1000 pages depending on the printer.

To define the capacity properly it is necessary know, for each workcenter, what will be the reference operation which determines the cycle. You can then define the data relative to the capacity.

Capacity per cycle (CA): determine the number of operations that can be done in parallel during a cycle.

Figure 7.20: *Working hours for a workcenter*

Generally the number defines the number of identical machines or people defined by the workcenter.

Time for a cycle (TC): give the duration in hour for that or the operations defined by a cycle.

Time before production (TS): give the wait in hours to initialise production operations. Generally this represents the machine setup time.

Time after production (TN): give the delay in hours after the end of a production operation. Generally this represents the cleaning time necessary after an operation.

Effective time (ET): is a factor that is applied to the three times above to determine the real production time. This factor enables you to readjust the different times progressively and as a measure of machine utilization. You can't readjust the other times because generally they're taken from the machine's data sheet.

The total time for carrying out X operations is then given by the following formula: ((C / CA) * TC + TS + TN_ * ET. In this formula the result of the division is rounded upwards. Then if the capacity per cycle is 6 it takes 3 cycles to realize 15 operations.

Multi-level routing

It is possible to define routing on several levels to support multi-level bills of materials. You can select the routing on each level of a bill of materials. The levels are then linked to hierarchies of bills of materials.

The second tab of the production order lets you define the links to analytical account to report the costs of the workcenter operations. If you leave the different fields empty Open ERP won't have any effect on the analytic accounts.

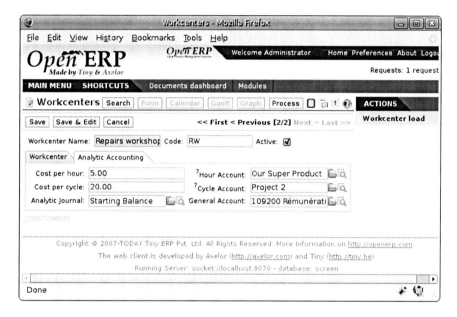

Figure 7.21: *Data about analytic accounts for a workcenter*

7.9.3 Routing

Routings define the assembly operations to be done in workcenters for manufacturing a certain product. They are usually attached to bills of materials which will define the assembly of products required for manufacture or for finished products.

A routing can be defined directly in a bill of materials or through the menu *Manufacturing → Configuration → Routings*. A routing has a name, a code and a description. Later in this chapter you'll see that a routing can also be associated with a stock location. That enable you to indicate where assembly takes place.

Figure 7.22: *Definition of a routing with three operations*

Subcontracting assembly

You'll see further on in this chapter that it is possible to link a routing and a stock location for the customer or the supplier. You do this after you've subcontracted the assembly of a product to a supplier, for example.

In the routing you must show the list of operations that must be done. Each operation must be done at a workcenter and possess a number of hours and/or cycles be done.

7.9.4 Impact on the production order

The routings are then attached to the bills of materials which are then also used to generate product order. On a production order you'll find assembly operations for manufacture on the **Operations** tab.

The times and the cycles shown in the production order are, in the same way as the materials, theoretical data. The user can change the values to reflect reality for manufacture.

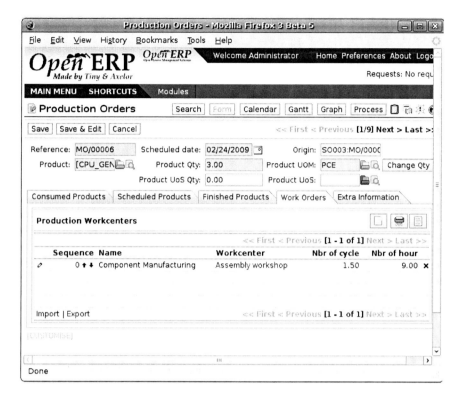

Figure 7.23: *Operations on a production order*

So if you use routings, Open ERP automatically calculates the operations required for the production order. If the workcenters are linked to analytic accounts, at the end of production, Open Erp will generate the analytic accounts representing the costs of manufacture. This will allow you to work out profitability per workcenter or manufacturing unit through analytic accounting.

But the routings also enable you to manage your production capacity. You will be able to leave the demand charts for the days / weeks / months ahead to validate that you don't forecast more than you are capable of producing.

To see a demand chart, list the workcenters using the menu *Manufacturing → Configuration → Workcenters*. Then select one or several workcenters and click on the action **Workcenter load**. Open ERP then asks you if you work in cycles or in hours and your interval is calculated (by day, week or month).

Theoretical times

Once the routings have been clearly defined, you determine the effective working time per assembly worker. This is the time actually taken by the assembly worker for each operation. That enables you to compare the real working time in your company and work out the productivity per person.

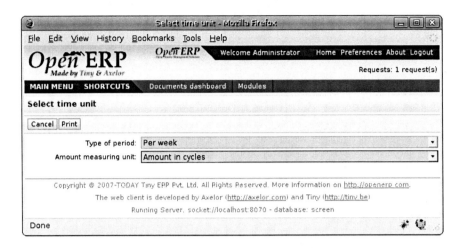

Figure 7.24: *Charge by workcenter*

7.9.5 Work operations

A production order defines the use of the products defined in the Bills of Materials, and the operations defined in the routing. You've seen how to handle manufacturing production as a top-level process, but some companies prefer to have finer-grained control of operations where instead of specifying just the production process itself, they enter data on each constituent production operation.

7.9.6 Management of operations

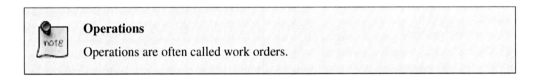

Operations

Operations are often called work orders.

To work using work orders you must install the optional module `mrp_operations`. Once the module is installed you'll find a new menu called *Manufacturing → Operations → Operations* to be carried out. The assembly workers must then encode each step operation by operation and, for each step, the real working time for it.

Operations must then be carried out one by one. On each operation the operator can click on **Start operation** and then **Close Operation**. The time is then worked out automatically on the operation between the two changes of status. The operator can also put the operation on hold and start again later.

The following process is attached to each operation.

Thanks to this use by operation, the real working time is recorded on the production order.

The production order is automatically put into the state 'Running' once the first operation has been started. That consumes some raw materials. Similarly the production order is closed automatically once the last operation is completed. The finished products are then made.

Figure 7.25: *List of operations to be carried out.*

7.10 Events and barcodes

If the company wants to work with barcodes in manufacturing you can work on each operation using events. Here are some examples of events for an operations:

- Starting an operation,

- Pausing an operation,

- Restarting an operation,

- Closing an operation,

- Cancelling an operation.

You place barcodes on the production orders on the machines or operators and a form of barcodes representing the events. To print barcodes select the events using the menu *Manufacturing → Configuration → Codes from start to finish*. Then click for printing the barcodes for the selected events. You can do the same for printing barcodes for the workcenters using the menu *Manufacturing → Configuration → Workcenters*.

Using the system these operations don't need data to be entered on the keyboard. To use these barcodes, open the menu *Manufacturing → Barcode events*. You must then scan, in order:

1. The barcode of the production order,

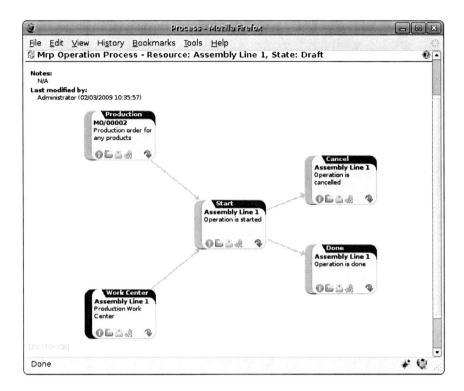

Figure 7.26: *Process for handling an operation*

2. The workcenter used,

3. The event code.

Open ERP then applies the events to the relevant operation.

7.10.1 Subcontracting manufacture

In Open ERP it is possible to subcontract production operations (for example painting and item assembly) at a supplier's. To do this you must indicate on the relevant routing document a supplier location for stock management.

You must then configure a location dedicated to this supplier with the following data:

- **Type of location** : Supplier,

- **Address of Location** : Select an address of the subcontractor partner,

- **Type of linkage** : Fixed,

- **Location of linkage** : your Stock,

- **Lead time for linkage** : number of days before receipt of the finished product.

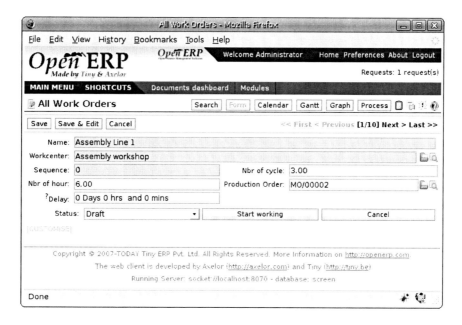

Figure 7.27: *Capturing events for work orders*

Then once the manufacture has been planned for the product in question, Open ERP will generate the following steps:

Delivery of raw materials to the stores for the supplier,

Production order for the products at the suppliers and receipt of the finished products in the stores.

Once the production order has been confirmed, Open ERP automatically generates a delivery order to send to the raw materials supplier. The storesperson can access this delivery order using the menu *Stock Management → Incoming Products*. The raw materials will then be placed in stock at the supplier's stores.

Once the delivery of raw materials has been confirmed, Open ERP activates the production order. The supplier uses the raw materials sent to produce the finished goods which will automatically be put in your own stores. The confirmation of this manufacture is made when you receive the products from your supplier. It's then that you indicate the quantities consumed by your supplier

Subcontract without routing

If you don't use routing you can always subcontract work orders by creating an empty routing in the subcontract bill of materials.

Production orders are found in the menu *Manufacture → Production Orders → Production Orders to start*. A production order is always carried out in two stages:

1. Consumption of raw materials.

2. Production of finished products.

Depending on the company's needs, you can specify that the first step is confirmed at the acknowledgment of manufacturing supplier and the second at the receipt of finished goods in the warehouse.

7.11 Treatment of exceptions

The set of stock requirements is generated by procurement orders. Then for each customer order line or raw materials in a manufacturing order, you will find a procurement form. To review all the procurement orders use the menu *Manufacturing → Procurement orders*.

In normal system use, you don't need to worry about procurement orders because they're automatically generated by Open ERP and the user will usually work on the results of a procurement: a production order, a task or a supplier order.

But if there are configuration problems, the system can remain blocked by a procurement without generating a corresponding document. For example, suppose that you configure a product **Procure Method** as `Make to Order` but you haven't defined the bill of materials. In that case procurement of the product will stay blocked in an exception state `No Bill of Materials defined for this product`. You must then create a bill of materials to unblock the problem.

Possible problems include:

- No bill of materials defined for production: in this case you've got to create one or indicate that the product can be purchased instead.

- No supplier available for a purchase: it's then necessary to define a supplier in the second tab of the product form.

- No address defined on the supplier partner: you must complete an address for the supplier by default for the product in consideration.

- No quantity available in stock: you must create a rule for automatically procuring (for example a minimum stock rule) and put it in the order, or manually procure it.

Some problems are just those of timing and can be automatically corrected by the system. That's why Open ERP has the two following menus:

- *Manufacturing → Automatic Procurement → Procurement Exceptions → Exceptions to correct,*

- *Manufacturing → Automatic Procurement → Procurement Exceptions → Temporary exceptions.*

If a product must be 'in stock' but is not available in your stores, Open ERP will make the exception in 'temporary' or 'to be corrected'. The exception is temporary if the system can procure it automatically, for example if a procurement rule is defined for minimum stock.

If no procurement rule is defined the exception must be corrected manually by the user. Once the exception is corrected you can restart by clicking on **Retry**. If you don't do that then Open ERP will automatically recalculate on the next automated requirements calculation.

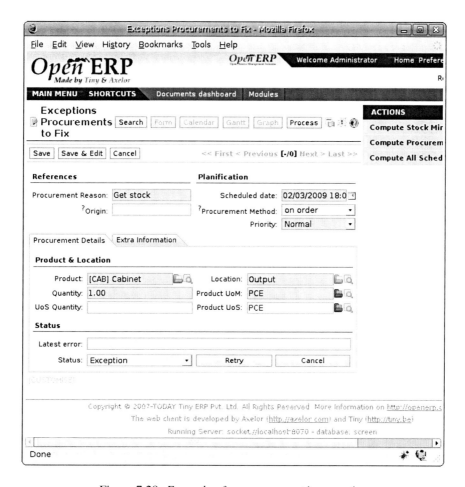

Figure 7.28: *Example of a procurement in exception*

7.12 Manual procurement

To procure internally, you can create a procurement order manually. Use the menu *Manufacturing → Procurement Orders → New Procurement* to do this.

The procurement order will then be responsible for calculating a proposal for automatic procurement for the product concerned. This procurement wll start a task, a purchase order form the supplier or a production depending on the product configuration.

It is better to encode a procurement order rather than direct purchasing or production, That method has the following advantages:

The form is simpler because Open ERP calculates the different values from other values and defined rules: purchase date calculated from order date, default supplier, raw materials needs, selection of the most suitable bill of materials, etc

The calculation of requirements prioritises the procurements. If you encode a purchase directly you short-circuit the planning of different procurements.

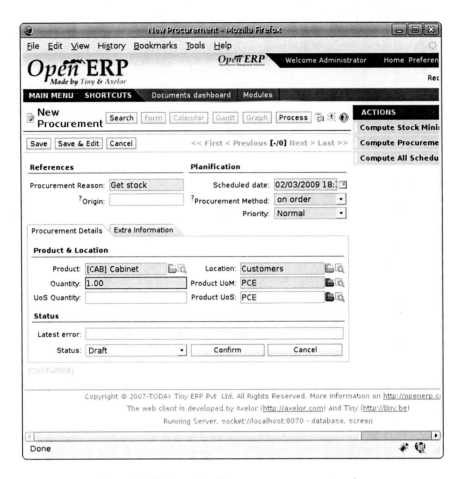

Figure 7.29: *Encoding for a new procurement order*

Shortcuts

On the product form you have an **ACTIONS** shortcut button **Create Procurements** that lets you quickly create a new procurement order.

7.13 Management of waste products and secondary products

For the management of waste you must install the module `mrp_subproduct`. The normal behaviour of manufacture in Open ERP enables you to manufacture several units of the same finished product from raw materials (A + B > C). With waste management, the result of a manufacture can be to have both finished products and secondary products (A + B > C + D).

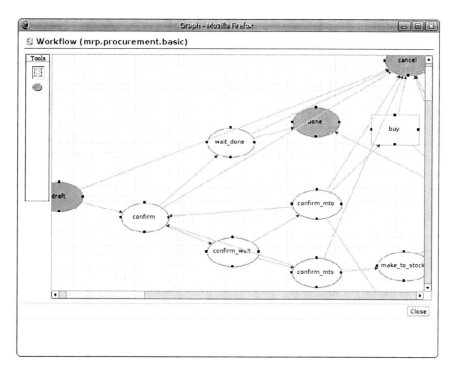

Figure 7.30: *Workflow for handling a procurement, a function of the product configuration*

> **Waste material**
>
> In Open ERP waste material corresponds to secondary products that are a by-product of the main manufacturing process. For example, cutting planks of timber will produce other planks but these bits of timber are too small (or the offcuts may have value for the company if they can be used elsewhere).

If the module `mrp_subproduct` has been installed you get a new field in the Bill of Material that lets you set secondary products resulting from the manufacture of the finished product.

When Open ERP generates a production order based on a bill of materials that uses secondary product you pick up the list of all products in the the third tab of the production order 'Finished Products'.

Secondary products enable you to generate several types of products from the same raw materials and manufacturing methods – only these aren't used in the calculation of requirements. Then if you need the secondary products Open ERP won't ask you to manufacture another product to use the waste products and secondary products of this manufacture. In this case you should enter another production order for the secondary product.

Figure 7.31: *Definition of waste products in a bill of materials*

Services in Manufacturing

Unlike most software for production management, Open ERP manages services as well as stockable products. So it's possible to put products of type **Service** in a bill of materials. These don't appear in the production order but their requirements will be taken into account.

If they're defined as **Make to Order** Open ERP will generate a task for the manufacture or a subcontract order for the operations. The behaviour will depend on the supply method configured on the product form **Buy** or **Produce**.

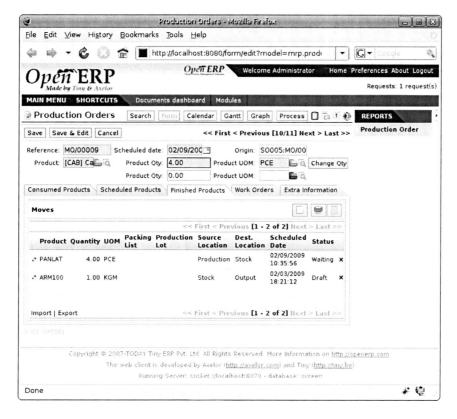

Figure 7.32: *A production order producing several finished products*

7.14 Management of repairs

The management of repairs is carried out using the module `mrp_repair`. Once it's installed this module adds new *Manufacturing → Repairs* menus under the Manufacturing menu for creating repair jobs and reviewing repairs in progress.

In Open ERP a repair will have the following effects:

- Use of materials: items for replacement,

- Production of products: items replaced from reserved stock,

- Quality control: tracking the reasons for repair,

- Accounting entries: following stock moves,

- Receipt and delivery of product from and to the end user,

- Adding operations that can be seen in the product's traceability,

- Invoicing items used and/or free for repairs.

7.14.1 Entering data for a new repair

Use the menu *Manufacturing → Repairs → New Repair* to enter a new repair into the system. You'll see a blank form for the repair data, as shown in the figure *Entering data for a new repair* below.

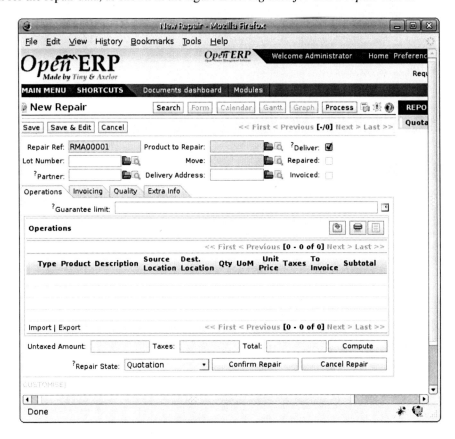

Figure 7.33: *Entering data for a new repair*

Start by identifying the product that will be repaired using the product lot number. Open ERP then automatically completes fields from the selected lot – the partner fields, address, delivery location, and stock move.

If a warranty period has been defined in the product description, in months, Open ERP then completes the field **Warranty limit** with the correct warranty date.

You must then specify the components that you'll be adding, replacing or removing in the operations part. On each line you must specify the following:

Add or remove a component of the finished product:

- Product Component,

- Quantity,

- Unit of Measure

- Price of Component,

- Possible lot number,

- Location where the component was found,

- To invoice or not.

Once the component has been selected, Open ERP automatically completes most of the fields:

- **Quantity** : 1,

- **Unit of Measure** : unit for managing stock defined in the product form,

- **Component Price** : calculated from the customer list price,

- **Source location** : given by the stock management,

- **To invoice or not** : depends on the actual date and the quarantee period.

This information is automatically proposed by the system but you can modify it all yourself.

You can also encode additional charges in the second tab of the repair - applicable list price, address and type of invoice, as well as additional line items that need to be added to the repair bill.

The third tab, Quality, is for encoding information about the quality: internal notes, notes for the quotation, corrective actions and preventative actions for example.

7.14.2 Repair workflow

A defined process handles a repair order – both the repair itself and invoicing the client. The figure *Process for handling a repair* shows this repair process.

Once a repair has been entered onto the system, it is in the 'draft' state. In this state it has no impact on the rest of the system. You can print a quotation from it using the action 'Print Quotation'. The repair quotation can then be sent to the customer.

Once the customer approves the repair, use the menu *Manufacturing → Repairs → Repairs in quotation* to find the draft repair. Click to confirm the draft repair and put it into the running state. You can specify the invoicing mode in the second tab:

- no invoicing,

- invoicing before repair,

- invoicing after repair.

You can confirm the repair operation or create an invoice for the customer depending on this state.

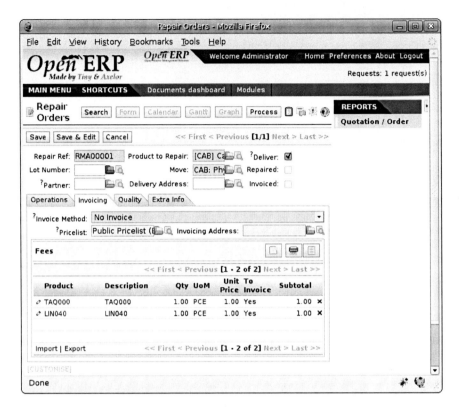

Figure 7.34: *Repair form, second tab*

7.14.3 Invoicing the repair

When the repair is to be invoiced, an invoice is generated in the draft state by the system. This invoice contains the raw materials used (replaced components) and any other costs such as the time used for the repair. These other costs are entered on the second tab of the repair form.

If the product to be repaired is still under guarantee, Open ERP automatically suggests that the components themselves are not invoiced, but will still use any other defined costs. You can override any of these default values when you're entering the data.

The link to the generated invoice is shown on the second tab of the repair document.

7.14.4 Stock movements and repair

When the repair has been carried out, Open ERP automatically carries out stock movements for components that have been removed, added or replaced on the finished product.

The move operations are carried out using the locations shown on the first tab of the repair document. If a destination location has been specified, Open ERP automatically handles the final customer delivery order when the repair has been completed. This also lets you manage the delivery of the repaired products.

For example, take the case of the cabinet that was produced at the start of this chapter. If you have to replace

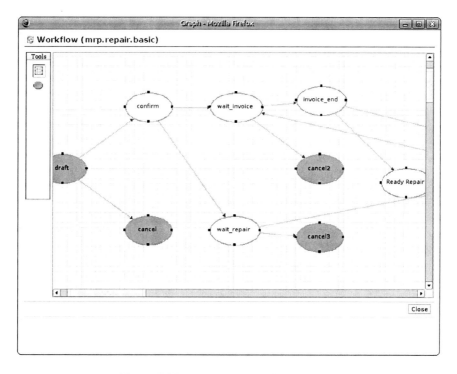

Figure 7.35: *Process for handling a repair*

the shelf PANLAT, you must enter data for the repair as shown in figure *Repair of a shelf in a cabinet*.
In this example, you'd carry out the following operations:

- Removal of a PANLAT shelf in the cabinet and put the faulty shelf in the location *Defective Products*,

- Placement of a new PANLAT shelf that has been taken from stock.

When the repair is ready to be confirmed, Open ERP will generate the following stock moves:

- Put faulty PANLAT into suitable stock location *Default Production > Defective Products*,

- Consume PANLAT: *Stock > Default production*.

If you analyze the traceability of this lot number you'll see all the repair operations in the upstream and downstream traceability lists of the products concerned.

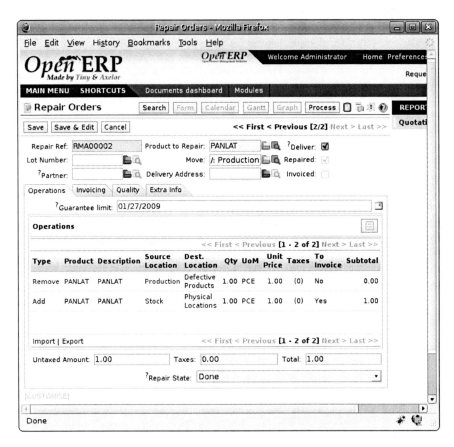

Figure 7.36: *Repair of a shelf in a cabinet*

Part IV

Process Management

This part of the book contains a single chapter, *Process*. It is concerned with something that is rather special in Open ERP - the management and visualization of cross-company processes and document workflows.

In combination with the documentation, this visualization can show exactly where a document (such as a Sales Order) has reached in its process, how it generates other documents (such as an Invoice), and the technical detail of its own workflow (which can be seen in both the GTK client and the web client).

Process

8

If you have reached this far in the book, your mind may well be reeling with the number of new documents (based on business objects) and processes that you need to encounter to model and manage your business.

Open ERP's process module, which is installed automatically when a process-aware module is installed, shows you cross-functional processes and technical workflows for those nodes in the process that have them. This visualization is invaluable for documentation - but it also goes a step further. You can modify processes and workflows and even generate entirely new processes and workflows for your various document types.

If your starting point is a specific document, such as an invoice or order, then you will also be shown the exact position of that document on its process and workflow diagrams.

For this chapter you should start with a fresh database that includes demonstration data, with `sale` and its dependencies installed and no particular chart of accounts configured. `process` is one of those dependencies. Also install some of the `hr` modules for the second example in this chapter, such as `hr_attendance`, `hr_contract`, `hr_holidays`, and `hr_holidays_request`.

8.1 The integration of processes into the management system

Processes are at the heart of a company: they form a structure for all activities that enable the company to function effectively. A company's human dimension is often disconnected from its processes at the moment, preventing individual employees' aspirations from being directed towards a collective objective.

From a mapping process, integrating management and the changing needs of each employee becomes very useful for the fulfillment of each. Based on that, each employee becomes aware of his own personal contribution to the company's value chain. This representation also helps an employee's own personal management because it shows his place and his role in the overall process, very often over several departments.

The system of 'Corporate Intelligence' will also be highly useful to system implementers who, after studying the requirements, have to formalize a company's processes to put them into operation in Open ERP.

8.1.1 Examples of process

To understand the aims of the system of Corporate Intelligence (process) better, you'll now see an overview of the functions available to you in a the study of two processes:

- A customer order quotation,

- The engagement of a new employee.

8.1.2 Following a customer sales order

The example *Example of a process handling a customer order quotation* shows the process for handling a customer sales order. Use the menu *Sales Management → Sales Orders* to list all orders, then choose Order SO001 – you can either check the checkbox to its left, or you can open the order itself by clicking the order date to the left of its name in the list.

To view the process for that specific order, click the **Process** button at the top right of the list or form. The process for this order is shown in the window, and the current state of this document can be seen by looking for the node whose left edge is colored maroon rather than grey.

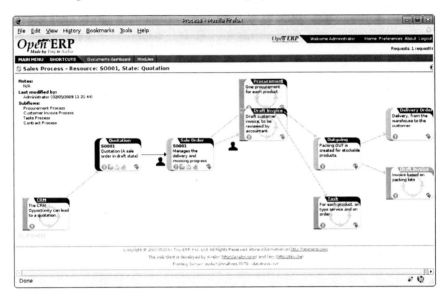

Figure 8.1: *Example of a process handling a customer order quotation*

This order is in the Quotation state. The whole of some nodes is greyed out because the selected document will never enter into that state, such as invoicing based on deliveries (the order is in an invoicing mode that's based on orders, not deliveries).

The process is completely dynamic and based on that specific sale order document. You can click each of the process nodes (**Quotation**, **Sale Order**, **Procurement**, **Draft Invoice**, **Outgoing Products**) using one of the links or icons on it:

- Obtaining the documentation and the corresponding process in the quality manual, using the **Help** (or **Information**) icon,

- Opening the corresponding Open ERP document, using the **Open** icon,

- Printing the document, using the **Print** icon,

- Printing the technical workflow by using the Gears (or **Print Workflow**) icon.

- Obtaining the documents that an employee needs to carry out the process by clicking the green arrow icon,

---

- Seeing the menu that Open ERP uses to get the document by hovering over the green arrow icon.

Returning to the process diagram, note that you can also get more information about the transitions between nodes by hovering the mouse cursor over a transition:

- A description of the transition,

- A list of the roles that can carry out the transition,

- The actions available to you from the state.

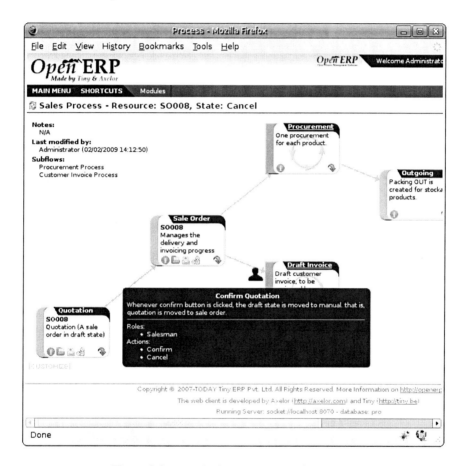

Figure 8.2: *Detail of a transition in the process*

Confirm quotation SO001 by clicking on the icon of a person beside the maroon-colored transition that takes the document from quotation to order. Then click the **Confirm** button. The process automatically moves on to the next state and updates its references to some new delivery reservations that you've just created (see the third tab **History** for a reference to the Packing List PACK13).

This dynamic response is extremely useful for learning about the software. It gives you a high-level view of the different actions carried out and their results.

During order processing, the salesperson can quickly:

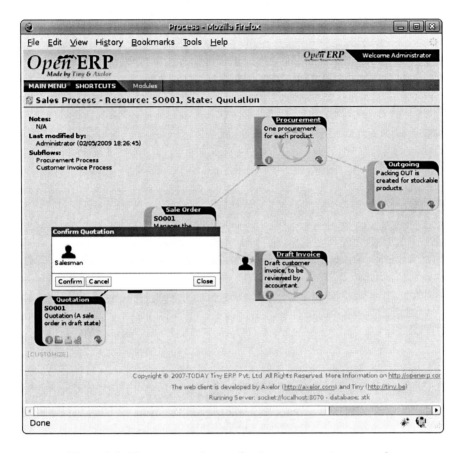

Figure 8.3: *The process after confirming a process into an order*

- Print the corresponding delivery note,

- Zoom into the invoice to see payment details,

- Get examples of the necessary documents (such as quotation types, export documents, and fax to confirm the order with the customer).

Create a draft invoice by starting the next step on your own.

It should be clear that this system of user processes gives you great visibility of the company's overall functions. Each process individually reflects the specific situation of the company and its documents.

8.1.3 New employee induction

Open the employee form for Fabien Pinckaers from the menu *Human Resources → Employees → All Employees*. Click the **Process** button to open the detailed process of engagement.

You can immediately see things that might interest the HR manager. On a single screen she has all of the documents about the selected employee. She can then zoom into each document to look at employee holidays,

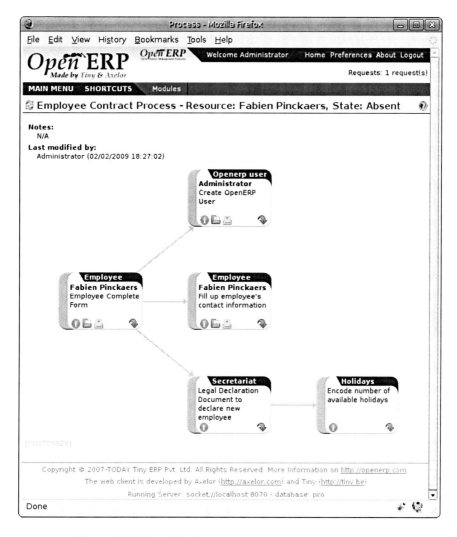

Figure 8.4: *Example of a process engaging a new employee*

associated documents, or the user account in the system.

It's also a great help for day-to-day management. When a new employee is engaged, an HR manager - or anyone else with a suitable role - can complete each node in the corresponding process, such as:

- Entering his address,

- Creating his user account in the system,

- Sending any mandatory employment documents to the relevant government departments,

- Declaring the required insurance documents,

- Setting meal preferences, perhaps,

- Entering statutory public holidays into the system.

You can click on each node to open the corresponding form in Open ERP. Some actions aren't owned by Open ERP, such as contacts with government offices and insurance companies. In this case click on the document icon to get the documents to be completed and posted or faxed to the institutions:

- Fax for insurance declarations,

- Statutary forms for government departments.

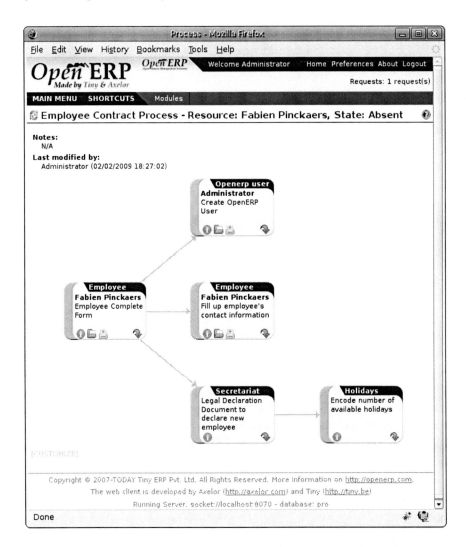

Figure 8.5: *Example of a process required for the declarations for a new employee*

The system of *Corporate Intelligence* gives you a complete overview of all the company's processes. So if you click on the node to the left it will start the recruitment process of selecting and interviewing new employees if the necessary modules have been installed.

8.2 Workflows and User Processes

Workflows are used to define the behaviour of a given document. They are used by developers and system implementers to determine which object should execute which actions and at which moments. These are principally technical processes defined in a vertical way on the lifecycle of a complete object (represented by a document). Changing a workflow will have a direct impact on the behaviour of the software in response to user actions. You handle all possible exceptions there so that the software is robust.

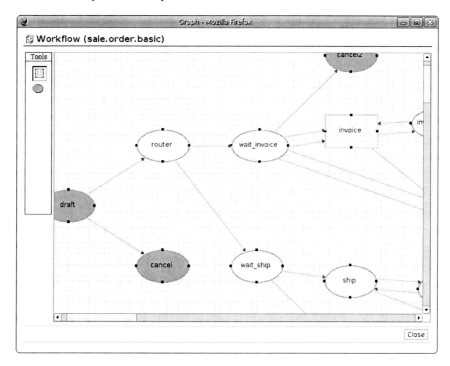

Figure 8.6: *Example of a workflow handling a customer order*

Unlike workflows, user processes represent workflows across all of a company and its documents. They are used by end users to locate an action for more complete handling. A change of user process won't have any effect on the software but will show the user another way of working on a given problem.

Processes are used by end users to help them understand the problems which haven't been handled in Open ERP. You can find actions that have no influence on the software, such as "Telephone customer to thank him", and "Send a fax to reassure him". As well as providing user help, processes provide functions such as:

- integration with Open ERP help and the company's quality manual,

- showing the user menu for finding a specific document.

User processes are thus connected to technical workflows. If you modify the software's behaviour with a workflow, the changes will be directly visible in the user processes that are based on the modified document. So if you add new required roles for certain transitions on a workflow they will automatically be shown in the process corresponding to the modified document.

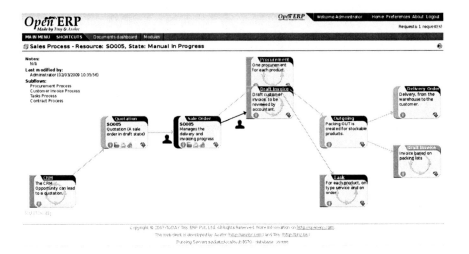

Figure 8.7: *Example of a process handling a customer order*

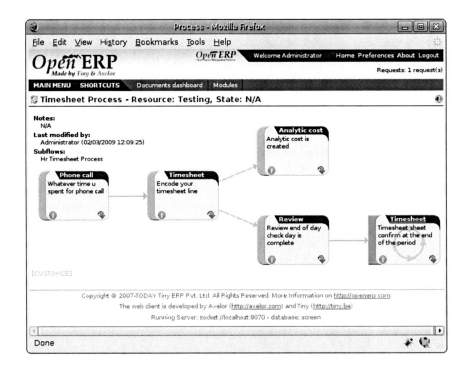

Figure 8.8: *Relationship between workflow and user process*

To get maximum benefit from the power of user processes and the workflow engine, Open ERP provides an integrated workflow editor and user process editor. This enable you to modify them through the client interface.

You'll only work with the process editor in this chapter. If you want to test the workflow editor click on the link to the bottom left of a document and select the menu *Customize → Manage Workflows*. Open ERP opens a graphical editor to modify the workflow for the selected document type.

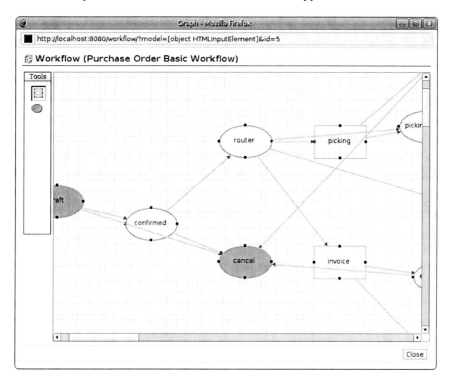

Figure 8.9: *Workflow editor modifying the behaviour of invoices*

The workflow editor is only available in Open ERP's web client at the time of writing. If you have the GTK client you can use the menus in *Administration → Low Level Objects → Workflow Items*. These are text-based not graphical.

8.2.1 Using processes effectively

Regardless of which Open ERP screen you're in you can call up a process on the current document by clicking the **Process** icon. Depending on the document you can have several processes defined using it, Open ERP then asks you to choose which one of them you want.

For example if you are in a meeting form, Open ERP will ask you to choose from the processes it knows about that involve such forms:

- processes for selecting and inducting new employees,

- tracing customer orders in pre-sales,

- processes for visiting customers and handling expenses.

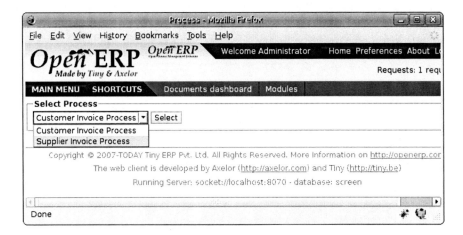

Figure 8.10: *Button for entering a user process from a form*

The element colored red shows the active process for the selected document. Elements in grey are the states that the selected document won't go through because of its configuration. You can use the different icons to open the document, print it, or get its documentation.

Some states have an image inside of arrows formed into a circle. These show that the state refers to another process. To go to this other process you can click on the title of the state. For example you can click on the invoice in the customer order management workflow to see in detail how that invoice is handled.

Finally, you can place your mouse for a second over a transition (hover over a transition) to get a help balloon appearing about this transition. Open ERP then shows you:

- A description of the transition,

- The actions you can take at this step,

- The roles you need to make anything happen from this step.

If you click on the transition, Open ERP opens a dialog box with buttons that enable you to change the document state. These are the same buttons that you see on the active document form. They enable you to confirm an order directly from the process and then see the consequences in real time at a macro level.

8.2.2 Defining your own user processes

Use the menus under *Administration* → *Customization* → *Enterprise Processes* to define new processes or modify existing processes. When entering a process, Open ERP shows you the list of states available for that process.

You can add a new state or modify an existing state. A state can be associated with an object (whose instances are represented by documents). If that is the case, choose it in the case object. You can set an expression

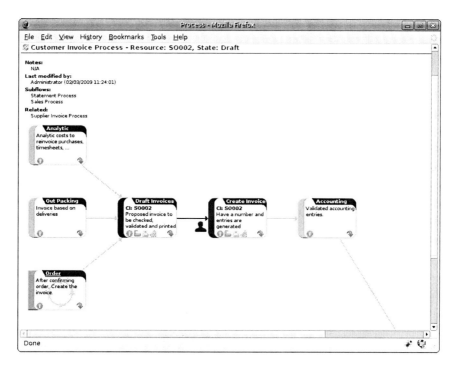

Figure 8.11: *A state that refers to another workflow*

that shows if the object can be found in that state or not. Expressions are in Python format. For example for the quotation state choose the object `sale.order` and set the following expression `object.state == 'draft'`.

You can also link to a menu so that users can learn which menu to use to access objects in a state. You can set the conditions in which this object is in a greyed-out state in the second tab **Conditions**. These expressions, too, are encoded in Python format.

Once the node has been defined you should set the transitions leaving this object. For each transition you can:

- Give the leaving and destination states,
- Set up a list of buttons that start various transitions in the process,
- Map between workflow transitions and the document that's selected,
- Put an explanatory notice in different languages.

The organization and quality of a company is typically related to its maturity. A mature company is one where processes are well established, and where staff don't waste much time searching for documents or trying to find out how to do their different tasks.

From this need for effective organization and explicit quality improvement, have appeared numerous tools:

- The ISO9001 quality standard,

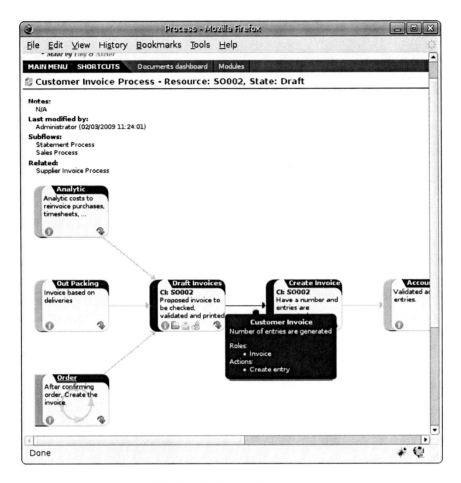

Figure 8.12: *Detail of a transition in a workflow*

- Business Process Management (BPM) tools,

- Use Case workflows, and formalized standards such as UML,

- The company Quality Manual.

The problem is that these tools are usually quite separate from your management system and often reserved for the use of just a few specific people in your company. They're treated separately rather than put at the heart of your management system. When you ask company staff about ISO9001 they usually see it as a constraint rather than a helpful daily management tool.

To help the company meet its quality requirements and to form these processes into assistance integrated with everyday work, Open ERP supplies a 'Corporate Intelligence (r)' tool that enables you to put company processes at the heart of your management system.

The system enables:

- new employees to learn how to use the software by graphically and dynamically discovering how each document and action works,

Figure 8.13: *Form for defining a process*

- easy access to the all the links to a document and everything that's attached to it,

- people to see both a high-level map and the detail of all a company's processes,

- access to a graphical model and integrated quality manual for rapid access that depends on the work context,

- use of a knowledge base and capitalization of that knowledge for all of the company's actions in the form of interactive processes,

- an employee to become more aware of his role in the whole environment.

Figure 8.14: *Screen for defining a process transition*

Part V

System Administration and Implementation

After you've tested and evaluated Open ERP, you'll need to configure it to match the software to your company's needs. Its flexibility enables you to configure the different modules, adapting them to your industry or sector of activity.

Designed for ERP project managers, this part of the book deals (in *Configuration & Administration*) with the administration and configuration of the system, giving you powerful tools for integrating the software in a company and driving and tracking the project, taking account of different problems, a range of supplier types, and (in *Implementation Methodology*) implementation risks, and the options available to you.

Configuration & Administration 9

This chapter is for the administrators of an Open ERP system. You'll learn to configure Open ERP to match it to your company's needs and those of each individual user of the system.

Open ERP gives you great flexibility in configuring and using it, letting you modify its appearance, the general way it functions and the different analysis tools chosen to match your company's needs most closely. These configuration changes are carried out through the user interface.

Users can each arrange their own welcome page and their own menu, and you can also personalize Open ERP by assigning each user their own dashboard on their welcome page to provide them with the most up to date information. Then they can immediately see the information most relevant to them each time they sign in.

And Open ERP's main menu can be entirely reorganized. The management of access rights lets you assign certain functions to specific system users. You can also assign roles, which define the part that each system user plays in the workflows that move system documents from state to state (such as the ability to approve employee expense requests).

For this chapter you should start with a fresh database that includes demonstration data, with `sale` and its dependencies installed and no particular chart of accounts configured.

 Configuration, Parameterization, Personalization, Customization

The word *personalization* is sometimes used in this book where you might expect to find *configuration* or *customization*.

Customization generally refers to something that requires a bit of technical effort (such as creating specialized code modules) and creates a non-standard system.

Configuration is less radical – it's the general process of setting all the parameters of the software to fit the needs of your system (often called *parameterization* or *setup*). Configuration is also, by convention, the name of the sub-menu below each of Open ERP's top-level menus that is accessible only to the administrative user for that section.

Personalization is just that subset of configuration options that shapes the system to the particular operational and/or stylistic wishes of a person or company.

Using the *OpenOffice.org Report Designer* module you can change any part of any of the reports produced by the system. The system administrator can configure each report to modify its layout and style, or even the data that's provided there.

The OpenOffice.org Report Editor

The OpenOffice.org plug-in enables you not only to configure the reports of the basic products in Open ERP but also to create entirely new report templates. When the user uses Open ERP's client interface, OpenOffice can create a report template that has access to all the data available to any Open ERP document type.

You can easily create fax documents, quotations, or any other commercial document. This functionality enables you to considerably extend the productivity of your salespeople who have to send many proposals to customers.

Finally, you'll see how to import your data into Open ERP automatically, to migrate all of your data in one single go.

For this chapter you should start with a fresh database that includes demo data, with `sale` and its dependencies installed and no particular chart of accounts configured.

9.1 Creating a Configuration Module

It's very helpful to be able to backup your specific configuration settings in an Open ERP module dedicated just to that. That enables you to:

- automatically duplicate the configuration settings by installing the module in another database,

- reinstall a clean database with your own configuration in case you have problems with the initial configuration,

- publish your specific configuration to benefit other companies in the same industrial sector,

- simplify migrations, if you have modified some elements of the basic configuration, there's a risk in returning them to their original state after the migration, unless you've saved the modifications in a module.

Start by installing the module `base_module_record` in the usual way. Then start recording your actions using the menu *Administration → Modules Management → Modules Recording → Start Recording*. Manually make all your configuration changes through the user interface as you would normally (such as menu management, dashboard assignments, screen configuration, new reports, and access rights management – details of some of these possibilities are described later in this chapter).

Once you've done all this, go to the menu *Administration → Modules Management → Modules Recording → Save Recorded Module*.

Contributing to the development of Open ERP

Once your personal configuration has been saved into a module, install the module `base_module_publish`. This gives you a new possible action **Publish Module** in the menu *Administration → Modules Manage → Modules*.

Use this function to publish your module on the official Open ERP site. It could then be reused by other companies that have the same needs as yours. You could then yourselves benefit from improvements made by these same companies in future.

Don't forget to create a user account beforehand on http://openerp.com.

Open ERP then creates a ZIP file for you containing all of the modifications you made while you were carrying out your configuration work. You could reinstall this module on other databases and/or publish it online to help other companies. This could turn out to be useful if you want to install a test server for your company's users and give them the same configuration as the production server.

To install a new module saved in ZIP file form, use the menu *Administration → Modules Management → Import a new module*.

9.2 Configuring the menu

Open ERP's menu organization isn't subject to any restriction, so you can modify the whole structure, the terminology and all access rights to it to meet your specific needs in the best possible way. However, before you do all that and just as you would for any other customizable software, you should balance both the benefits you see in such changes and the costs, such as the need to train users, to maintain new documentation and to continue the alterations through subsequent versions of the software.

This section describes how to proceed to change the structure of the menu and the welcome page, to configure the terminology of the menus and forms in the user interface and for managing users' access rights to the menus and the various underlying business objects.

9.2.1 Changing the menu

As administrator, and using the web client, select a menu item (but don't click it). Click on the line containing *Administration → Translations → Import/Export → Export a Translation File* (but not on the string `Export a Translation File` itself) and click the **Switch** button to bring up the menu item as an editable form (you can do the same using the GTK client – there you select the line and click the **View** button instead).

You could now edit this form (**but don't do that, read the next paragraph first!**) – change its **Parent Menu**, which moves the entry to a different part of the menu system; edit its **Menu** name to change how it appears in the menu tree, or give it a new **Icon**. Or you could give it a new **Action** entirely (but this would lose the point of this particular exercise).

Instead of editing this form, which is the original menu entry, duplicate it. With the web client you must first make the form read-only by clicking the **Cancel** button, then you click the **Duplicate** button that appears (in the GTK client, click *Form → Duplicate* from the top menu). The form that remains is now the duplicate entry, not the original.

To move this duplicate entry, change the **Parent Menu** field by deleting what's there and replacing it with another menu that everyone can see, such as **Tools** or **Human Resources**, and make sure that the entry moves to the end of the menu list by replacing the **Sequence** with 99 . You can experiment with icons if you like. Save the form and then click **Main Menu** to see the results.

Duplicating the menu

If you're planning to modify a menu you should duplicate it first. In this way you'll always keep a link to the original menu that works if you need it to.

9.2.2 Personalizing the welcome page for each user

When you sign into Open ERP for the first time, a welcome page appears. In a minimal system, such as that created in the original `openerp_ch02` database before it was expanded in *Guided Tour*, and in the `openerp_ch03` database, you only get the main menu – the same as you get by default when you click the *Main Menu* button. As you add functionality to your database you get more choices for the welcome page, with different dashboards automatically assigned to various company roles as they're created in the demonstration data.

The administrator can change both the welcome page and the main menu page individually for each user of the system, and can adapt Open ERP to each role in the company to best fit the needs of everyone.

To make modifications for a particular user, edit the user configuration again in *Administration → Users → Users*. Open the form for a particular user, and select different menu entries for the two fields **Home Action** and **Menu Action**.

The **Home Action** is the menu item that is automatically opened when you first sign on, and is also reached when you click the **Home** link in the top right toolbar of the web client. There you can choose any page that you'd reach through any menu – one of the dashboards could be most useful. The **Menu Action** is the one you reach through the **Main Menu** button in the web client (the **Menu** button in the GTK client). You can choose the main menu and the dashboards there.

Actions on the administrator's menu

It's very easy to change the welcome page and the menu of the different users. However, you shouldn't change the main administrator's menu because you could make certain menus completely inaccessible by mistake.

9.2.3 Assigning default values to fields

You can quite easily configure the system to put default values in various fields as you open new forms. This enables you to pre-complete the fields with default data to simplify your users' work in entering new documents.

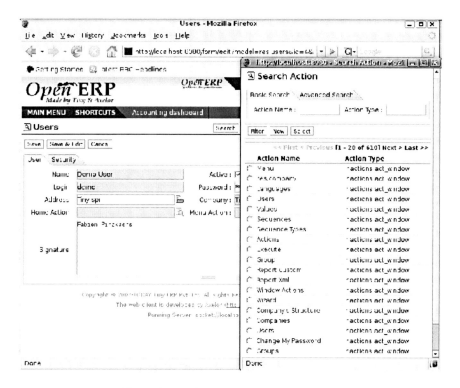

Figure 9.1: *Selecting a new welcome page*

- If you're using the web client hold `Ctrl` down and Right-Click at the same time (that's a mouse right-click while the mouse pointer is in the field and the Control key is held down on the keyboard).

- If you're using the GTK client, you just need to right-click the mouse while the pointer is in the field.

An administrator has the choice of making the default work just for that user, or for all users of the database.

To check this new configuration, open a new partner form: the field **Country** should now contain the entry `New Zealand`.

This is a very powerful feature! An administrator can use this functionality to redefine the behavior of your whole system. You can test that in database `openerp_ch13` by opening up a new **Purchase Order** form, clicking the second tab **Purchase Shippings**, selecting `From Picking` in the **Invoicing Control** field and then making that the default.

From that moment on, you'd automatically create draft purchase invoices only when goods are received, so you could very easily restrict your accountants from paying any invoices that turn up until you were sure you had received the goods. It wouldn't stop anyone from selecting another method of invoice control, but they'd start with the default definition.

Figure 9.2: *Inserting a new default value*

9.2.4 Changing the terminology

You can use Open ERP's language translation functionality to substitute its standard terminology with terminology that fits your company better. It's quite straightforward to adapt the software with different terms specific to your industry. Moreover, this can strengthen acceptance of your new Open ERP system, because everybody will be able to retain their usual vocabulary.

You can do this one of two ways:

- translate them in a CSV file, which gives you a global overview of all of the system terms so that you can search and replace specific occurrences everywhere,

- translate the phrases directly in the client, which means that you can change them in their context, and that can be helpful to you while you're translating.

The same approach is used to translate terms that haven't been created yet. This can be useful, for example, with modules that haven't yet been translated into English or any other language that you want.

Translation through a CSV file

To translate or modify all of the system's phrases you first have to export a translation file in CSV form. And to do that, you have to install a language into Open ERP. To load a translation that already exists in Open ERP use *Administration → Translations → Load an Official Translation* choose a language and then click **Start Installation**.

Then export it using *Administration → Translations → Import/Export → Export a Translation file. Select the language, then the :guilabel:'CSV File* format, then one or more (or all) modules. Click **Get File** to start the download process, then click the small **Save** icon to save the file somewhere. A French translation would be named `fr_FR.csv` by default, but you can name it whatever you like.

UTF-8 format

The CSV file is encoded in the UTF-8 format. Make sure that you retain this format when you open the file in a spreadsheet program because if you **don't** retain it you risk seeing strange character strings in place of accented characters.

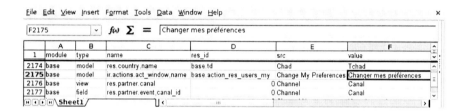

Figure 9.3: *CSV translation file with a translation in view*

The file contains six columns: **module** , **type** , **name**, **res_id**, **src**, and **value**. You have to ensure that the first line, which specifies these column names, remains untouched.

The **src** field contains the base text in English, and the **value** field contains a translation into another conventional language or into a specialist technical phrase. If there's nothing at all in the **value** field then the English translation will automatically be used on the the form you see.

Where should you modify the text?

Most of the time, you will find the text that you want to modify in several lines of the CSV file. Which line should you modify? Refer to the two columns **type** (in column B) and **name** (in column C). Some lines have the name **ir.ui.menu** in the **name** column which shows that this is a menu entry. Others have **selection** in the **type** column, which indicates that you'd see this entry in a drop-down menu.

You should then load the new file into your Open ERP system using the menu *Administration → Translations → Import/Export → Import a Translation file*. You've then got two ways forward:

- you can overwrite the previous translation by using the same name as before (so you could have a special 'standard French' translation by reusing the **Name** Français and **Code** fr_FR),

- you could create a new translation file which users can select in their **Preferences**.

If you're not connected to the translated language, click **Preferences**, select the language in **Language** and finally click **OK** to load the new language with its new terminology.

> **Partial translations**
>
> You can load a selection of the lines in a translation file by deleting most of the lines in the file and then loading back only the changed ones. Open ERP then changes only the uploaded lines and leaves the original ones alone.

Changes through the client interface

You can also change labels and other screen items on screen in the web client. To do that, open the form that you want to translate, then click the **Translate this resource.** icon to its top right. You then have the choice of translating:

- the data in the system (contained in the **Fields**),
- the field titles (the **Labels**),
- all of the **Action** buttons to the right of the form (the **Relates** option),
- the terms used in the form **View**.

You can modify any of these.

The procedure is slightly different using the GTK client. In this you just right-click on a label or button with the mouse. You can choose to translate the item itself or the whole view.

This method is simple and quick when you only have a few entries to modify, but it can become tiresome and you can lose a lot of time if you've got to change some terms across the whole system.

In that case it would be better to use the translation method that employs a CSV file.

> **Tacking account of translations**
>
> In the GTK client the modified terms aren't updated immediately. To see the effects of the modifications you must close the current window and then reopen the form.

9.3 User Login

> **Managing Passwords**
>
> If you let users change their passwords for themselves you'll have no direct control over the password they choose. You should have a written policy about password strength to try to maintain a level of security in your system.

Managing users through LDAP

With the `users_ldap` module, user accounts can be managed through an LDAP directory that can be made common to various different company resources.

Connection parameters for the LDAP directory are then registered with the company definition. You can provide a user profile template there from which new users are automatically created during their first connection to Open ERP.

LDAP

The LDAP protocol (Lightweight Directory Access Protocol) enables you to manage common directories for various different resources through your standard TCP/IP network.

This enables users in the company to have the same username and password to access all their applications (such as email and intranet).

9.4 Managing access rights

One of the most important areas in configuring Open ERP is how to manage access rights to the information in it.

You're planning to put everything significant to your business into the system, but most of your staff need see only part of it, and may need to change even less of it. Who should have rights to what, and how do you manage that?

Open ERP's approach to rights management is highly flexible. Each user can belong to one or more groups, and the group(s) you belong to determine(s):

- the visibility of each menu item and

- the accessibility of each table in the database.

For example, the group `Stock` may only be given access to some of the menus in *Stock Management*, and may have no access to any of the accounting information. Each system user who works in Stores is given membership of the `Stock` group. If some users also work elsewhere, they'd also be given membership of other groups.

Open ERP users can also belong to various roles. Just as group gives a user access rights, each role determines the user's duties. This is managed at the level of workflows, which form the company's business processes.

9.5 Groups and Users

To configure access rights you'd start by defining the groups. It's important for the groups to be representative of your company's job functions rather than of its individual employees.

So if your finance director is also your sales director, you should create both a Finance Director group and a Sales Director group, even though they're both the same person, and would both be assigned to this user in practice. This gives you flexibility for the future.

You should also create groups within a departmental areas that have different levels of access rights. For example, if you create a `Sales Director` group and a `Sales` group avoid assigning exactly the same rights to each group. The first could see all the of reports, while the second could be restricted to seeing quotations. You could either make the `Sales Director` a member of both groups, and give the Sales Director group a limited set of extra rights, or give the `Sales Director` group all the rights it needs for a Sales Director to belong only to this one group. You should choose the scheme that gives you most flexibility and then stick with it to maintain consistency.

Flexibility in managing access

To give yourself flexibility, you can ensure that a trusted staff member (perhaps a director or someone in accounts, or even the system administrator) is given wide rights to use the system, and is authorized by the management to carry out specific tasks for people.

9.5.1 Access rights for menus

To get a feel for rights management in Open ERP you'll create a new `Stock1` group, with access to the *Stock Management* menu items. You'll then create a stores person user who's a member of the `Stock1` group.

To create a new group, use the menu *Administration → Users → Groups*. Enter the group name Stock1.

Then to create a new user linked to this, use *Administration → Users → Users* to enter the following:

- **Name** : `Stores Person`,
- **Username** : `stores`,
- **Password** : `stores`,
- **Company** : `<your company>`,
- **Action** : `Menu`,
- **Menu Action** : `Menu`.

In the second tab of the user form, **Security** , add the `Stock1` group that you just created.

Save the user, then go into the menu *Administration → Security → Grant Access to Menus* to get a list of menus. Filter this list using the search field **Menu** to get the *Stock Management* menu item. In the form describing the menu, add `Stock1` into the **Groups** field. While you're at it, also add the `admin` group there. From now on, only members of the `Stock1` group and the `admin` group will be able to see this menu item in their main menu list.

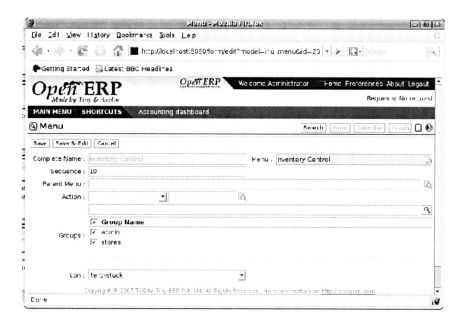

Figure 9.4: *Groups that have access to the Stock Management menu*

Menu hierarchy

Since menus are hierarchical there is no need to hide access to lower menus: once you've configured *Stock Management* this way, all lower-level menus become invisible to members of other groups.

Security

This method of managing access to menus doesn't guarantee that users are prevented from reaching hidden business objects in the system in other ways. For example, hiding the Invoices menu won't prevent people reaching invoices through purchase and sales orders, or by guessing the URL.

For effective security management you must use the methods for managing access rights to objects presented in the following section.

Initial access configuration

In the initial configuration, Open ERP's admin user, a member of the admin group, is given access to the Configuration menu in each section of the main menu. This is a general convention. For example, *Partners → Configuration* is visible in the administrator's menu amongst the other Partner menu items, but only those other menu entries are visible to other users. Similarly, the main menu entry *Administration* is, by convention, visible only to users who are members of the admin group.

9.5.2 Access Rights to Objects

The menu access rights determine who can access which menu, but doesn't define what you can do once you're in the menu.

Access controls on the objects give you the possibility of defining what your users have the right to do with your data when they get access to it. Access control of objects is structured the same way as access to menus.

Object

An object represents a document in the system. Objects are linked to database tables and also have additional concepts, such as the functions of fields, inheritance from other objects, and class methods that give them behavior.

If no group is assigned to an object, all users can access it without any restriction of any sort. Conversely, when an access control is defined for an object, a user must be a member of a group owning appropriate access rights to have any sort of access to that object.

You must always ensure that you don't lock the `admin` group out of any objects that control administration and configuration options, such as the `ir.model.access` model.

You can manage four access modes on objects independently:

- **Read access** : members of the group can read the data in the object,
- **Create access** : members of the group can create a new record in the object,
- **Write access** : members of the group can modify the contents of records in the object,
- **Delete access** : members of the group can delete records from the object.

To configure access rights on a Open ERP objects, use the menu *Administration → Security → Access Controls → Access Controls List* and click **New** or choose one there and click **Edit**. You give a **Name** to the access control, select a **Group**, and the object (**Model**), then check the checkbox corresponding to each of the four **Access** modes.

If you don't specify any group in the access rules, the rule is applied to all groups. So to remove access to an object for all users you could create a rule:

Figure 9.5: *Access control to invoices for the Finance/Admin group*

- which is defined for a specific object,

- which is linked to no group,

- for which none of the four access options is checked.

You can then create additional rules on the same object to give specific rights to certain groups.

9.5.3 Modification history

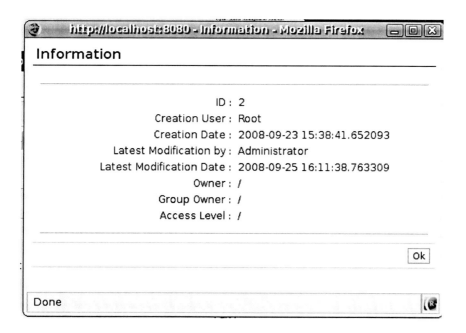

Figure 9.6: *Partner Record history*

Each record in a Open ERP database carries a note of its history. You can find out who it was created by and when that occurred, and who last modified it and when that occurred. Click the **View Log** icon at the top right of any form in the web client (but only when it's read- only, not when it's editable) to display a dialog box showing this information, as shown in the figure *Workflow for order SO005*. It can help you identify who to contact if there are any problems with the data in the records.

> **Audit Trail**
>
> Open ERP has an Audit Trail module `audittrail` which can be used to track any or all of the changes to one or more objects. It should be used with care, because it can generate huge amounts of data in the live database, but can be an invaluable tool.

9.6 Configuring workflows and processes

Workflows represent the company's different document flows. They're completely configurable and define the path that any individual Open ERP object (such as an order) must follow depending on the conditions (for example an order over a certain value must be approved by a sales director, otherwise by any sales person, before the delivery can be triggered).

The figure *Workflow for order SO005* shows the standard workflow for an order. You can show it from the GTK client starting with *Sales Management → Sales Order → All Sales Order*. Select an order, then go to the top menu *Plugins → Execute a plugin → Print Workflow* to show the menu below.

In the web client you can reach a workflow from the associated cross-company process (the process itself is reached by going to the sales document and then clicking the **Process** button above it), Chapter *Process* provides all of the information needed to create and modify technical workflows and cross-company processes.

9.6.1 Assigning roles

Users can be linked to several roles specifying their duties in certain phases of different workflows accompanying the various documents. For example, if a user has taken the role of services manager he takes on the task of approving holiday requests from his staff. So his role will be integrated in the holiday request workflow.

Role definition is done in *Administration → Users → Roles Structure → Roles*, the same way you define groups, except that roles can be hierarchical: a parent role has the same influence as all of its child roles (for example, the sales director would be able to do all of the things that have been defined for a sales person, as well as anything defined specifically for the sales director group, if the sales director has been made a parent of the sales group).

Once the roles have been defined, you can add them into the workflow transitions using the **Role** field. This means that users who have the required role can make the transitions in the workflow, which enable them to pass from one activity to another (for example confirming an order or an invoice).

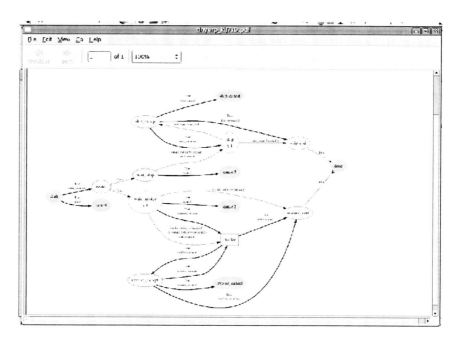

Figure 9.7: *Workflow for order SO005*

9.7 Configuring reports

Open ERP has two distinct report types:

- Statistical reports: these are calculated data, often represented in the form of lists or graphs. These reports are dynamic and you can navigate through the data that comprise the figures through the client interface.

- Report documents: they're used to print system documents. The result is usually a PDF generated by a selection made on the screen. Furthermore, Open ERP enables you to open these reports in OpenOffice.org to edit in any changes you want before sending them to your customer.

Because of the power of the Open ERP engine, these two types of report can be created or modified without needing any development and this can be done directly in the client interface of Open ERP or from OpenOffice.org.

9.7.1 Managing statistical reports

Many reports are configured in advance in Open ERP. You can find them in the *Reporting* submenus under each main menu entry.

You can also install more new reports using various different modules whose name usually starts with `report_`.

Modeling a new report

Open ERP gives you the possibility of developing your own analyses to meet your specific needs. To define a new analysis of the system's data you should install the module `base_report_creator`. This enables you to create complex queries on the database, in a simple and visual way.

Once the module is installed, create a new report using the menu *Dashboards → Configuration → Custom Reports*.

Give a **Report Name** to your new report and select the objects that you're going to analyze. For example, select the three following objects: **Partner**, **Sale Order**, **Sale Order line**.

Then turn to the second tab **View parameters** to select the views that you want in your report. Select `Tree` in the **First View** and `Graph` in the **Second View**. You can choose the type of graph displayed using the **Graph View** fields. You could also select `Calendar` as a view if you were going to add the **Date** field in your report.

> **The MS Excel plug-in**
>
> The Microsoft Excel plug-in enables you to connect to Open ERP and automatically extract the selected data. You can then apply formulas and graphs to make your own dashboards of measures directly in Excel. The .xls file can be saved and, when it is reopened, it reconnects to Open ERP to refresh the different lists and graphs with live data.

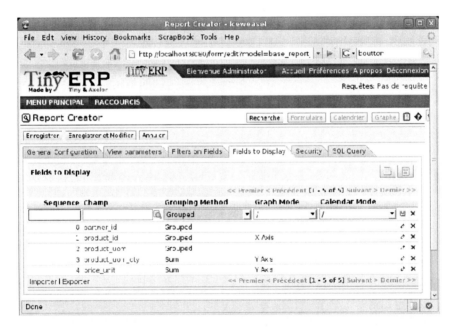

Figure 9.8: *Fields selected for the analysis of sales by customer and by product (plugin_excel.png)*

In the third tab **Fields to Display** you can add filters on all the fields of the selected objects (**Filters on Fields**). To do that, use the button **Add Filter** at the top of the form. For the moment, don't add a filter.

In the fourth tab you must indicate which of the fields in the list you want to be shown in your report (**Fields to Display**). Complete the screen along the lines of the figure below.

1. The **Sequence** field gives the order of the fields displayed.

2. **Field** the second column enables you to select a field from any of the three objects you selected in the first tab.

3. **Grouping Method** the third column lets you to determine the grouping operation that is to be applied to this field:

   - **Grouped** [enables you to group document entries with the same value in this] field.
   - **Sum** : gives the sum of values in this field.
   - **Minimum** : gives the minimum of all the values that appear in this field.
   - **Maximum** : gives the maximum of all the values that appear in this field.
   - **Average** : gives the arithmetic average of all the values in this field.

4. **Graph Mode** the fourth column, determines if the field will appear in the graph view and, if so, on which axis (X or Y).

5. **Calendar Mode** the fifth column, enables you to specify if the field can be the basis of a calendar view.

You can now **Save** the report you defined. Click on the **Open Report** button to the right of the form to get the requested analysis.

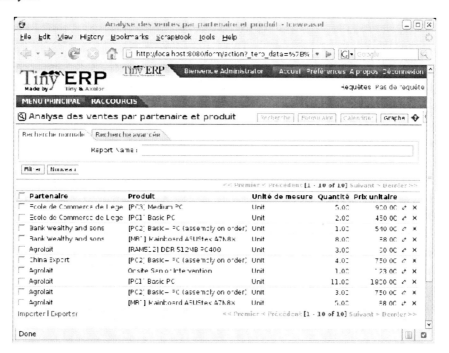

Figure 9.9: *Analyzing sales by partner and by product in list view*

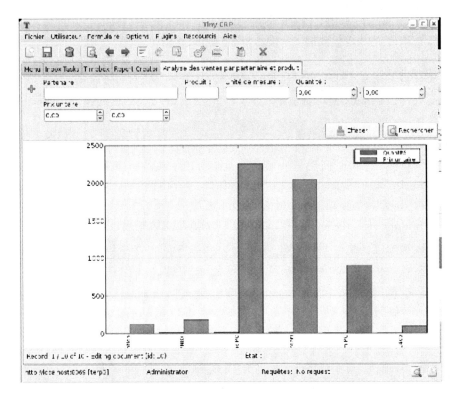

Figure 9.10: *Analyzing sales by partner and by product in graph view*

Configuring the dashboards

A dashboard is a selection of reports previously defined in Open ERP. You can choose from hundreds of predefined reports and, for each report, indicate its position on the dashboard.

Just like fields on reports, the **Sequence** field determines the order in which views appear in the dashboard.

Once the dashboard has been defined through the menu *Dashboards → Configuration → Dashboard definition* you can use the **Create Menu** button to create a menu entry for your dashboard anywhere in the menu system.

9.7.2 Managing document templates with OpenOffice.org

To configure your printable documents in Open ERP, use the module `base_report_designer`.

The OpenOffice.org Writer plug-in

You can create your own reports in just a few minutes using the OpenOffice.org Writer plug-in. This tool can give your team a big productivity improvement. Using it, you can create templates for all of your company's documents, reducing the work of creating and laying out data and customer documents.

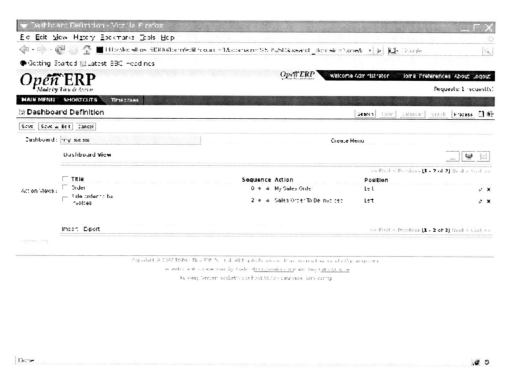

Figure 9.11: *Definition of a new dashboard*

The system is both simple and powerful, because it gives you the benefits of all of the layout facilities offered by OpenOffice.org Writer as well as all of the data and calculation provided by Open ERP. You could create or modify reports directly from OpenOffice.org and then use them in Open ERP.

> **Independence from OpenOffice.org**
>
> OpenOffice.org is only used to generate new document templates. The system administrator is the only person who has to install it.
>
> Once the document templates have been defined the users don't need it to carry out their normal work. They can use either Microsoft Office or OpenOffice.org as they choose.

The OpenOffice.org plug-in enables you to search for fields in Open ERP and integrate them into your document templates. You can use data loops in tables or sections, enabling you to attach several lines to an order, for example.

Once the new report has been defined it appears directly in the Open ERP client for the system users.

There are two modes of using reports:

- make the report produce a PDF document with data in it reflecting the selected record (for example, an invoice).

- make the report open a document for modification in OpenOffice.org, with data in it reflecting the selected record. This enables you to modify the document in OpenOffice.org before sending it to the customer (such as with a Quotation).

The personalized reports are stored in the Open ERP database and are accessible to everyone who has rights to use your database without any need for the installation of OpenOffice.org on their own computers. The document modifications are applied to a single database.

Installing the OpenOffice.org module

You should install two components before using the report editor:

- the module `base_report_designer` – first in your Open ERP installation if it's not already there, and then in the Open ERP database, you want to use it in.

- the OpenOffice.org Report Designer in the OpenOffice.org installation on your system administrator's computer.

You start by installing the module `base_report_designer` just like all the other Open ERP modules.

To install the OpenOffice.org extension, look for the file `openerpreport.zip` supplied with the *Report Designer* distribution. Check that OpenOffice.org is properly installed on your computer and that you have administration rights for installation.

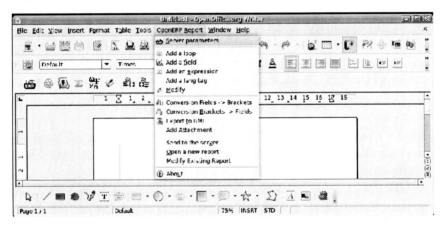

Figure 9.12: *Menu Open ERP Report in OpenOffice.org Writer*

Start OpenOffice.org Writer, select *Tools → Package Management...* to open the Package Management dialog box and then search for the `openerpreport.zip` file to install it. Then close the application and restart Writer: a new menu appears in the top menu bar – **Tiny Report** or **Open ERP Report**.

Connecting OpenOffice.org to Open ERP

Select *OpenERP Report → Server parameters* in the top menu of OpenOffice.org Writer. You can then enter your connection parameters to the Open ERP server. You must select a database `demo_min` in which you've already installed the module `sale`. A message appears if you've made a successful connection.

Modifying a report

The report editor lets you:

- modify existing reports which will then replace the originals in your Open ERP database,

- create new reports for the selected object.

To modify an existing report, select *OpenERP Report* → *Modify Existing Report*. Choose the report:menuselection:*Request for Quotation* in the **Modify Existing Report** dialog box and then click **Save to Temp Directory**.

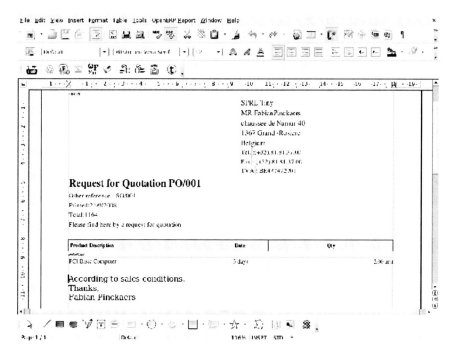

Figure 9.13: *Modifying a document template*

OpenOffice.org then opens the report in edit mode for you. You can modify it using the standard word processing functions of OpenOffice.org Writer.

The document is modified in its English version. It will be translated as usual by Open ERP's translation system when you use it through the client interface, if you've configured your own setup to translate to another language for you. So you only need to modify the template once, even if your system uses other languages – but you'll need to add translations as described earlier in this chapter if you add fields or change the content of the existing ones.

Older reports

The older reports may not all have been converted into the new form supported by Open ERP. Data expressions in the old format are shown within double brackets and not in OpenOffice.org fields.

You can transform an old report format to the new format from the OpenOffice.org menu *OpenERP Report → Convert Bracket–Fields*.

From the Open ERP toolbar in OpenOffice.org it's possible to:

- connect to the Open ERP server: by supplying the connection parameters.

- add a loop: select a related field amongst the available fields from the proposed object, for example Order lines . When it's printed this loop will be run for each line of the order. The loop can be put into a table (the lines will then be repeated) or into an OpenOffice.org section.

- add a field: you can then go through the whole Open ERP database from the selected object and then a particular field.

- add an expression: enter an expression in the Python language to calculate values from any fields in the selected object.

Python Expressions

Using the Expression button you can enter expressions in the Python language. These expressions can use all of the object's fields for their calculations.

For example if you make a report on an order you can use the following expression:

'%.2f' % (amount_total * 0.9,)

In this example, amount_total is a field from the order object. The result will be 90% of the total of the order, formatted to two decimal places.

You can check the result in Open ERP using the menu *Sales Management → Sales Orders → All Orders*.

Creating a new report

The general template is made up of loops (such as the list of selected orders) and fields from the object, which can also be looped. Format them to your requirements then save the template.

The existing report templates make up a rich source of examples. You can start by adding the loops and several fields to create a minimal template.

When the report has been created, send it to the server by clicking *OpenERP Report → Send to server*, which brings up the **Send to server** dialog box. Enter the **Technical Name** of sale.order , to make it appear beside the other sales order reports. Rename the template as Sale Order New in **Report Name**, check the checkbox **Corporate Header** and finally click **Send Report to Server**.

To send it to the server, you can specify if you prefer Open ERP to produce a PDF when the user prints the document, or if Open ERP should open the document for editing in OpenOffice.org Writer before printing. To do that choose PDF or SXW (a format of OpenOffice.org documents) in the field **Select Report Type**.

9.7.3 Creating common headers for reports

When saving new reports and reports that you've modified, you're given the option to select a header. This header is a template that creates a standard page header and footer containing data that's defined in each database.

The header is available to all users of the Open ERP server. Its template can be found on the file system of the server in the directory addons/custom and is common to all the users of the server. Although reports attach information about the company that's printing them you can replace various names in the template with values from the database, but the layout of the page will stay common to all databases on the server.

If your company has its own server, or a hosted server, you can customize this template. To add the company's logo you must login to the Open ERP server as a user who's allowed to edit server files. Then go to the addons/custom directory, copy your logo across (in a standard graphical file format), then edit the file corporate_rml_header.rml in a text editor. Text in the form <image file="corporate_logo.png" x="1cm" y="27.4cm" width="6cm"/> should be put after the line <!-logo-> to pick up and display your logo on each page that uses the corporate header.

9.8 Importing and exporting data

Every form in Open ERP has a standard mechanism for importing data from a CSV file through the client user interface. That's the same format as used in the language translations.

>
> **Forms and Lists**
>
> You have access to the Import and Export functions in the web client on a single form view in read- only mode – you can't reach Import or Export in any other view or when the form is editable. If you're using the GTK client you can find the functions from the top menu *Form → Import...* and *Form → Export....*

The CSV file format is a text format compatible with most spreadsheet programs (such as OpenOffice Calc and Microsoft Excel) and is easily editable as a worksheet. The first line contains the name of the field in the form. All the subsequent lines are data, aligned in their respective columns.

9.8.1 Exporting Open ERP data to CSV

Start exploring Open ERP's use of the CSV format by exporting a modestly complex set of data, the partners and partner addresses in the demonstration data.

Go to *Partners → Partners* for the list of partners and then scroll to the bottom of the list to click the **Export** link. This pops up the **Export Data** dialog box. Select the following fields:

- **Name**,

- **Contact Name** under the **Contacts** menu,

- **City** under the **Contacts** menu.

You can either select and add them one at a time, or Ct... ...click ... ...
order in which you select them is the order in which the ... 'll be displayed.

Then click **Export** and save the resulting `data.csv` f... ... somewhere ... perhaps y... . You
can open that file in a spreadsheet program or a text edi...

You'll see that you have a list of partners, with the name and city of each partner's contacts ... In the
couple of cases where there is more than one address, the partner name is left out. So it is important to note
that the order of entries is critical - do not sort that list!

List limits

There is a limit to the number of items you can export in the clients - it's the
number you can actually see and that is limited to a maximum of 100 in the web
client, but is arbitrary in the GTK client.

So if you want to export everything, use the GTK client. Set the export limit to
an arbitrarily large figure (using the **+** button to expose the **Parameters** and **Limit**
fields), then click *Form → Export data...*, set up the fields to export, and then
prepare to wait.

9.8.2 Importing CSV data to Open ERP

Use this export file as a template for an import file by deleting all of the data and using new data (here you'll
just import new data alongside the demonstration data, but the principle is the same for a blank database).

For example, to import partners with several contacts for which you specify a name and a city, you would
create the following CSV file from the export file:

Table 9.1: Example of importing partner address fields

Name	Contacts/Contact Name	Contacts/City
Whole Globe Technologies	Graham Global	Athens
	Wanda World	Rome
	Emerson Earth	New York
Miles A Minute		

From the list of partners, click the **Import** button and then in the **Import Data** window click **Open** to search
for and import the new `data.csv` file. The web client automatically matches column names but the GTK
client requires that you click the **Auto detect** button.

You'll get a dialog box showing that you have imported 2 objects, and you can see the new partners and partner
addresses when you refresh the list on screen.

9.8.3 The CSV format for complex database structures

When you import data you have to overcome the problem of representing a database structure in `.csv` flat files. To do this, two solutions are possible in Open ERP:

- importing a CSV file that's been structured in a particular way to enable you to load several different database tables from a single file (such as partners and partner contacts in one CSV file, as you have just done above),

- importing several CSV files, each corresponding to a specific database table, that have explicit links between the tables.

Server-side importing

You can also import CSV data in through the server interface. The file format is the same, but column headings differ slightly. When importing through the user interface it checks that the column heading names match the names seen in the forms on the user interface itself. In contrast, when importing through the server the column heading names must match the internal names of the fields.

Start by building the header of the CSV file. Open the import tool on the object that you're interested in and select the fields that you want to import into your Open ERP database. You must include every field that's colored in blue because those fields are required (unless you know that they get filled by default with an appropriate value), and also any other field that's important to you.

Use the field names as the column names in the first line of your CSV file, adding one field per column. If your CSV file has these names in the first line then when you import your CSV file, Open ERP will automatically match the column name to the field name of the table. When you've created your CSV file you'll do that by clicking the **Nothing** button to clear the **Fields to Import**, then select your CSV file by browsing for a **File to import**, and then clicking the **Auto Detect** button.

To import CSV data that matches your database structure, you should distinguish between the following types of field in the Open ERP interface: *many-to-many* fields (between multiple sources and destinations), *many-to-one* fields (from multiple sources to a single destination), and *one-to- many* fields (from a single origin to multiple destinations).

Foreground table

Each of these types is described in relation to a foreground table – the table whose entry form you're viewing and whose entries would be updated by a simple CSV file.

Just because one of these relation fields appears on the foreground table, does not mean that there is an inverse field on the related table – but there may be.

So there is *no* one-to-many field in the User form to reflect the many-to-one **user_id** Salesman field in the Partner form, but there *is* a many-to-one **partner_id** Partner field in the Partner contact form to reflect the one-to-many **child_ids** Partner contacts field in the Partner form.

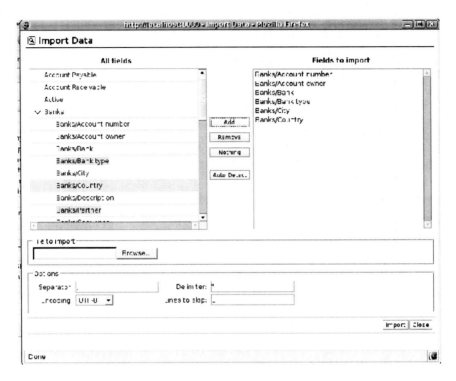

Figure 9.14: *Selecting fields to import using a CSV file*

Have a look at the screenshots below to see the differences.

Figure 9.15: *A many-to-one field: a salesperson linked to a partner*

Figure 9.16: *A many-to-many field: partner categories*

All of the other fields are coded in the CSV file as just one text string in each column.

Many-to-one fields

Many-to-one fields represent a relationship between the foreground table and another table in the database where the foreground table has a single entry for the other table. Open ERP tries to link the new record in the

Figure 9.17: *A one-to-many field: partner contacts*

foreground table with the field in the other table by matching the field values.

Field identifiers

If you're working on the server side you can use identifiers rather than the names of resources to link tables. To do this you import the first file (for example, Products) with a column named **id** in your CSV file that contains a unique identifier for each product. This could be an incrementing number.

When you import other files which link to the first table, you can use the identifier in preference to the names (so, for example, when you're saving inventory you can use product:id instead of the product name). You then don't need any complex conversion to create links between the two tables.

This considerably simplifies the importation of another database into Open ERP. You just create a linking id column for each table that you're importing that contains the identifier used in the first table.

Many-to-many fields

Many-to-many fields are handled just like many-to-one fields in trying to recreate the relationship between tables: either by searching for names or by using identifiers.

There are several possible values in a single many-to-many field. Therefore a partner can be given several associated categories. You must separate the different values with a comma.

One-to-many fields

One-to-many fields are a bit different. Take as an example the **Partner Contacts** field in the Partner form, which contains all of the linked contacts.

To import such a field you don't have to link to an existing entry in another table, but can instead create and link to several partner contacts using the same file. You can then specify several values for different fields linked to that object by the one-to-many field. Each field must be put in a column of the table, and the title of that column must be expressed in the form field_one-to- many/field_linked-object. The partner data you imported earlier took that form.

Symmetry in relation fields

Depending on the structure of your data it can be easier to use the one-to-many form or the many- to-one form in relating two tables, so long as the relevant fields exist on both ends of the relationship.

For example, you can:

- import one partner with different contact in a single file (one-to-many),

- import the partners first, and then contacts with the field linking to the partner in a many-to- one form).

9.8.4 Another example of a CSV import file

To illustrate data importing, you can see another example below. First import partner categories, and then import some partners and their contacts along with links to the categories just created. Although you can create new contacts at the same time as creating partners (because you can do this for *one-to-many* relations), you can't create new categories this way (because they use *many-to-many* relations). You must create new categories in a separate step.

Partner categories

Start by creating partner categories in a CSV file:

1. Create the following table in your spreadsheet program:

Table 9.2: Partner categories file

	Column A	Column B
Line 1	Category Name	Parent Category
Line 2	Quality	
Line 3	Gold	Quality
Line 4	Silver	Quality
Line 5	Bronze	Quality

On the first line, **Category Name** and **Parent Category** are the column titles that correspond to field names in the **Partner category** form.

Column A is for the different partner categories and **Column B** indicates if that category has a parent category. If **Column B** is blank then the category sits at the top level.

2. Save spreadsheet file in CSV format – separated by commas – and name the file `categories.csv`.

3. In Open ERP, select *Partners → Configuration → Categories → Edit Categories*.

4. Click **Import** (to the bottom left of the list) to bring up the **Import Data** dialog box, in which you'll find the ist of fields that can be imported.

5. Click **Browse...** on the **File to import** field and select the CSV file you just created, `categories.csv` Then click **Auto Detect** to atch the column names in the CSV file with the field names available in:guilabel:*Partner Categories*.

6. Click **Import** at the bottom-right of the dialog box to load your data. You should get the message 4 `objects imported` in a new dialog box. Close both this and the **Import Data** dialog box to return to the original page.

7. Click *Partners → Partners by category* to view the tree of categories, including the new `Quality` branch that you loaded.

New partners

Here's how to create new partners with more than one contact, as you did before, and how to link them to these new categories:

1. Enter the table below into your spreadsheet program.

Table 9.3: Partner data file - partners.csv

	Column A	Column B	Column C	Column D
Line 1	Name	Categories	Contacts/Contact Name	Dedicated Salesman
Line 2	Black Advertising	Silver,Gold	George Black	Administrator
Line 3			Jean Green	
Line 4	Tiny sprl		Fabien Pinckaers	Administrator

2. The second line corresponds to the creation of a new partner, with two existing categories, that has two contacts and is linked to a salesman.

3. Save the file using the name `partners.csv`

4. In OpenERP, select *Partners → Partners* then import the file that you've just saved. You'll get a message confirming that you've imported and saved the data.

5. Verify that you've imported the data. A new partner should have appeared (`NoirAdvertising`), with a salesman (`Administrator`), two contacts (`George Black` and `Jean Green`) and two categories (`Silver` and `Gold`).

9.8.5 Exporting data in other forms

Open ERP's generic export mechanism lets you easily export any of your data to any location on your system. You're not restricted to what you can export, although you can restrict who can export that data using the rights management facilities discussed above.

You can use this to export your data into spreadsheets or into other systems such as specialist accounts packages. The export format is usually in the CSV format but you can also connect directly to Microsoft Excel using Microsoft's COM mechanism.

Access to the database

Developers can also use other techniques to automatically access the Open ERP database. The two most useful are:

- using the XML-RPC web service,

- accessing the PostgreSQL database directly.

Module Recorder

If you want to enter data into Open ERP manually, you should use the Module Recorder, described in the first section of this chapter.

By doing that you'll generate a module that can easily be reused in different databases. Then if there are problems with a database you'll be able to reinstall the data module you generated with all of the entries and modifications you made for this system.

Implementation Methodology 10

You may have mastered the technical aspects of administering and using your enterprise management system, but you still have a great deal of work to do integrating Open ERP into your company. This work is more business-related and social in nature than technical.

The Open ERP implementation process encompasses several different phases: evaluation, planning, configuration, data migration, deployment, and user training, and affects both support and maintenance.

The management of ERP projects, and IT project management in general, are the subject of very many other books that you might want to investigate for yourself. The elements of the methodology presented here aren't intended to be an exhaustive review, just a brief overview of the different phases necessary to implement Open ERP in your company

Implementation

Implementation encompasses the whole process of integrating and deploying Open ERP, including evaluating it, establishing specifications, planning the deployment, the configuration of the software, loading data, installation and training the users. It doesn't generally extend to software customization, nor support and maintenance.

10.1 Requirements Analysis and Planning

Requirements analysis and planning are the keys to the success of an implementation. At this stage you should set up a management team to define the costs and benefits of the project, select a project team, and set out the detailed stages that will have to be carried out.

Open ERP is so easy to start using that it's not always obvious, particularly to IT staff, that a clear requirements plan is necessary for implementing the system successfully. The difficulty isn't particularly in installing the software nor in configuring it, but rather more about:

- knowing what to configure,

- deciding if you should adapt the software or perhaps change your method of working, for some of your specialized processes,

- forming teams that can specify and work on some of the changes,

- ensuring that your users are committed to the change.

ERP system implementation is a project carried out using information technology but it's a business project rather than an IT project in itself. The challenge of this type of project is in changing the behaviour of those involved at all levels of the enterprise.

People in the IT department will certainly be an integral part of the project but they should be managed by someone in a senior position who both understands the business impact across the organization and has experience of technical projects. Ideally the project manager should know the company well, both its specific quirks and its different standard cross-company processes.

If the enterprise doesn't have its own IT group, you're probably better off opting for an SaaS offer. This means that you subcontract all the difficult technology, from the installation of the server to its maintenance, all the while being assured of the installation of a robust architecture with its redundancy, backed-up servers, and separation of authentication and data.

10.1.1 Planning methods

Planning methods vary in their degree of complexity, formality and level of automation. It's not the intention of this chapter to steer you towards one method or the other.

Open ERP's menus are organized to lead you through an implementation in a sensible order, so that information that has to be entered first is encountered first in the menu system. Forms are also organized so that if you enter data in the natural order you'll get later fields completed automatically by the earlier ones where possible. And demonstration data illustrates how Open ERP's functional areas are linked from one to the other

The menus themselves hint at several helpful implementation suggestions, for example the submenus of *Administration* → *Configuration* are useful for the configuration of the software. New functions such as the Module Recorder enable you to significantly accelerate the configuration of data.

10.2 Deployment

As you've seen the complete architecture of Open ERP includes the following elements:

- a database server,
- an Open ERP application server,
- an Open ERP client-web server,
- several clients that access the Open ERP server: they can either be web clients if the client-web server is installed, or GTK clients.

Deployment

Deployment is the process of putting a Open ERP database into a production-ready state, where it can be used by everyone in your business for their daily work. You'd usually configure Open ERP and load data into it on one development system, train staff on that or another training system and deploy it onto a production system that has better protection against failure, better security and more performance.

10.2.1 Deployment Options

To deploy Open ERP in your company, several options are available to you:

- an SaaS (Software as a Service) or on Demand offer which includes the equipment, the hosting, the maintenance and the support on a system configured to your needs in advance,

- an internal installation, that you manage yourselves or have managed by an IT services company such as an Open ERP partner,

- hosting by a server supplier on which Open ERP is installed, which enables you to proceed to add adaptations on your server.

The first two approaches are the most commonly used.

The SaaS (Software as a Service) offer

SaaS is a complete package hosted at a supplier, that includes the following services: server hardware, hosting of the generic solution, installation and initial configuration, redundancy of the architecture, backups, system maintenance and support. It's also known as **On-Demand**.

It's provided in the form of a monthly subscription with a fixed price per user. You can find the detail of Tiny's SaaS packages at http://ondemand.openerp.com/.

SaaS packages don't permit you to develop specific modules to your needs. On the contrary, they offer a service at a set price based on standard software modules that contain few migration risks. SaaS suppliers are limited generally to the modules certified and validated by the original author and project manager, Tiny.

Here are the main advantages of an Open ERP SaaS solution:

- an unbeatable return on investment (cost of implementation: 0, cost of licenses: 0),

- costs that are controlled and without surprises (the offer includes maintenance, frequent migrations and support),

- a turnkey solution, installed in less than twenty-four hours,

- packages adapted and preconfigured for different sectors of activity,

- a very robust architecture guaranteed to have constant and permanent access, reachable from anywhere.

So this server is recommended for small companies with fewer than about fifteen employees.

Hosting by a supplier

At first sight a hosted Open ERP system appears similar to SaaS: it provides Open ERP from a remote installation through a web browser. But in general the similarities stop there.

To compare it with an SaaS package you should check if the hosting offer properly includes the following elements:

- server hardware,

- hosting,

- maintenance,

- future migrations,

- backups,

- server redundancy,

- telephone and email support,

- frequent updates to the modules.

Also get yourself up to speed on the following points:

- the version of Open ERP proposed,

- the costs of implementation (configuration, data loading, training),

- the cost of configuration (if it's proposed),

- the technology and the procedure used for securing your database,

- the technology and the procedure for preventing system faults,

- the technology and the procedure for restoring a faulty system,

- limitations on the number of users, the number of simultaneous users, and the size of the database,

- the level of support and its costs,

- the procedure used to update Open ERP (to fault-fixed versions)

- the procedure adopted for Open ERP upgrades (to versions that have both fault fixes and new functionality).

Calling such suppliers can be a good solution if you are willing to entrust all the technical specifications for the functioning of Open ERP to them, especially if you need to use customized or extension modules that aren't in the stable version released by Tiny.

Internal Installation

Large and medium-large companies typically install Open ERP using their own internal company resources. They usually prefer to have their own IT service in charge of maintenance.

Such companies can do the implementation work themselves internally, or turn to an Open ERP partner who will do the ERP implementation work or assist them with it. Generally companies prefer to adopt an intermediate solution which consists of:

1. Turn the initial implementation over to a partner to limit the risks and delays of integration. That enables them to be managed by experts and to obtain a high quality configuration.

2. Take charge of the simple needs for themselves once the software has been implemented. It's quite a lot more convenient for them to be able to modify the database tables, forms, templates and workflows internally than routinely depend on a supplier.

An internal installation will probably prove more costly than an SaaS package or hosted service. Even if you put yourself in charge of it all, you'll take quite a bit of time learning how to manage the implementation unless the team already has experience of Open ERP. This represents a significant risk.

However, an internal implementation can be particularly interesting where:

- you want to keep your data within your company,

- you think you want to modify your software,

- you want a specific package of modules,

- you'd like a very fast response time,

- you want the software to be available even if your Internet connection goes down.

These factors, and access to the resources needed to handle an implementation and the subsequent maintenance, are the reasons that large and medium-large companies usually do it for themselves, at least partly.

10.2.2 Deployment Procedure

The deployment of a version of Open ERP is quite simple when your server has been configured in your production environment. The security of the data will then be a key element.

When you've installed the server you should create at least two databases:

- a test or development database, in which the users can test the system and familiarize themselves with it,

- a production database which will be the one used by the company in daily use.

 Version numbering

Open ERP uses a version numbering model that comprises 3 numbers A.B.C (for example 4.2.2 or 5.0.0) where changes in the number A signify a major functional change, changes to number B signify an update that includes a batch of fault fixes and some new functionality, and the number C generally refers to some limited updates or fixes to the existing functionality.

The number B is special: if it's an odd number, (for example 4.3.2 or 5.1.0) it's for a development version which isn't designed for a production environment. The even numbers are for stable versions.

If you have prepared a data module for Open ERP (that is a module that consists just of data, not altered functionality), you should test it in your development version and check that it doesn't require any more manual adjustments. If the import runs correctly, it shows that you're ready to load your data in the production database.

You can use the Open ERP database backup procedure at different stages of configuration (see *Installation and Initial Setup*). Then if you've made a false step that you can't recover from you can always return to a prior state.

Since your data describes much of your company's value, take particular care both when you need to transfer it (in backups and across your network) and when you're managing the super-administrator password. Make sure that the connection between a PC client and the two servers is correctly secured. You can configure Open ERP to use the HTTPS protocol, which provides security for data transfer

HTTPS

The HTTPS protocol (Secured Hyper Text Transfer Protocol) is the standard HTTP protocol secured by using the SSL (Secure Socket Layer) or TLS (Transport Layer Security) security protocols. It allows a user to verify her identify to the site to which she wants access, using a certificate of authentication. It also guarantees the integrity and confidentiality of the data sent between the user and the server. It can, optionally, provide highly secure client authentication by using a numbered certificate.

The default HTTPS port is 443.

You could also use the PostgreSQL database directly to backup and restore data on the server, depending on access rights and the availability of passwords for the serve.

10.3 User training

Two types of training are provided by the Tiny company and its partners:

- Technical training in Open ERP: the objective of this intensive training is to enable you to develop your own modules by modifying and adapting the existing ones. It covers the creation of new objects, menus, reports and workflows, and also of interfaces with external software. It lasts for five days and is designed for IT people

- User training: this enables you to be productive as rapidly as possible in the use of Open ERP. All of the modules there are detailed with concrete examples and different exercises. For the sake of realism the training uses data for a fictitious company. This training also lasts for five days. It is designed for those responsible for an ERP project, who will then be capable of training employees internally.

Tiny's training calendar is available on the official Open ERP site by clicking the menu *Services → Training*. The training is delivered in either French or English depending on the course.

Both Tiny, the creators of Open ERP, and the Open ERP partners can also provide customized training. This, although more expensive, is focused on your own needs.

Your training needs depend on the type of deployment you've chosen. If you have opted for an SaaS development, technical training isn't very useful.

In summary, you should arrange both user training and self-paced training (perhaps based on this book series) if you can. Technical training is strongly advised if you see yourselves developing your own modules. Although it's not obligatory it gives you quite a time advantage in any serious Open ERP engagement.

10.4 Support and maintenance

It's when you actually use your ERP that you will obtain value from your investment. For that reason maintenance and support are critical for your long term success.

- Support aims to ensure that end users get the maximum productivity from their use of Open ERP by responding to their questions on the use of the system. Support can be technical or functional.

- Maintenance aims to ensure that the system itself continues to function as required. It includes system upgrades, which give you access to the latest functionality available.

Some partners offer preventative maintenance. This makes sure that all the specific developments for your system are revised and tested for each new version so that they remain compatible with the base Open ERP.

Tiny themselves have changed their support strategy from time to time. At the time of writing they propose a maintenance contract supplied either direct to the end user or through partners that guarantees a quick fix to any faults discovered in the covered code. Although you can expect these fixes to become available to all users of the code in time, maintenance guarantees quick attention. And you're likely to get quicker migration support to new upgrades.

If you haven't anticipated your needs with a preventive maintenance contract, the costs of migration after a few years can become significant. If special modules that you developed have been allowed to become too old you may eventually need a new development to your specifications.

10.4.1 Updates and Upgrades

There are four sources of code change for Open ERP:

- patches supplied by Tiny to correct faults: after validation these patches shouldn't cause any secondary effects,

- minor updates, which gather the fault corrections together in one package, and are generally announced with a modification of the version number, such as from 5.0.0 to 5.0.1,

- upgrades, which bundle both the fault corrections and the improvements to the functionality in a major release such as from 5.0.3 to 5.2.0.

- new functions generally released in the form of new modules.

You should establish a procedure with your supplier to define how to respond to changes in the Open ERP code.

For simple updates your maintenance team will evaluate the patches to determine if they are beneficial to the use of your Open ERP. These patches should be tested on an offline instance of Open ERP before being installed in your live production version.

The maintenance team would also take charge of regular updates to the software.

Patches and updates can only be installed if you have the necessary access to the Open ERP server. You must first install the patch or update and then restart the server using the command line: `-update=all` .

Once Tiny has released a new upgraded version your response should be a cautious one. If you're perfectly satisfied with the existing system it would be best to not touch the new version. If you want to have access to the new functionality supplied by an upgraded version, you have a delicate operation to carry out. Most upgrades require your data to be migrated because the databases before and after the upgrade can be a little different.

10.4.2 Version Migration

Open ERP has a system to manage migrations semi-automatically. To update specific modules, or the whole database, you only need to start the server with the argument:`-update=NAME_OF_MODULE` or `-update=all`(that's minor module changes).

New stable versions of Open ERP sometimes require operations that aren't provided in the automated migration. Tiny, the creator and maintainer of Open ERP, has a policy of supporting migration from all official stable releases to the latest. Scripts are provided for each new release of a stable version. These carry out the upgrade from the previous major version to the new major version.

Managers responsible for the migration between two versions of Open ERP will find the documentation and the necessary scripts in the directory `doc/migrate` of the Open ERP server.

The changes between version 4 and 5 made the migration process more difficult than in the past so there was a greater delay in the provision of migration assistance and more manual work than usual.

The procedure for migrating runs like this:

1. Make a backup of the database from the old version of Open ERP

2. Stop the server running the old version

3. Start the script called `pre.py` for the versions you're moving between.

4. Start the new version of the server using the option `-update=all`

5. Stop the server running the new version.

6. Start the script called post.py for the versions you're moving between.

7. Start the new version of the server and test it.

A migration is never an easy process. It may be that your system doesn't function as it did before or that something requires new developments in the functionality of the modules that have already been installed. So you should only move to a new version if you have a real need and should engage a competent partner to help if the version that you use differs greatly from the basic version of Open ERP.

Similarly you should take care that this migration does not incorrectly change any setting that has already been made. The main menu structure might have been modified in place without proper recording of the changes. So you could find that you're making the wrong assumptions about that structure when later loading data in that was recorded with the Module Recorder.

Conclusion

Open ERP has become established as the main free market-changing alternative for enterprise management systems in amongst software from giants such as SAP, Oracle and Microsoft, and from the small software developers in their own niches.

Until now only two main alternatives existed for systems that manage a company's information: install a proprietary ERP system, complete but usually overweight, inflexible, and expensive; or develop a solution internally, adapted to current needs but often expensive to develop, not integrated, and incomplete.

With its free business model, Open ERP combines the advantages of a complete ERP system with the flexibility of an in-house solution. The open source code, the project's general flexibility, and its hundreds of modules let you construct a solution from a selection of the modules already available and you can then freely update it as your needs evolve.

The results will be at the top end of what you might expect from any ERP system, let alone an Open Source system. The considerable gains in productivity, efficiency and visibility become apparent only a few months after implementation. And you can gain from increased operational quality even if you reduce your human resourcing intensity. Because there are fewer repetitive tasks for your staff to do, they can concentrate on higher added-value work. We frequently receive the gratitude of senior management who get better results from their business because they've adopted Open ERP.

You aren't alone

Many resources are at hand to accompany you on your Open ERP adventure.

Bypass the technical difficulties by using the "on demand" offer: Odoo. For a quick low-cost start you can make use of a month's comprehensive free trial of Tiny's Open ERP on demand offer, available at http://odoo.com. Using this you sidestep any technical difficulties and get a comprehensive set of system administration services, server hosting, configuration to your environment, maintenance, support and initial training.

An SaaS (Software As A Service) offer is suited to the needs of small enterprises that don't have very specific needs, and where the initial cost and the delay of implementation are critical factors.

To meet its objectives of minimal cost, the on demand package aims for highly automated standardized data migrations, minimal support load by training customers well, and a strict limit to the number of modules offered. So you can't use your own modules, and are limited to the standard modules that are included in various package levels.

Consult the available resources

Larger companies often prefer a more classic implementation path. Even though Open ERP's simplicity makes this task easier than with other systems, you can't hide the fact that a project implementation is complex and introduces big changes to a company.

So you can turn towards some of the different actors in this free software ecosystem to help you out:

- the community of users and developers,
- Tiny's Open ERP partner companies,
- the main project developers, Tiny, themselves.

The community of users and developers

The community, supported by Tiny, hosts a set of communication tools which can help you in your Open ERP investigation.

- **The forum** : http://openobject.com/forum

The forum enables you to discuss issues with other Open ERP users. It's very active and you have a good chance of receiving some form of response to your questions within twenty-four hours or so.

- **Online Documentation** : http://doc.openerp.com

You will find several information in this documentation: how to use Open ERP, how to develop on Open ERP and a list of available modules and their descriptions.

- **Launchpad** : https://code.launchpad.net/~openobject/

The most recent communication tool is the launchpad system, which now hosts all of Open ERP's source code (using the *bzr* source code control system) and is used for reporting faults. It's become the central location for Open ERP technology.

Open ERP partners

If you need contract-backed guarantees for implementing and maintaining Open ERP you can contact an official Open ERP partner. Open ERP partners offer various services such as user training, prototype installations, and change management services. The complete list of partners by country and by type can be found on the official Open ERP site: http://openerp.com/partners.html.

The main developer, Tiny

Finally you can call the main project developers, Tiny, who can help you in your Open ERP project. Tiny offers various services such as free demonstration days for the software, user training and technical training, support contracts, maintenance contracts and developments as required. Depending on the demand, they can also put you in contact with partners most aligned to your requirements.

- **The mailing list** : To keep up to date with all Open ERP's news you can subscribe to the mailing list using http://tiny.be/mailman/listinfo/tinyerp-announce.

To conclude, don't forget that Open ERP has more than four hundred modules available and that many of them haven't been covered in this book. So if you haven't found a solution to your problems here, look amongst those modules, talk to other Open ERP users on the forum, and don't hesitate to contact a partner.

Wishing you the greatest of success in your ERP project,

— Geoff Gardiner and Fabien Pinckaers.

Index

stock check, 144
Stock Management, 48, 129
Supplier Relationship Management, 49
support, 289
system
    administration, 24
    administrator, 24, 262

T

tender, 122
timezone, 27
Tiny ERP, 3
traceability
    downstream, 168
    upstream, 168
traceability (stock), 170
trading company, 106
training, 288
translation, 258

U

unit of measure, 139
UoM, 139
update, 289
upgrade, 289
user
    access, 31
    account, 21
    configuration, 31
    group, 31, 261
    role, 31
username
    password, 21

V

virtual
    stock, 142

W

warning, 90
waste products, 226
welcome page, 256
work operations, 219
work orders, 214
workcenter, 214
workcenter, cycle, 215
workflow, 235, 242, 266
    role, 266

X

XML-RPC, 10

Printed in the United States
151991LV00006B/2/P